The Big Lie

The Big Lie

EXPOSING THE NAZI ROOTS OF
THE AMERICAN LEFT

DINESH D'SOUZA

REGNERY
PUBLISHING
A Division of Salem Media Group

Regnery® is a registered trademark of Salem Communications Holding Corporation

Cataloging-in-Publication data on file with the Library of Congress

ISBN 978-1-62157-348-7
e-book ISBN 978-1-62157-536-8

Published in the United States by
Regnery Publishing
A Division of Salem Media Group
300 New Jersey Ave NW
Washington, DC 20001
www.Regnery.com

Manufactured in the United States of America

10 9 8 7 6 5 4 3 2 1

Books are available in quantity for promotional or premium use. For information on discounts and terms, please visit our website: www.Regnery.com.

Distributed to the trade by
Perseus Distribution
www.perseusdistribution.com

To my wife Debbie

One lifetime is too short

Contents

One

Return of the Nazis

Although fascism seems to be dead, it could have a second coming in different forms.[1]

Walter Laqueur, *Fascism: Past, Present, Future*

S ome of Sigmund Freud's most interesting cases involved people who did bad or destructive things and then shifted the blame onto others. Such cases are now standard in psychological literature. Psychologists today are quite familiar with patients who display selfish or vicious behavior and then attribute those qualities to their psychologist. It is also quite common in the course of therapy for patients with a morbid hostility toward a parent or sibling to become morbidly hostile toward the therapist. Following a term coined by Freud, psychologists call this phenomenon "transference."

Transference, in its wrongful assignment of blame and responsibility, is obviously a form of lying. A special case of transference involves "blaming the victim." In the relevant psychological literature, the perpetrator of some terrible action blames it not on himself but, incredibly, on the victim of the offense. Serial killers who target prostitutes, for example, might come to believe that the prostitutes deserve to be raped and murdered. "That woman was a whore. She had it coming." This enables the killer to consider himself a vengeful angel, an instrument of justice.

A good example of blaming the victim was the serial killer Ted Bundy. Earlier in life Bundy had been rejected by a woman who was a brunette. He developed an intense hatred toward her because she made him feel inferior and worthless. So he targeted young brunettes on college campuses to abduct and murder, in effect displacing his hate onto them and holding them responsible for what the other woman once did to him. In Bundy's mind, he had been unjustly rejected and victimized, and by a perverted process of displacement he held the women he killed responsible for this.[2]

Blaming the victim is a lie, but a lie of a special type. Normally lying is a distortion of the truth. This applies to transference in the general sense of the term: the qualities of the patient are shifted to the therapist. But when a perpetrator blames the victim, he does more than blame an innocent party. He blames the very party that is being directly harmed by his actions. Blaming the victim involves the perpetrator and victim exchanging places: the bad guy becomes a good guy and the good guy becomes a bad guy. This is more than a distortion of the truth; it is an inversion of it. It's a big, big lie.

The big lie is a term routinely attributed to Adolf Hitler. Supposedly Hitler used the term to describe Nazi propaganda. In his autobiography, *Mein Kampf*, Hitler contrasts the big lie with little or ordinary lies. "The great masses of the people," he writes, "more easily fall victim to the big lie than to a little one, since they themselves lie in little things, but would be ashamed of lies that were too big. Such a falsehood will never enter their heads, and they will not be able to believe in the possibility of such monstrous effrontery and infamous misrepresentation in others."[3]

Hitler, however, is not referring to his own big lies. Rather, he is referring to the lies allegedly promulgated by the Jews. The Jews, Hitler says, are masters of the big lie. Now recognize that *Mein Kampf* is a tireless recitation of libels and calumnies against the Jews. The Jews are accused of everything from being capitalists to being Bolsheviks, from being impotent to lusting after Nordic women, from being culturally insignificant to being seekers of world domination. The charges are contradictory; they cannot simultaneously be true.

Yet while lying about the Jews and plotting their destruction, Hitler accuses the Jews of lying and of plotting the destruction of Germany. Hitler employs the big lie even as he disavows its use. He portrays himself as a truth-teller and attributes lying to those he is lying about—the Jews. Could there be a more pathological case of transference, and specifically, of blaming the victim?

The big lie is now back, and this time it is about the role of fascism and Nazism in American politics. The political Left—backed by the mainstream of the Democratic Party—insists that Donald Trump is an American version of Hitler or Mussolini. The GOP, they say, is the new incarnation of the Nazi Party. These charges become the basis and rationalization for seeking to destroy Trump and his allies by any means necessary. The "fascism card" is also used to intimidate conservatives and Republicans into renouncing Trump for fear themselves of being branded and smeared. Nazism, after all, is the ultimate form of hate, and association with it, the ultimate hate crime.

In this book, I turn the tables on the Democratic Left and show that they—not Trump—are the real fascists. They are the ones who use Nazi bullying and intimidation tactics and subscribe to a full-blown fascist ideology. The charges that they make against Trump and the GOP are actually applicable to them. The self-styled opponents of hate are the actual practitioners of the politics of hate. Through a process of transference, leftists blame their victims for being and doing what they themselves are and do. In a sick inversion, the real fascists in American politics masquerade as anti-fascists and accuse the real anti-fascists of being fascists.

The Race Card

This is a topic I have not written about before. On two occasions, once in 1976 and again in 1980, Reagan offhandedly linked the Democratic Party with fascism. The media went into a predictable uproar, implying that once again the old cowboy was spouting gibberish. "Reagan Still Sure Some in New Deal Espoused Fascism" read the headline in the *Washington Post*.[4] When he said that, I had no idea what Reagan was talking about. But he knew; he came of age in the 1930s. He was there. He saw the affinities between fascism and the New Deal, affinities that I will elaborate in a subsequent chapter.

Only now, decades later, do I understand what Reagan was getting at. I wish he could have read this book; he would see that, far from being guilty of falsehood or exaggeration, he was guilty of massive understatement. But at the time, I like most of my fellow Republicans and conservatives was a victim of the progressive paradigm, embedded in all our institutions of culture, from academia to Hollywood to the media. In this case, the story that we had accepted, like suckers, was the idea that fascism and Nazism are inherently "right wing."

The Left is really good at inventing and disseminating these paradigms. When one of them falls, they simply reach for another. In my previous book and film, *Hillary's America*, I challenged another powerful leftist paradigm. This is the paradigm that the progressives and the Democrats are the party of emancipation, equality, and civil rights. I showed instead that they are the party of slavery and Indian removal, of segregation and Jim Crow, of racial terrorism and the Ku Klux Klan, and of opposition to the civil rights movement of the 1960s.

My goal was to strip away the race card from the Democrats—a card they had been successfully playing against Republicans for a generation. Incredibly the Democrats had taken full credit for the civil rights movement, even though Republicans are the ones who got it passed, and even though the opposition to it came almost entirely from the Democratic Party. Democrats accused Republicans—the party of emancipation and opposition to segregation, bigotry, and white supremacy—of being the party of bigotry and white supremacy.

Talk about transference. This was my introduction to the Left's political strategy of shifting the blame for racism onto the party that had historically opposed racism in all its forms. So successful were the

Democrats in this con that in 2005 a head of the Republican National Committee, Ken Mehlman, went around apologizing to black groups for sins that had actually been committed, not by the Republicans, but by the Democrats.[5] Equally astonishing, the Democrats have never admitted their racist history, never taken responsibility for what they did, never apologized for it, never paid one penny of restitution for their crimes.

What intrigued me most was how one can get away with such a big lie. The answer is you have to dominate all the large megaphones of the culture, from academia to the movies to the major media. With this cultural arsenal at their disposal, big liars can spin out falsehoods with the confidence that no one else has a large enough megaphone to challenge them. They can have their lies taught in classrooms, made into movies and TV shows, and reported in the everyday media as the unvarnished truth. This is how big lies come to be widely believed, sometimes even by the people who are being lied about.

Hillary's America was met with outrage on the Left, but no one could rebut a single fact in the book or movie. Even my most incriminating allegations proved invulnerable. I noted that, in 1860, the year before the Civil War, no Republican owned a slave; all the four million slaves at the time were owned by Democrats. Now this generalization could easily be refuted by someone providing a list of Republicans who owned slaves. The Left couldn't do it. One assiduous researcher finally sought to dispute me with a single counterexample. Ulysses S. Grant, he pointed out, once inherited a slave from his wife's family. I conceded the point but reminded him that, at the time, Ulysses S. Grant was not a Republican.

Fearful that they had no substantive answer to *Hillary's America*, the mainstream media went into complete denial. If you watched the major networks or public television, or listened to National Public Radio, you would have no idea that *Hillary's America* even existed. The book was Number One on the *New York Times* bestseller list and the movie was the top-grossing documentary of the year. Both were dense with material directly relevant to the ongoing election debate. Yet they were completely ignored by a press that was squarely in the Hillary camp.

Despite the failed fulminations and widespread denial, however, the book and movie had an effect. Many people credit it with motivating Republicans and persuading undecideds and thus helping Trump get to the White House. I have no idea how to measure this effect. I do know my book and film helped shape the election narrative. They helped expose Hillary as a gangster and the Democrats as her accomplices with a long history of bigotry and exploitation to account for. In the 2016 election, for the first time the Democrats could not drop the race bomb and get away with it.

Even after the election, it's now harder, as a consequence of the book and movie, for Democrats to play the race card. They tried, briefly, in attempting to halt the nomination of Jeff Sessions as Trump's attorney general. Decades ago, the charge went, he said some racist things. Yes, but what about Democrat Robert Byrd, "conscience of the Senate"? Decades ago, he had been a leader of the Ku Klux Klan. Yet the Clintons and Obama eulogized him when he died in 2010. The Democrats discovered, to their dismay, that their race card had become a dud. It no longer worked. Sessions sailed through.

So now the Democrats have moved from the big race card that no longer works to their biggest card—the Nazi card. Of course this is not an abandonment of the race card, because racism was intrinsic to Nazism. Hitler, in his unremitting hatred for the Jews—a hatred based not on what they did or even on their religion but simply because of their racial and biological identity—is the ultimate racist.

Consequently, the Democrats hope not merely to sustain the Nazi allegation against Trump and the GOP but also to salvage the race card in a new form. My objective, now as before, is to do to the new Nazi paradigm what my previous book did to the old race narrative, namely, blow it out of the water. Here I refute their bogus narrative, expose their big lie, and pin the Nazi tail precisely where it belongs—on the Democratic donkey.

Reductio Ad Hitlerum

The topics of Nazism and fascism must be approached with the greatest care, not only because they involve massive suffering and loss of life, but also because the terms themselves have been so promiscuously used and abused in our culture. Nowhere was this better illustrated than in the response of several Hollywood figures to Trump's election and inauguration.

"I feel Hitler in these streets," fumed actress Ashley Judd. Singer John Legend charged that Trump's "Hitler-level" rhetoric could turn America into Nazi Germany. According to a tweet by RuPaul, on November 8, 2016, "America got a giant swastika tattooed on her forehead." Actress Meryl Streep said her criticism of Trump had produced a "terrifying" response. "It sets you up for all sorts of attacks and armies of brownshirts…and the only way you can do it is if you feel you have to…. You don't have an option."[6]

This is Streep doing her best Dietrich Bonhoeffer imitation. Yet exactly how were these brownshirts attacking her? Turns out their attacks were on Twitter and other social media. No one actually beat her up. Real brownshirts would have. So too, RuPaul probably knows that in Nazi Germany a male drag queen like him would have been sent to a concentration camp and euthanized. If he actually believed America had become Nazi Germany, one might expect him to immediately leave the country. Somehow RuPaul knows, and we all know, he's perfectly safe here.

Some conservatives are unruffled by the Left's application of the fascist label to Trump. Historian Victor Davis Hanson bemusedly recalls that Ronald Reagan and George W. Bush were both, at one time or another, likened by the Left to Hitler. Daniel Greenfield tracked the Hitler analogy back to Goldwater and Nixon in his online *FrontPage Magazine* article titled, "Every Republican Presidential Candidate is Hitler." One of my own books, *The End of Racism*, so agitated David Nicholson of the *Washington Post* that he heard "the tread of heavy jackboots, faint and far away, but steadily approaching."[7] These examples confirm Hanson's point that comparing something to the Nazis generally means nothing more than this is something of which the Left strongly disapproves.

Scholars have complained that terms like Nazi and fascist have become virtually meaningless in popular culture. Many years ago the philosopher Leo Strauss, himself a refugee from Nazi Germany, deplored what he termed the *Reductio ad Hitlerum*, by which he meant the tendency to refute whatever one doesn't like by associating it with Hitler. The reasoning goes like this: Hitler didn't like modern art, so criticism of modern art is an evil reminiscent of the Nazis. Hitler detested communism; therefore anti-communists are continuing in the Hitler mode. All of this, Strauss suggested, is pure foolishness.

In California, where pure foolishness is abundant, we hear of "food Nazis," "health Nazis," and "surf Nazis." Nazism, in these cases, appears to be a positive quality, indicating commitment. Historian Anthony James Gregor, a leading scholar of Italian fascism, says that fascism is routinely attributed to people who are avowedly Christian, who seek lower levels of taxation, who oppose further government regulation, who are skeptical about global warming, and who seem indifferent to the fate of endangered species. "Unhappily," he writes, "the term Fascism has been dilated to the point where its cognitive use has become more than suspect."[8]

But the fascist and Nazi charge against Trump and the Republicans cannot be so easily dismissed. In fact, it is not in the same category as the dismissive tropes of Reagan as Hitler or Bush as Hitler. For one, the contemporary charge is far more widespread. Both before and after the election, the Nazi analogy wasn't merely a taunt; it was used as a description. It is now the central organizing theme of Trump coverage in media and academia, and other issues, from immigration to foreign policy to trade, are subsumed under its banner.

For writer Chris Hedges, Trump's presidency is "the dress rehearsal for fascism," which presumably means that fascism, although not here yet, is right around the corner. In the same vein, Ben Cohen saw in Trump "the beginnings of a fascist state." Deepak Malhotra insists in *Fortune* that Trump represents "the specter of homegrown fascism." Andrew

Sullivan warned in the *New Republic* that Trump has "destroyed the Republican Party and created what looks like a neofascist party in its place." Aaron Weinberg of HuffPost diagnosed the "slow crawl of Hitler's fascism." Writing in Salon, historian Fedja Buric sought to strike a note of nuance, insisting, "Trump's not Hitler, he's Mussolini." MSNBC host Rachel Maddow revealed that "I've been reading a lot about what it was like when Hitler first became chancellor…because I think that's possibly where we are." Legal scholar Juan Cole described the result of the election in this way: "How the US went fascist." Documentary filmmaker Ken Burns termed Trump "fascistic" and "Hitleresque." The most over-the-top reaction came from Sunsara Taylor, an activist from a group called Refuse Fascism, who appeared on Tucker Carlson's show to say of Trump, "He's more dangerous than Hitler ever could have been."[9]

Second, the fascist and Nazi charge is endorsed by leading lights in the Democratic Party. Democratic presidential candidate Martin O'Malley accused Trump of taking a "fascist appeal right into the White House." In reference to Trump, Bernie Sanders invoked relatives who died in the Holocaust as a result of "a lunatic…stirring up racial hatred." Invoking the dark memory of "history's worst authoritarians," Senator Elizabeth Warren insisted Trump poses a "serious threat."[10] While Obama and Hillary did not play the fascist or Nazi card, they did not distance themselves from or repudiate it. Nor has any other authority figure in the Democratic Party. How can they disavow it? This is now the motto of the Democratic Left's opposition to Trump.

Third, some foreign leaders seemed to accept that Trump is a fascist, perhaps even a Nazi. In Britain, Labor Member of Parliament Dennis Skinner warned that if his country continued its alliance with America in the wake of Trump's election, it would be walking "hand in hand" with a fascist. In Canada, the New Democratic Party leader Tom Mulcair used the fascist label to describe Trump's temporary travel ban. Two former Mexican presidents, Enrique Calderon and Vicente Fox, likened Trump to Hitler, with Fox noting that Trump's speech at the Republican convention reminded him "of Hitler addressing the Nazi party." These comments give international affirmation to what the American Left says here, and some of it could have implications for U.S. diplomatic relations.[11]

Fourth, some prominent Republicans and conservatives echoed the leftist accusation. At a donor event, former GOP gubernatorial candidate Meg Whitman compared Trump to Hitler and Mussolini. Former New Jersey Republican governor Christine Todd Whitman said of Trump's campaign slogans, "This is the kind of rhetoric that allowed Hitler to move forward." Writing in the *New York Times*, sometime conservative columnist Ross Douthat concluded Trump is a "proto-fascist." Neoconservative historian Robert Kagan had no reservations whatever. "This is how fascism comes to America." After the election, Senator John McCain, the GOP's presidential nominee in 2008, said of Trump's criticism of the media that this is how the dictators of the twentieth century got started.[12] This is unprecedented. When multiple people in your own party say you're a fascist, that makes it seem that you're a fascist.

The Left mobilizes a battery of experts to back up its equation of Trump and the GOP with fascism and Nazism. *Slate* interviewed Robert Paxton, a leading historian of fascism, on the parallels between Trump on the one hand, and Mussolini and Hitler on the other. Bill Maher trotted out historian Timothy Snyder who linked Trump's rise with that of Hitler. "In my world, where I come from, it's the 1930s." Hitler biographer Ian Kershaw made the same point to a British newspaper. "Parallels to the dark period between the two world wars are not to be overlooked." And historian Ron Rosenbaum, author of *Explaining Hitler*, explained Trump as having come to power with "views coming out of a playbook written in German. The playbook is *Mein Kampf.*"[13]

Finally, the fascist charge against Trump isn't a throwaway line; the Left advances a plethora of reasons to back up this accusation. Historian John McNeill took to the *Washington Post* to grade Trump on "the 11 attributes of fascism." Writing on the website Alternet, Kali Holloway declared, "Trump is an eerily perfect match with a famous 14 point guide to identify fascist leaders."[14] This time, the Left and the Democrats seem confident they can make the fascist label stick, and in this way permanently discredit Trump and his supporters.

"Not Our President"

What interests me here are not the Left's reasons for comparing Trump to the fascists and Nazis—I deal with those in the next chapter—but what the comparison is intended to accomplish. Clearly, it seeks to make Trump's presidency illegitimate. This notion—that even if Trump won fair and square, he somehow doesn't deserve to be president—was first circulated even before the election. Hillary and Obama never treated Trump as a legitimate nominee.

Once Trump was elected, the Democratic Left launched an unprecedented crusade to prevent his assuming office. They demanded recounts, which are reasonable when the margins are very close, as they were in the 2000 Bush-Gore election. But Trump's margins were significant in all the crucial states in question. There was a recount or two, and Trump ended up gaining a few votes.

Then the Left sought to discredit Trump's win by highlighting that Hillary won the popular vote. Again, this seems like an odd thing to focus on when U.S. elections are not decided by popular vote. The American political system is designed to balance individual representation and state representation. This is for the purpose of preventing large states from monopolizing power. Consequently, the Electoral College gives larger states more electors but ensures that smaller states also have enough electoral clout to make a difference.

It's not important to decipher the precise rules of the system. The main point is that this is a democratic system and these are the longstanding, agreed-upon rules of the game. In this respect, the rules of the Electoral College are like the rules of a tennis match, which is decided not by points but by sets. Does it make sense, in a match with a final score of 6–4, 6–4, 0–6, 1–6, 6–4 that the loser, despite winning only two sets out of five, nevertheless be awarded the prize on the grounds that he won more overall points than the winner? This is absurd. Trump prevailed by the rules of the game, and his win is clearly undiminished by the observation that Hillary would have won under some other set of rules.

Next the Left sought to directly pressure electors not to choose Trump in the Electoral College. Electors reported being inundated, harassed, even threatened. While most of this was pure desperation—and the effort ultimately failed—Peter Beinart in the *Atlantic Monthly* made a convoluted argument about why "the electoral college was meant to stop men like Trump from being president." No matter what the voters decided, Beinart insisted electors should vote against Trump on the grounds that he is an "irresponsible demagogue" and his victory created a "national emergency."[15]

Finally, the Left sought to discredit the election by saying the Russians rigged it. They rigged it, supposedly, by hacking into Hillary's private server. No proof was ever provided that the Russians did this. And why would the Russians prefer Trump over Hillary? One of Trump's first actions in office was to launch a military strike against Russia's ally Syria. So the very concept of the Russians weighing the scales in favor of Trump makes little sense.

But even if the Russians hacked Hillary's server, they weren't the ones who chose Trump over Hillary. The American voters did. So whatever evidence the Russians may have unearthed, in the end it was the American people who determined the value of that evidence. They are the ones who judged it sufficiently incriminating to give Hillary the boot.

Once Trump fired FBI Director James Comey, the Left—which had criticized Comey's role in the election—went into high dudgeon, generating such a furious storm of accusation that former FBI Director Robert Mueller was named special counsel to investigate potential collusion between the Trump team and Russia. While Mueller's charge was to objectively uncover the facts, the undisguised agenda of the Left is to use the probe to impede Trump's performance, increase pressure for his impeachment, and (if all goes according to plan) to force his resignation.

As all this was going on, I scratched my head over the Left's unembarrassed effort to suppress the valid result of a free election. Then I realized that Mussolini and Hitler, too, came to power through a lawful—or at least quasi-lawful—process. Neither Mussolini nor Hitler staged a coup. The blackshirts marched on Rome in an atmosphere of chaos and Mussolini was invited by King Victor Emmanuel III to form a new government.

Although he never won a popular majority of German voters, Hitler was the head of the largest party in Germany in 1933 when he was made chancellor by President Paul von Hindenburg. A few weeks later the German parliament, the Reichstag, approved the Enabling Act essentially transferring its power to Hitler. Democracy, in other words, paved the way for these despots to seize power. Consequently, for leftwingers who view Trump in the same light as Hitler and Mussolini, an election victory is no justification for allowing an American fascist or Nazi to come to power.

Now it must be said that when a major political party basically rejects the outcome of a free election, we are in uncharted territory. This happened in the United States once before, of course, in 1860, when the same party, the Democrats, refused to accept the election of Abraham Lincoln. The result was a bloody civil war.

Not since Lincoln has an American president faced greater resistance to his legitimacy than Trump. Even so, despite some loose talk about California leaving the union, America is not facing a serious secession movement of the kind that developed in the South in 1860–1861. What we're seeing, rather, is a breakdown of confidence, among the losers of the 2016 election, in the democratic process itself. From their point of view, how could democracy have produced such a frightening and preposterous result?

Nearly seventy Democratic lawmakers refused to attend Trump's inauguration, an unprecedented violation of democratic etiquette that would have provoked massive media outrage had Republicans done it to, say, Bill Clinton or Barack Obama. And just weeks into his presidency, even before Trump had done anything that could remotely be considered unconstitutional, Democratic Congresswomen Maxine Waters and Tulsi Gabbard raised the issue of impeachment. Columnist Richard Cohen even suggested the need for a "constitutional coup"—basically an assembly of elected officials who, according to Cohen, have the authority to remove from office a president whom they deem "unable to discharge the powers and duties of his office."[16]

Even more scandalous, a former Obama defense official, Rosa Brooks, raised the possibility of the U.S. military refusing to obey Trump's orders and perhaps even ousting him from office. If Trump ordered the military to do something that the generals deemed insane, Brooks said, then they might refuse to obey it. And if Trump insisted, Brooks implied, they might have to get rid of him by military coup. A similar argument had been made before the election in the *Los Angeles Times* by James Kirchick of the Foreign Policy Initiative. Kirchick concluded his article, "Trump is not only patently unfit to be president, but a danger to America and the world. Voters must stop him before the military has to."[17]

While rarely stated explicitly, there were also calls for Trump's assassination. Shortly after Trump's election, British journalist Monisha Rajesh wrote, "It's about time for a presidential assassination." Lars Maischak, a historian at Fresno State University, tweeted, "To save American democracy, Trump must hang." At the Women's March in Washington, D.C., singer Madonna ranted, "Yes, I'm angry. Yes, I'm outraged. And I have thought an awful lot about blowing up the White House." Comedian Kathy Griffin notoriously posted a photo of her posing with an image of a bloody, decapitated Trump, resulting in a fire storm of protest that forced her to apologize. The rapper Snoop Dogg released a music video for a song called "Lavender" in which he aims a handgun right at the head of a clown dressed as Trump and pulls the trigger, popping out a red and white flag that reads BANG. Another rapper, Big Sean, spoke of murdering Trump with an icepick.[18] It's hard to know how seriously to take any of this, but one can only imagine the reaction if anyone talked this way about Trump's predecessor Obama.

A similar breakdown of confidence in the democratic process was instrumental in the fascist rise to power in Italy in the 1920s and the Nazi ascent in Germany in the early 1930s. Notice that we are talking about early fascism and Nazism. Today when we think about Mussolini or Hitler it is in terms of World War II. It is impossible to think about Nazism, for example, without also thinking of the Holocaust. But of course this is not how the Italians or the Germans first experienced the fascists and the Nazis.

Nobody is saying that Trump today is Hitler circa 1945. Trump has not started a world war or annexed or invaded other countries, and he has certainly not exterminated six million Jews. This is not the basis of the progressive Democratic critique of Trump. Rather, they liken him to pre-war Mussolini and Hitler, and they warn that, unchecked, he may end up doing horrific things just as those two men eventually did.

In the early 1920s and 1930s, however, it was the fascists and the Nazis who scorned parliamentary democracy with its cumbersome and, to their way of thinking, unworkable rules. These were the parties that declared democratically elected leaders illegitimate and openly backed strategies to oust them from power. So who is doing that in America? Not Trump. Rather, it is the progressive Democrats who continue to question the validity of Trump's presidency. It is the progressives today who refuse to accept the results of election rules and procedures. They are the ones reacting, as the fascists and Nazis did, against what they perceive to be a malfunctioning democratic system.

Then there is the issue of violence. As every scholar of fascism and Nazism knows, the fascists and Nazis gloried in it. They were not alone in this: their political rivals, the socialists and the communists, also believed in violence. Naturally this was a recipe for street bloodbaths. The early days of fascism and Nazism saw routine confrontations between the rival political groups. In Italy, Mussolini's blackshirts fought hand-to-hand with the socialists. Quite a few people were killed in those street battles.

Hitler describes in *Mein Kampf* how his brownshirts would come to political events, typically held in bars and beer halls, armed with bats and sticks. The communists might outnumber us, he writes, but in order to stop our meetings they are going to have to kill us. In Hitler's account there are blows raining and combatants falling to the ground and there he is, continuing with his speech, refusing to be cowed by the mayhem around him.[19]

These confrontations from early fascism and Nazism remind me of the showdowns between the Left and Trump supporters during the campaign. I do not mean merely that the latter are reminiscent of the former. I mean that the anti-Trump protesters view themselves as waging an anti-fascist struggle. Their posters liken Trump to Hitler and Mussolini. One standard depiction is Trump with a Hitler mustache. Another is side-by-side depictions of Trump and Mussolini. The protesters call themselves anti-fascists or Antifa for short.

The election period was dominated by these heated and sometimes violent confrontations. Interestingly they all occurred at Trump rallies; there were no incidents at Hillary rallies. In one case, Trump had to cancel a rally in Chicago because even the police couldn't manage the chaos. In San Jose, leftists pelted Trump supporters with eggs, leading to heated exchanges, including pushing and shoving and blows. While this sort of thing was commonplace in Italy and Germany during the early twentieth century, it has not been seen in American politics since the frenetic outbursts of the 1960s.

Trump himself seemed impatient with the disrupters. In one case he said of a protester, "I'd like to punch him in the face." Of another he said, "In the good old days, they'd have knocked him out of here so fast." Trump once offered to pay the legal fees of supporters who got into scuffles with protesters. Yet never once did Trump urge the disruption of Hillary's rallies. His general stance was, "We have some protesters who are bad dudes. They are really dangerous and they get in here and start hitting people." When a group of Latino protesters attempted to disrupt a rally Trump held in Miami, he told his crowd, "You can get them out, but don't hurt them."[20]

Later a group called Project Veritas released videotaped evidence that the Hillary campaign and leftist groups had paid protesters to provoke violence at Trump rallies. Still, the mainstream media blame the violence on Trump. The argument seemed to be that even when the Left started it, the violence was a natural and justifiable response to Trump's incendiary rhetoric. The media portrayed the Antifa disrupters as heroic resisters trying to block the rise of Nazism in America.

I want to focus on post-election violence because that is very unusual in America. After all, the election is over and the president has been elected. Nevertheless, there were massive protests and disruptions at Trump's inaugural events. These protests were organized by a mélange of groups, the most prominent of which seemed to be one called Refuse Fascism. According to one of its fliers, "It is the fascist character of the Trump/Pence regime which renders it illegitimate and a peril to humanity." The group's call to resistance was signed by, among others, actor Ed Asner, activist Bill Ayers, comedians Margaret Cho and Rosie O'Donnell, and author Alice Walker.[21]

Police braced for a stormy inauguration week, and they were right to come prepared. The trouble started at the DeploraBall, an independently organized soiree by Trump supporter Mike Cernovich, who is accused of being "alt-right." Hundreds of protesters gathered outside, shouting "Nazi scum" and holding up "Alt-Reich" signs as guests walked in. Two men, one in a Hitler mask and the other in a Mussolini mask, held up signs that said, "Trump is Alt-Right with us." When the Trump supporters yelled back at the protesters, the atmosphere became unruly and the leftist protesters threw bottles at DeploraBall attendees and police.[22]

The official inauguration itself drew a much stormier response from the Left. Dressed in black with many wearing masks, the protesters hurled rocks, bricks, and chunks of concrete, smashing storefronts including a downtown McDonald's, Bank of America, and Starbucks. Using garbage bins and newspaper boxes, they set fires in the middle of the street. They also overturned cars and burned them. Members of Black Lives Matter chained themselves to fences at security checkpoints, forcing the Secret Service to close those areas down.

With helicopters hovering overhead, police used chemical spray and noise grenades to drive the protesters back, but when one police SUV attempted to drive through the crowd, protesters pelted it with rocks, smashing the vehicle's rear window. Leftist activists engaged in clashes with police, who finally dispersed them with pepper spray. More than two hundred people were arrested. Interestingly, eleven of them were journalists, who were supposedly there as media but who also seem to have taken part in the rioting.[23]

Around the same time, hundreds of masked resisters showed up at the University of California at Berkeley to prevent a Trump supporter, Milo Yiannopoulos, from speaking. They tore down rows of police barricades, smashed windows, battered ATMs, and threw firecrackers at police. They were joined by several hundred demonstrators, students and leftists from the larger Bay Area, carrying signs with such slogans as THIS IS WAR. The group organizing the protest was called By Any Means Necessary and it described itself as an anti-fascist organization.

The protesters released a statement saying they were fighting to stop "a major fascist operative" from invading their campus. "Let's be clear: Milo Yiannopoulos is not engaging in free speech. He is consciously spearheading the Nazification of the American University."[24] In reality, Yiannopoulos is a conservative provocateur and comedian. He also is flamboyantly gay, proclaims himself a "Dangerous Faggot," and calls Trump "daddy." While he bashes Islam for its vicious suppression of women and homosexuals, he has no association with fascism or Nazism. I can only imagine how he would have fared in Hitler's Germany. Even so, from the resisters' viewpoint, Milo was the Nazi and they were protecting their community from Nazism.

The disrupters had no intention of being peaceful. Their clearly stated objective was to keep Milo out. Police couldn't handle a disruption on this scale so the event was cancelled. Watching the protesters in their all-black attire, with their faces covered, some of them brandishing rods and sticks, I could not help but think of the Italian blackshirts and the Nazi brownshirts, parading the streets with their helmets, bats, brass knuckles, and chains. The surrealism of the atmosphere at Berkeley in a sense reflected the surrealism that has characterized American politics since the beginning of the election season.

So here we have an irony. The Berkeley protesters, like the Trump protesters in D.C., view themselves as anti-fascists. They are there in their masks and with their gear, they say, in order to stop fascism. Yet they are the ones who are enforcing censorship by blocking a speaker from speaking on a campus. They are also the ones lawlessly preventing Trump supporters from attending inauguration events. While the Trump people do their own thing, the leftists are the ones who are in their faces, harassing the Trump supporters, threatening them, breaking and burning things, and engaging in skirmishes with the cops. How, then, is it that the alleged fascists seem to be acting in a peaceful and lawful manner and the anti-fascists seem to most closely resemble the fascists they are supposedly resisting?

A Rationale for Violence

At first, I thought I was merely witnessing the shocked aftermath of a shocking election. The Left did not expect Trump to win. As late as October 20, 2016, the *American Prospect* published an article, "Trump No Longer Really Running for President," the theme of which was that Trump's "real political goal is to make it impossible for Hillary Clinton to govern." The election result was, in the words of columnist David Brooks, "the greatest shock of our lifetimes."[25] Trump won against virtually insurmountable odds, which included the mainstream media openly campaigning for Hillary and a civil war within the GOP with the entire intellectual wing of the conservative movement refusing to support him. Initially I interpreted the Left's violent upheaval as a stunned, heat-of-the-moment response to the biggest come-from-behind victory in U.S. political history.

Then I saw two things that made me realize I was wrong. First, the violence did not go away. There were the violent "Not My President's Day" rallies across the country in February; the violent March 4 disruptions of Trump rallies in California, Minnesota, Tennessee, and Florida; the April anti-Trump tax rallies, supposedly aimed at forcing Trump to release his tax returns; the July impeachment rallies, seeking to build momentum for Trump's removal from office; and the multiple eruptions at Berkeley.[26]

In Portland, leftists threw rocks, lead balls, soda cans, glass bottles, and incendiary devices until police dispersed them with the announcement, "May Day is now considered a riot." Earlier, at the Minnesota State Capitol, leftists threw smoke bombs into the pro-Trump crowd while others set off fireworks in the building, sending people scrambling in fear of a bomb attack. Among those arrested was Linwood Kaine, the son of Hillary's vice presidential candidate Tim Kaine.[27] More of this, undoubtedly, is in store from the Left over the next four years.

What this showed is that the Left was engaging in premeditated violence, violence not as outbreak of passion but violence as a political strategy. Many on the Left justified the violence and made the case for why it was right. How, then, in a democratic society, can citizens insist they are warranted in preventing others from speaking and in disrupting the results of a democratic election?

According to Jesse Benn, writing in *HuffPost*, Trump is a twenty-first century fascist. Moreover, "Trump doesn't exist in a vacuum. He's the natural consequence of Republicans' longstanding embrace of racism...and using immigrants as scapegoats." The rise of fascism, he says, is not a "typical political disagreement between partisans." Fascists historically have only been stopped by "violent insurrection." To believe otherwise, he insists, is to "risk complicity in a new era of fascist politics in the United States."[28]

Writing in the *Atlantic Monthly*, Vann Newkirk insisted that since "democratic institutions have not stopped the rise of Trump...why should people who he proposes to victimize and marginalize trust democratic institutions to protect them?" Trump's very agenda, Newkirk argues, is based on violence: the violence of wall building, the violence of deportation, the violence of keeping people out of America because of their religion, the violence of "punishing women for abortions." Consequently, a vote for Trump is "a vote for a wide promulgation of violence." Facing a fascist threat to their lives and liberties, protesters have no choice but to use force to protect themselves. The only way to stop the violence is for Trump to give up his agenda or for his supporters to replace him with "someone less violent."[29]

Writing in the *Nation*, Natasha Lennard begins with the premise that since Trump represents fascism, "it is constitutive of fascism that it demands a different sort of opposition." Lennard argues it makes no sense to fight fascism with argument; rather, fascism can only be stopped with physical force of the kind used by the militant brigades fighting Franco in Spain or the communist groups that fought Nazis in the 1920s and early 1930s. Anti-fascists, she concludes, are committed to stopping fascists from speaking: "the essential feature of anti-fascism is that it does not tolerate fascism; it would give it no platform for debate."[30]

Writing in *Salon* during the election season, activist Chauncey DeVega began by admitting that "in a functioning democracy, political violence should almost always be condemned." In this case, however, DeVega was willing to make an exception because Trump is a "political arsonist" who is also "on the wrong side of history." According to DeVega, leftist violence is "a response to the threats both overt and implied of physical and other harm made by Donald Trump and his supporters against undocumented Hispanic immigrants, black Americans, other persons of color and Muslims." Carefully note DeVega's language: even if Trump's people are not actually violent, if they are seen to make "overt or implied threats," then the Left is warranted in using actual violence against them.[31]

These sentiments were also echoed in activist Kelly Hayes's article titled, "No Welcome Mat for Fascism: Stop Whining About Trump's Right to Free Speech."[32] Indeed the entire argument of all these writers can be summed up in a single phrase, "No free speech for fascists." This phrase—it turns out—goes back to the 1960s, where it was used by the New Left in protests against the Vietnam War. The inspiration for that slogan came from a Berkeley professor named Herbert Marcuse, who is largely forgotten today, but who was a guru of the 1960s radicals and whose basic arguments are now at the center of the contemporary political debate.

Marcuse argued that the Left is the party of tolerance, but tolerance is not for everybody; it is only for tolerant people. In Marcuse's view, the

Left must not be tolerant of the intolerant. Intolerant people, according to Marcuse, are basically fascists. They refuse to respect the democratic process, so why should they be accorded the respect they withhold from others? Marcuse argued that far from putting up with these right-wing fascists, the Left should repress them, shout them down, even beat them up or kill them. Basically, the Left should destroy fascism by any means necessary, or else the fascists would destroy them.

Marcuse's argument echoes Hitler himself, who said that either the Nazis would destroy the Jews or the Jews would destroy the Nazis. "If they win," Hitler wrote, "God help us! But if we win, God help them!" Marcuse was himself a refugee from Nazi Germany. He fled the brutality of the Nazis. But at the same time he saw the effectiveness of the Nazis in routing enemies and in bringing fellow Germans into submission. Basically Marcuse argued that in order to defeat Nazism in America, it was necessary for the Left to use Nazi tactics.

By Nazi tactics I'm not referring merely to violence by angry students and activists. I am also referring to what the Nazis called *Gleichschaltung*. The term itself means "coordination" and it refers to the Nazi effort to use intimidation across the cultural institutions of society to bring everyone into line with Nazi priorities and Nazi doctrine. Progressives in America are using their dominance—actually their virtual monopoly—in the fields of academia, Hollywood, and the media to enforce their own *Gleichschaltung*.

They do this not merely through the type of blatant propagandizing and outright lying that would do Joseph Goebbels proud, but also through the relentless battering and forced exclusion of dissident voices from their cultural institutions, so that theirs is the only point of view that is communicated to the vast majority of students and citizens. Again, from the point of view of the Left such intimidation and exclusion is warranted because it is right and proper for anti-fascists to use repression against those they deem fascists.

This whole modus operandi—which Marcuse termed "repressive tolerance" and which is encapsulated in the no-free-speech-for-fascists doctrine—is now at the heart of our political debate. It raises two important questions. First, is it true that fascists do not deserve to be heard and that it is justifiable to deny them their civil and constitutional rights? Second—the bigger question—is it true that the people whom the Left calls fascists and Nazis are actually fascists and Nazis?

The Real Fascists

These are the questions I intend to answer in this book. The first question I defer to my final chapter, where I answer it with a resounding no. Interestingly enough, leftists should like my answer, because what I am basically saying is that we should not deprive them of their civil and constitutional rights. They are the real fascists, but even so, they deserve the full protection of the constitution and the laws. At the same time, I agree with the principle that fascists cannot be fought in the normal way. It takes special resolution to defeat a movement so vicious and perverse. What we need to defeat the Left is nothing less than *Denazification*, and at the end of this book I show how this can be done.

Having sort of given away the answer, I now turn to the other and larger question: who are the real fascists in American politics? This question is rarely asked in a serious way, and I want to give credit to two worthy predecessors who earlier ploughed this ground. The first is the economist Friedrich Hayek whose book *The Road to Serfdom*, first published in 1944, made the startling claim that Western welfare-state democracies, having defeated fascism, were themselves moving inexorably in the fascist direction.

Hayek identified fascism as a phenomenon of the Left, a cousin of socialism and progressivism. And he warned, "The rise of fascism and Nazism was not a reaction against the socialist trends of the preceding period but a necessary outcome of those tendencies." While Hayek's book was written in a pedantic, measured tone, appealing to progressives to learn from one who had witnessed firsthand the rise of fascism in Europe, progressive scholars immediately set about reviling Hayek, with one, Herman Finer, accusing him of displaying a "thoroughly Hitlerian contempt for the democratic man."[33]

If you spotted, in this reaction, the familiar progressive ploy of seizing the Hitler card and playing it right back against Hayek, then you are beginning to see how the big lie works. Here is Hayek making a case for how progressives are moving in the direction of Hitler, and without answering this charge and with no supporting evidence whatever, the Left turns around and accuses Hayek of being like Hitler.

Jonah Goldberg received pretty much the same treatment for his important book *Liberal Fascism*. Goldberg argues, "What we call liberalism—the refurnished edifice of American progressivism—is in fact a descendant of and manifestation of fascism." Goldberg argues that fascism and communism, far from being opposites, are "closely related historical competitors for the same constituents." Goldberg terms progressivism a "sister movement of fascism" no less than communism, displaying a "family resemblance that few will admit to recognizing."[34]

Goldberg traces innumerable links between progressivism and fascism, spelling out the left-wing laundry list in both the platforms of Mussolini and Hitler, and then showing their parallel in modern American progressivism. Goldberg uses a broad brush, even detecting an odor of fascism in modern progressive environmentalism, vegetarianism, holistic medicine, and child care policies. Even though he occasionally overdoes his fascist comparisons, his book is well worth reading for its originality and comprehensiveness. Once again, the Left set upon Goldberg with a vengeance, charging him with being, of all things, a fascist.

Hayek and Goldberg are the starting point for my book. But I go much further and delve into areas of inquiry untouched by them. Hayek, for example, asserted that fascism and Nazism emerged out of the Left but he never showed how this occurred. Drawing on the work of scholars like Anthony James Gregor, Renzo De Felice, and Zeev Sternhell, I tell the riveting story of how fascism and Nazism both emerged out of a debate within socialism. The problem began when the central prophecies of Marxism failed to occur. This created a massive crisis within the Left, and essentially Marxism split into two camps: the first became Leninism and Bolshevism, and the other became fascism and Nazism.

Goldberg associates the American Left with fascism, but he does not dare make an equivalent link with Nazism, probably because he doesn't want to risk associating the Left with genocide and concentration camps. This is where my book actually takes off. As Goldberg well knows, fascism and Nazism are two different things. Hitler virtually never referred to himself as a fascist, and Mussolini never ever called himself a Nazi or a National Socialist. I intend to show that there are deep and profound connections not just between the Left and fascism but also between the Left and Nazism.

In some ways the progressive Democrats are even closer to the German Nazis than to the Italian fascists. The Italian fascists, for example, were much less racist than the Democratic Party in the United States. There are no parallels for the costumed racial terrorism of the Democratic Party-backed Ku Klux Klan in Italy, although one can find such parallels in Nazi Germany. Democratic policies of white supremacy, racial segregation, and state-sponsored discrimination were also alien to Italian fascism but right at home in the Third Reich.

Here, for instance, is a passage from Robert Paxton's *The Anatomy of Fascism*: "It may be that the earliest phenomenon that can be functionally related to fascism is American: the Ku Klux Klan." Long before the Nazis, Paxton points out, the Klan adopted its racial uniform of robes and hoods and engaged in the type of intimidation and violence that offered "a remarkable preview of the way fascist movements were to function in interwar Europe."[35] If this seems like a surprising concession by a progressive, Paxton protects his political side by not mentioning that during this period the Ku Klux Klan was the domestic terrorist arm of the Democratic Party.

The racism of the Democratic Party in America not only preceded the racism of the Nazis, it lasted far longer—more than a century compared to the twelve years of Nazi rule in Germany. The Democratic Party's racism after the Civil War was preceded by the Democratic Party's defense of slavery and its support of policies for the relocation and extermination of American Indians. We think of concepts like "genocide" and "concentration camps" as unique to Nazism, but what term other than genocide can we use to describe Democratic president Andrew Jackson's mass relocation of the Indians? Didn't Jackson and his allies systematically seek to dispossess, disinherit, and dismember the Indians as a people? Using the official United Nations definition of genocide, I show that he did.

Moreover, what is the slave plantation if not a special type of concentration camp? This may seem like an outrageous analogy. How can anyone compare a forced labor system, however unjust, to Nazi camps designed and used to kill people? But as we will see, the concentration camps were also work camps. In the German camps and on the Democrat-run plantations, forced labor was employed with "human tools" solely with regard to productivity and with little if any regard for the lives of the workers who were, in both cases, considered inferior and even subhuman. The analogy between two of the worst compulsory confinement and forced labor systems in human history is not merely legitimate; it is overdue.

Moreover, this whole issue has been raised to a completely new level since the publication of historian Stanley Elkins's path-breaking book *Slavery*. Elkins not only drew an elaborate comparison of the plantation as a "closed system" akin to a concentration camp, he also showed that slavery produced personality types eerily similar to those described by Nazi camp survivors. So the point is that even on some of the institutions and practices uniquely associated with the Nazis—from genocide to the concentration camp—the Democrats in a sense got there first.

Learning from Hitler

In this book I will show what the Left learned from the Nazis, and also what the Left taught the Nazis. It turns out that the Left provided the Nazis with some very important policy schemes that the Nazis then murderously implemented in Europe. Hitler, for instance, specifically said he intended to displace and exterminate the Russians, the Poles, and the Slavs in precisely the way Americans in the Jacksonian era had displaced and exterminated the native Indians. The Nazi Nuremberg Laws were directly modeled on the segregation and anti-miscegenation laws that had been implemented decades earlier in the Democratic South.

Forced sterilization and euthanasia aimed at eliminating racial "defectives" and producing a "superior" Nordic race were two additional schemes the Nazis got from American progressives. This is not my view of the matter; it is the Nazi eugenicists' view of the matter. In the early twentieth century, eugenics and social Darwinism were far more prevalent in America than they were in Germany. Margaret Sanger and her fellow progressive eugenicists didn't get their ideas for killing off undesirables—or preventing their births—from the Nazis; the Nazis got them from their American counterparts who dominated the field of international eugenics. So there is a two-way traffic between Nazism and the American Left.

This is a story that deeply implicates the heroes of American progressivism: Woodrow Wilson, Franklin D. Roosevelt, and John F. Kennedy. Wilson was a veritable progenitor of American fascism. I call him a proto-fascist. In addition, he was a racist who was almost single-handedly responsible for the revival of the Ku Klux Klan, the organization that, according to historian Robert Paxton, is the closest American precursor to a Nazi movement.

As we will see, Franklin D. Roosevelt was an avid admirer of Mussolini who sought to import Italian fascist schemes to America. FDR also collaborated with the worst racist elements in America, working with them to block anti-lynching laws and exclude blacks from New Deal programs and name a former Klansman to the Supreme Court. Mussolini, for his part, praised FDR's book *Looking Forward* and basically declared FDR to be a fellow fascist. Hitler too saw FDR as a kindred spirit and the New Deal was widely praised as an American form of fascism in the Nazi Party's official newspaper *Volkischer Beobachter* and other Nazi publications.

JFK toured Nazi Germany in the 1930s and came back effusive with praise of Hitler and his theory of Nordic superiority. "I have come to the conclusion," JFK wrote in his diary, "that fascism is right for Germany and Italy." Touring the Rhineland, JFK echoed Nazi propaganda at the time. "The Nordic races appear to be definitely superior to the Romans." Hostility toward Hitler, JFK insisted, stems largely from jealousy. "The Germans really are too good—that's why people conspire against them." Even though JFK fought in World War II, he retained a soft spot for Hitler as late as 1945, when he described him as the "stuff of legends…Hitler will emerge from the hate that now surrounds him and come to be regarded as one of the most significant figures to have lived."[36]

These incriminating facts are known to many progressive scholars. But after Word War II, as this group came increasingly to dominate the academy—a dominance that was fully consolidated by the late 1960s—the progressives recognized how crushing it would be if Americans knew about the actual record of progressivism and the Democratic Party. What if people, especially young people, knew the links between revered progressive figures like Wilson, FDR, and JFK on the one hand, and the hated Mussolini and Hitler on the other? Such knowledge would not merely topple progressive heroes from their pedestal. Basically it would be the end of progressivism and the Democratic Party.

So progressives decided to tell a new story, and this is the story that has now become our conventional wisdom. In this story, the very fascism and Nazism that were, from the outset, on both sides of the Atlantic, recognized as left-wing phenomena now got moved into the right-wing column. Suddenly Mussolini and Hitler became "right-wingers," and the people who supposedly brought them to power became "conservatives." The Left, then, became the glorious resisters of fascism and Nazism.

To make this story work, fascism and Nazism had to be largely redefined. The big problem was that Mussolini and Hitler both identified socialism as the core of the fascist and Nazi *weltanschauung*. Mussolini was the leading figure of Italian revolutionary socialism and never relinquished his allegiance to it. Hitler's party defined itself as championing "national socialism." So the progressives had to figure out how to move these avowed left-wingers to the Right, and how to get the "socialism" out of "national socialism." This was not an easy task.

How to do it? Taking a cue from the Marxists, the Left resolved as early as the 1960s to suppress altogether the fact that fascism and Nazism were systems of thought. According to the left-wing historian Denis Mack Smith, "Italian fascism originated not as a doctrine but as a method, as a technique for winning power, and at first its principles were unclear even to its own members." Historian Ruth Ben-Ghiat, who is extensively quoted in the media linking Trump to fascism, insists nevertheless that fascism is "one of those words that is very hard to define precisely" because "fascism was all about contradictions, and this kind of ambiguity has remained in fascism."[37]

In reality, such nonsense can only be sustained by refusing to take seriously the fascists themselves. As historian Anthony James Gregor writes, "Under the crabbed influence of the Marxist analysis of fascism, fascist statements are never analyzed as such. They are always 'interpreted.' Fascists are never understood to mean what they say. As a consequence, there has been very little effort, to date, to provide a serious account of fascism as an ideology."[38] Instead the Left identified fascism with amorphous tendencies that could just as easily be applied to numerous other political doctrines: authoritarianism, militarism, nationalism, and so on.

Think about this: we know the name of the philosopher of capitalism, Adam Smith. We also know the name of the philosopher of Marxism, Karl Marx. So, quick, what is the name of the philosopher of fascism? Yes, exactly. You don't know. Virtually no one knows. My point is that this is not because there were no foundational thinkers behind fascism—you will meet them in this book—but rather that the Left had to get rid of them in order to avoid confronting their unavoidable socialist and leftist orientation. So—as with *Hillary's America*—the progressives agreed among themselves to say, "let's all pretend that none of this exists, shall we?" This is the big lie in full operation.

If statism and collectivism are at the core of fascism, national socialism adds another explosive ingredient—anti-Semitism. This much is well known. What the progressives have carefully disguised, however, is the degree to which Nazi anti-Semitism grew out of Hitler's hatred for capitalism. Hitler draws a crucial distinction between productive capitalism, which he can abide, and finance capitalism, which he associates with the Jews. For Hitler, the Jew is the unproductive money-grubber at the center of finance capitalism, the entrepreneurial swindler par excellence. This hardly sounds "right-wing"; in fact, with some slight modification, it echoes progressive rhetoric about greedy Wall Street investment bankers. Thus progressives realized the necessity of hiding the true basis of Hitler's anti-Semitism, and to do this, anti-Semitism itself had to be redefined.

As you can see, we are dealing with a big, big lie—a lie that keeps getting bigger, and one that encompasses many smaller lies—so I have my work cut out for me. But we need to understand the big lie in all its dimensions in order to be free of it. Once we are free of it, the Left is finished. Their power over us is gone. They had the race card and now they have the Nazi card, but they have no other cards left. If they lose this one, they lose their moral capital and are exposed for what they are—the bigoted, thuggish, self-aggrandizing thieves of our lives and liberties. They are the true descendants of Mussolini and Hitler, and in defeating them we can finally lay to rest the ghosts of fascism and Nazism.

Two

Falsifying History

Propaganda is always a means to an end.
The propaganda that produces the desired results is good
and all other propaganda is bad.[1]

Joseph Goebbels, Nazi Minister of Propaganda

This chapter exposes the falsification of history that supports the accusation that Trump and the GOP are twenty-first century fascists and Nazis. The falsification is the product of seventy years of progressive deception and cover-up. The deception involves highlighting the incidental features of Mussolini and Hitler and pretending that they represent fascism at its core. The cover-up involves hiding the real essence of fascism—including the very name of the leading philosopher of fascism—because once that essence is exposed, it becomes obvious that Trump and the GOP cannot possibly be fascist, and that, on the contrary, fascism and Nazism are both ideologies of the Left. Indeed, we will see startling parallels between the central themes of twentieth-century fascism and Nazism and those of twenty-first-century American progressivism.

Before we get into this topic, it's important to clear up what we mean by the terms "Left" and "Right." The political use of the two terms dates back to 1789 and the French Revolution. In the National Assembly in Paris, the partisans of the Revolution sat on the left side and their opponents sat on the right. This is how we got our original "left-wing" and "right-wing." The term "right-wing" in this context refers to defenders of the Ancien Régime who wanted France to return to the governing alliance of throne and altar that had preceded the revolution. "Conservative" became a description of the old guard who wanted to conserve the monarchy and the prerogatives of the established church against revolutionary overthrow.

So right away we have a problem: if this is what "right-wing" and "conservative" mean, then there are no right-wingers or conservatives in America. America has never had either a monarchy or an established church. Modern American conservatives have no intention to introduce either. In what sense, then, are modern conservatives right-wing? What is it that American conservatives want to conserve?

The answer is pretty simple. They want to conserve the principles of the American Revolution. So while the French Right opposed the French Revolution, the American Right champions the American Revolution. If it seems paradoxical to use the terms "conserve" and "Revolution" in the same sentence, this paradox nevertheless defines the modern-day conservative. The American Revolution was characterized by three basic freedoms: economic freedom or capitalism, political freedom or constitutional democracy, and freedom of speech and religion. These are the freedoms that, in their original form, American conservatives seek to conserve.

As the founders understood it, the main threat to freedom comes from the federal government. Our rights, consequently, are protections against excessive government intrusion and intervention. That's why the Bill of Rights typically begins, "Congress shall make no law." By placing fetters or restraints on the federal government, we secure our basic rights and liberties. The objective of these rights and liberties is for Americans to devote their lives to the "pursuit of happiness." Happiness is the goal and rights and liberties are the means to that goal. Right-wingers in

America are the ones who seek to protect the rights of Americans to pursue happiness by limiting the power of the central state.

"An elective despotism," Jefferson said, "is not what we fought for."[2] Jefferson's Democratic-Republican Party preceded our current two-party system, but his sentiment is one that American right-wingers and conservatives would heartily endorse. Even elected governments do not have unlimited power. They must operate within a specified domain; when they go beyond that domain, they become a threat to our freedom and, in this respect, tyrannical. We are under no more obligation to obey an elected tyranny than the founders themselves were obliged to obey the tyrannical authority of the British Crown.

By limiting state power, conservatives seek among other things to protect the right of people to keep the fruits of their own labor. Abraham Lincoln, America's first Republican president, placed himself squarely in the founding tradition when he said, "I always thought the man who made the corn should eat the corn." Lincoln, like the founders, was not concerned that private property or private earnings might cause economic inequality. Rather, he believed, as three of the founders themselves wrote in *Federalist Paper* No. 10, that "the protection of different and unequal faculties of acquiring property" is the "first object of government."[3]

American conservatives also seek to conserve the transcendent moral order that is not specified in the Constitution but clearly underlies the American founding. Consider, as a single example, the proposition from the Declaration of Independence that we are all "created equal" and endowed with "inalienable rights" including the "right to life." This means for conservatives that human life is sacred, it has a dignity that results from divine creation, it is so precious that the right to life cannot be sold even with the consent of the buyer and seller, and finally that no government can violate the right to life without trespassing on America's most basic moral and political values.

So much for the political Right, what about the Left? The Left in America is defined by its hostility to the restrictions placed by the founders on the federal government. That's why leftists regularly deplore constitutional restraints on government power, proclaiming the Constitution woefully out of date and calling for us to adopt instead a "living Constitution"—a Constitution adapted to what the Left considers progressive. Indeed many leftists today use "progressive" as their preferred political label. They used to call themselves "liberal," a term which refers to liberality or freedom; now they use "progressive," a term which identifies them with the future as opposed to the past.

Progress by itself is a vacant term; we need to know what progressives mean when they use it. What they mean is progress toward greater federal power and federal control. The progressives, in other words, are champions of the power of the centralized state. Two very bad words in modern progressivism are "state's rights." Progressives are happiest when the federal government is running things, and when they are in charge of the federal government. That's what ensures "progress"; any setbacks to this program represent "reaction" and "regress." No wonder leftists term conservatives who resist expanding government power as "regressive" or "reactionary."

But why does state power have to be so centralized? While the founders viewed the government as the enemy of rights, the progressive Left regards the federal government as the friend and securer of rights. Moreover, progressives distrust the free-market system and want the government to control and direct the economy, not necessarily nationalizing or taking over private companies, but at least regulating their operations and on occasion mandating their courses of action.

In addition, the Left seeks government authority to enforce and institutionalize progressive values like federally funded abortion and equal treatment of gays and transsexuals. From its abortion stance alone we see that the Left rejects the idea of a transcendent moral order as firmly as it rejects the conservative principle of an inalienable right to life. So if "Right" in America means a limited, nonintrusive government with a wide scope for the individual pursuit of happiness, "Left" in America means a powerful centralized state that implements leftist values and is controlled by the Left.

Introducing the Lie

Equipped with our understanding of Left and Right, let's now begin our investigation of whether Trump and the GOP are somehow allied with fascism and Nazism, and if not, who is. There is no point in beginning with the various pundits like Bill Maher, Chris Matthews, Michael Kinsley, or Chris Hedges who have, in their own vulgar fashion, equated Trump with Hitler. It seems obvious that none of them knows anything about fascism beyond cocktail-party blather. Typical is Matthews who termed Trump's firing of FBI Director James Comey a "whiff of fascism" even though the president has every right to replace his FBI director, as Bill Clinton did.[4] I pass over the others in silence.

But things become interesting when a major progressive scholar of fascism gets involved. So I begin with two interviews from historian Robert Paxton, author of *The Anatomy of Fascism*, followed by a telling quotation from that book. The first interview is with left-wing radio host Amy Goodman, who seemed quite exercised by Trump re-tweeting a Mussolini quotation. The quotation read, "It is better to live one day as a lion than 100 years as a sheep." When asked to recant, Trump refused. "It's a very good quote," he said. "What difference does it make whether it's Mussolini or somebody else?" Here is Trump's trademark fearlessness. He regards the quotation by itself as benign and refuses to be scared off by the supposedly radioactive association with Mussolini. Paxton drily comments of Trump, "I think he's quite tolerant of these kinds of political oratory." Elsewhere in the conversation, Paxton notes that, just like Hitler, "Not so very long ago Trump was a guaranteed laugh line. He was considered a buffoon. All you had to do was to show the hair and call him 'the Donald' and everyone kind of snickered."[5] So the buffoon-to-power transition supposedly links Trump with the führer.

In his second interview, with Isaac Chotiner of *Slate*, Paxton gets more substantive. "The use of ethnic stereotypes and the exploitation of fear of foreigners is directly out of a fascist's recipe book. Making the country great again sounds exactly like the fascist movements. Concerns about national decline, that was one of the most prominent emotional states evoked in fascist discourse, and Trump is using that full-blast. An aggressive foreign policy to arrest the supposed decline. That is a fascist stroke." There is a lot here, and I will deal with it presently, but I would like to point out that there are many other American presidents who have talked about national decline, promised to restore the country, and promoted an aggressive foreign policy without being accused of reading out of the fascist recipe book.

Then Paxton continues, "I read an absolutely astonishing account of Trump arriving for a political speech and his audience was gathered in an airplane hangar and he landed his plane at the field and taxied up to the hangar and got out. This is exactly what they did in 1932 for Hitler's first election victory. I suppose it was accidental, but wow, that is an almost letter-perfect replay of a Hitler election tactic." So Trump is guilty of Hitler election tactics because he landed in a plane and there were people gathered at the hangar? Instead of content linking Trump to fascism, Paxton concluded with the observation that Trump "even looks like Mussolini in the way he sticks his lower jaw out."[6] No comments from Paxton on whether Trump has the same affection for Italian food that Mussolini did.

Finally, I turn to a passage in *The Anatomy of Fascism* where Paxton, having dutifully noted the collapse of Hitler's and Mussolini's regimes in World War II, speculates whether fascism might come to America and, if so, what it might look like. "The language and symbols of an authentic American fascism," he writes, "would have little to do with the original European models. They would have to be as familiar and reassuring to loyal Americans as the language and symbols of the original fascisms were familiar and reassuring to many Italians and Germans. No swastikas in an American fascism, but Stars and Stripes and Christian crosses. No fascist salute, but mass recitations of the pledge of allegiance."[7]

Notice what Paxton is communicating in this passage and in the two preceding interviews. As a good progressive, he is giving the left-wing outlets in the media what they want. He does some appropriate hemming and hawing—at one point, he notes that Trump's individualism is not entirely consistent with fascism—but he still confirms that Trump is, on the balance, a kind of fascist and proto-Nazi. He definitively links fascism with the patriotic displays of the American Right. Yet he makes no mention of limited government or capitalism or any of the core defining features of American conservatism.

At no point does Paxton suggest that there is anything about Obama or Hillary that mirrors fascism or Nazism. Fascism is an Italian term that means "groupism" or "collectivism." The *fasci* in Italy were groups of political activists who got their name from the *fasces* of ancient Rome—the bundles of rods carried by the lictors to symbolize the unified strength of the Romans. The core meaning of the term *fascism* is that people are stronger in groups than they are as individuals.

Paxton of course knows this, but he thinks it's better not to mention it. In fact, not once does he even hint that fascism might be a phenomenon of the political Left. And throughout these interviews we are struck by how little Paxton actually tells us about fascism, about what it is. Not once does he cite a fascist thinker who gives us the fascist understanding of fascism—all we get is the progressive interpretation that seems to move quickly from a few generalities like national decline and patriotism to its resolute conclusion.

Again, I'm not saying Paxton doesn't know better. We can see from his book that he does. He knows the relevant documents; he references them. He is familiar with the fascist intellectuals; he cites them. That is what makes his performance so intriguing. While knowing better, Paxton is telling ignorant people just enough to confirm their prejudices, while maintaining his scholarly bona fides. In the end, I want to suggest, Paxton is knowingly participating in the big lie.

So this is how the big lie is disseminated: wily academics like Paxton lay the intellectual foundation, and the media and Hollywood then say, "Look, here's a guy who actually knows his stuff confirming that our political hit is justified." Interestingly Paxton's field is neither Nazism nor Italian fascism; it is Vichy France. Anthony James Gregor is the greatest living authority on fascism, and Stanley Payne recently published a definitive book on the history of fascism. Yet the progressive media never approaches them for interviews.

Why? Here is a direct quotation from Gregor's *The Ideology of Fascism*: "The movement itself was not conservative. It was revolutionary. Its clear intention was to destroy all the social, economic and political artifacts of classical liberalism." And here is a quote from Payne: "The nucleus that eventually founded fascism in Italy did not stem from the right-wing nationalists but from the transformation of part of the revolutionary left."[8] From a leftist point of view, this is very inconvenient. So why interview Gregor or Payne when they are likely to directly contradict what the Left is attempting to prove? That's why they found Paxton, because Paxton was willing to play their game. They offer him academic celebrity, and he tells them what they want to hear. This is how the big lie works.

Trump's Fascist Rating

Now let's turn to some alleged characteristics of fascism and Nazism that are invoked by the Left to prove that Trump (and sometimes the GOP and conservatives) resembles fascists and Nazis. In each case, we'll see that the claim is completely false and that Trump's fascism rating is close to zero. What makes the falsehoods doubly interesting is that, in most cases, they are double lies. What I mean by this is not merely that Trump and the GOP aren't what the Left makes them out to be, but fascism and Nazism aren't what the Left makes them out to be either. So the accused is literally innocent on two counts: he didn't do what he's accused of doing, and what he's accused of doing is not the criminal offense that is alleged. I'm going to deal with the biggest charge first and then take up the other ones.

Racism and xenophobia: this is the hot-button charge. Every comparison between Trump and the Nazis goes here. Elizabeth Warren explains Trump's rise as the product of "an ugly stew of racism." Historian James Whitman warns that "white nationalism lives in the White House." Jeet

Heer charges in the *New Republic* that Trump's "racism and xenophobia" display his "fascist roots" that are not his alone but "lie in the Republican Party." Along the same lines, leftist writer Michael Tomasky traces a "direct and indisputable" line from "racist and xenophobic movements" to "Trump's GOP," concluding, "They're supporting Trump as white people because they feel he will protect their white privilege."[9]

Yet the evidence for Trump's racism and xenophobia is sorely lacking. Perhaps the strongest basis for the charge is that the Left has uncovered some white supremacists and anti-Semites who say they back Trump. One of them, Richard Spencer, held a notorious rally during which he and his few dozen supporters cried out, "Hail Trump." Spencer seems here to be doing his best Hitler imitation. Yet if these racists and anti-Semites endorse Trump, Trump himself doesn't endorse them. The best the Left can show is that Trump has retweeted some statements by white nationalists even though the statements themselves are benign. I retweet people all the time without knowing much about them. The conventions of social media do not require that we check out the backgrounds of the people that we retweet.

Over the course of American history many racists voted for Lincoln—who actively courted the anti-immigrant, Know-Nothing vote—and Wilson and FDR, who actively sought the votes of avowed racists. It doesn't follow that Lincoln, Wilson, and FDR were racists. As I've shown in my previous work, Lincoln clearly wasn't a racist. Later in this book I'll prove independently that Wilson was a racist and FDR was in bed with the worst racists in America. My point here is simply that the racist vote by itself doesn't make its beneficiary a racist.

Obviously, the question still remains: why do these guys like Trump if Trump isn't a racist like them? One possible answer is that these are jobless guys, losers in society, some of them total imbeciles. Whatever they call themselves—fascists or something else—frankly I don't believe they are fascists or know much about fascism. Hitler would have sent most of them straight to the gas chambers. (Let's recall that one of the earliest categories of people Hitler euthanized were the so-called "imbeciles.") It's quite possible that these guys voted for Trump because they expect him to bring back unskilled jobs. So even if Trump is not a racist, it's still possible that racists would like him for reasons that have nothing to do with racism.

Is Trump a racist and xenophobe because he "hates immigrants" and once called a Hispanic federal judge a "Mexican"? Yes, I know the judge in question is a U.S. citizen of Mexican descent. I'm a U.S. citizen of Asian and Indian descent, so that would be like calling me an "Asian Indian." If someone intends to insult me by calling me that, I'm not offended; what's the big deal? Even for those who are thin-skinned, Trump was at worst being somewhat insensitive. Insensitivity is not the same thing as bigotry.

Trump's statements about Muslims cannot be termed racist for the simple reason that Islam is a religion, not a race. Can they, however, be termed xenophobic or anti-Muslim? Certainly the Muslims themselves don't seem to think so. In May 2017, Trump visited Saudi Arabia, the most devout Muslim country in the world, and he received a hero's welcome. Trump's reception in the region contrasts sharply with the reception Obama received. Despiste Obama's craven kowtowing to Islam, he was routinely treated with contempt and suspicion by America's Muslim allies in the region.

Let's consider Trump's executive order banning travel to America from several Muslim-majority countries. These countries happen to be breeding grounds for terrorists. They are also countries where the vetting of people, some of whom have been displaced from their homes and communities, is especially difficult. John Locke says that whatever other tasks a government undertakes—whether humanitarian or otherwise—its primary duty is to protect its own citizens from foreign and domestic thugs. That isn't fascism; it's classical liberalism.

Similarly, classical liberalism holds that a liberal society is a social compact among citizens who agree to come together for certain benefits and protections that they seek in common. In exchange for these protections and privileges, they give up the exercise of some of their natural rights. The point here is that natural rights belong to everyone, but civil and constitutional rights are the product of a social compact. It follows, therefore, that civil rights belong only to citizens. Aliens who are not part of the American social compact don't have any constitutional rights. Again, Trump's denial that illegal aliens have a constitutional right to be here is in the mainstream of the liberal tradition.

Trump isn't against "immigrants" for the simple reason that illegal aliens are not immigrants. Leftists in Congress and the media routinely conflate legal and illegal immigrants as in New York Governor Andrew Cuomo's comical rant, "We are all immigrants," and in this *New York Times* front-page headline: "More Immigrants Face Deportation Under New Rules."[10] According to this leftist narrative, my wife Debbie (an immigrant from Venezuela) and I (an immigrant from India) should be living in fear. But this is a lie, and Cuomo and the editors of the *New York Times* know it. Trump has no intention to send us packing to our countries of origin. Trump's distinction is between legal immigrants and lawbreakers who seek to circumvent the immigration process.

This is not a racial distinction. Trump has never said that America is a white man's country or that brown or black people should not emigrate here. Most immigrants today come from Asia, Africa, and South America, and Trump seems fine with that. Contrast Trump's position with that of Hitler. The Jews of Germany were legal immigrants or descended from legal immigrants. They were German citizens. Yet Hitler did not consider them to be true Germans. The Nuremberg Laws stripped Jews of their German citizenship. So for Hitler the line was not between legal and illegal immigrants. It was not even between immigrants and native-born Germans. Rather, it was a racial line between Nordics or Aryan Germanic people on the one hand, and Jews and other non-Aryan "inferiors" on the other.

Finally, anti-Semitism. During the campaign, Trump ran an ad condemning the "global power structure" for "stripping our country of its wealth" and "putting money into the pockets of a handful of large corporations and political entities." Senator Al Franken responded, "When I saw the ad, I thought that this was something of a German Shepherd dog whistle. It had an Elders of Zion feeling to it, an international banking conspiracy to it." Franken here is invoking the notorious anti-Semitic tract *The Protocols of the Elders of Zion* to charge that Trump is anti-Semitic. In the same vein, David Denby in the *New Yorker* and Peter Dreier in the leftist journal the *American Prospect* both compare Trump to the notorious anti-Semitic radio demagogue from the 1930s: Father Charles Coughlin.[11]

What Denby and Dreier fail to mention is that Charles Coughlin was a rabid leftist. Dreier actually calls Coughlin "right-wing" because "he used his radio program to promote anti-Semitic conspiracy theories and to support Adolf Hitler and Benito Mussolini." But this of course begs the question: were Hitler and Mussolini right-wing? In the course of this book you will see me definitively show that they were not. Dreier is simply making an *argumentum ad ignorantium*—an argument based on the ignorance of his audience. In sum, he's relying on the big lie.

Denby portrays Coughlin as an opponent of FDR, noting that he "could not stop FDR from triumphing politically." Denby omits that in 1932 Coughlin was an enthusiastic supporter of FDR and a ferocious critic of President Hoover and the Republicans. In the 1932 presidential election, Coughlin presented the country with a simple choice: "Roosevelt or Ruin." Given Coughlin's mammoth radio audience, he is widely credited with helping FDR get elected.

Later Coughlin broke with FDR—this is what Denby is referring to—but only because he considered FDR to have sold out some of his own principles. In 1935 Coughlin founded the National Union of Social Justice to put pressure on FDR from the Left. In his newspaper—tellingly named *Social Justice*—and on his radio show, Coughlin inveighed against Roosevelt for failing to nationalize the Federal Reserve and the banks and for other alleged concessions to the capitalist class.

Trump can't be a modern-day Father Coughlin because Father Coughlin was a man of the far Left. In fact, Coughlin's anti-Semitism is in stark contrast with Trump's philo-Semitism. And in Trump's case, his pro-Jewish stance is hardly a surprise. He has a Jewish daughter-in-law, a Jewish son-in-law who is also one of his closest advisers, a daughter on whom he dotes who converted to Judaism, and Jewish grandchildren.

As we can see from his April 2017 Holocaust remembrance speech and his May address at Israel's Yad Vashem memorial, Trump is unapologetically pro-Jewish and pro-Israel in a way that his predecessor Barack Obama never was. In the words of Israel's prime minister, Netanyahu, "There is no greater supporter of the Jewish people and the Jewish state than President Donald Trump."[12] In sum, Trump is no racist, he is no xenophobe, and he is no anti-Semite.

Characteristics of Nazism

Now it's time to deal with the other characteristics that are said to establish Trump's association with fascism and Nazism.

Insanity: One of the oddest things regularly asserted about Trump is that he is literally insane. Columnists Andrew Sullivan and Paul Krugman are the two most insistent peddlers of this thesis; Rosie O'Donnell echoed it. Two Democratic congressmen have introduced legislation to take the nuclear football out of Trump's hands, and one of them, Ted Lieu, has a second bill in Congress requiring Trump to get psychiatric counseling.[13] Why this insistence on Trump being a loon? The underlying connection is with Hitler and Mussolini. A whole generation of progressive commentary insists that these two were insane. What else would make them kill so many millions of people and launch a world war?

But Trump is clearly not insane. He has certainly never been diagnosed with any kind of mental illness. He is highly successful in business. He has a dedicated wife and extremely well brought up children. He got himself elected, and now he's handling the most extreme opposition with aplomb. Clearly there's a method to his madness. Nor were Hitler and Mussolini insane. Evil, yes, but not insane. Cold-blooded murder does not make you crazy. There are innumerable killers in prison and on death row who aren't insane. (In fact, if they were, they would be "not guilty by reason of insanity.") Conversely there are innumerable insane people in asylums who haven't harmed anyone. So enough with the insanity nonsense. It's a too-easy way to dismiss Trump and a too-easy way to avoid confronting the real evil of Hitler and Mussolini.

Reactionary: Trump and the GOP are routinely described as a "reactionary," and the label is equally used to discredit conservatives. The classic text here is leftist scholar Corey Robin's *The Reactionary Mind*, which identifies the American Right with the "fighting nostalgia" that Hitler and Mussolini appealed to. Although the book was published in 2012, Matt Feeney termed it just days before the 2016 election as "the book that predicted Trump."[14] So in this view Trump and conservatives are, just like the fascists and Nazis, extreme reactionaries.

The reactionary charge is convenient for the Left because it associates conservatism and fascism with the past, and distinguishes it from progressivism, which is obviously concerned with the future. What makes the charge believable on the surface is that Trump, like most conservatives, seems to want America to get back to the good old days. Isn't that what Hitler promised to do? Wasn't his Third Reich a reactionary attempt to restore the First Reich of Charlemagne and the Second Reich of Bismarck?

Perhaps, but Trump's promised restoration is concerned with bringing back jobs. It is also about making government smaller and less bureaucratic. It is not about repealing progress in America on civil rights or women going to work. It is not about sending gays back into the closet. So, too, modern conservatism is about restoring the ideals of the founders, not the actual agrarian, undeveloped world in which the founders lived. So the Right seeks to apply old principles—which it considers enduring or permanent truths—in our situation today to create a better future. There is nothing reactionary about that.

Nor were Mussolini's fascism or Hitler's National Socialism reactionary in the classic sense. "All of Hitler's political ideas," Stanley Payne writes in *A History of Fascism*, "had their origin in the Enlightenment." Historian Richard Evans wrote that "none of the voters who flocked to the polls in support of Hitler" sought "to restore a lost past. On the contrary, they were inspired by a vague yet powerful vision of the future."

This vision invoked symbols from the past, but it "did not involve just looking back, or forward, but both."[15]

One of the groups that most strongly supported fascism in Italy was the self-designated Futurists. Led by Filippo Marinetti, the futurists championed fast cars and new technologies and viewed themselves as being on the cutting edge of both the sciences and art. This was the group that encouraged fascism and Nazism to use new advances in technology and up-to-date techniques of media and propaganda. Historian Zeev Sternhell concludes that far from being reactionary, "The conceptual framework of fascism...was nonconformist, avant-garde and revolutionary in character."[16]

The fascists and the Nazis sought to create a new man and a new utopia freed from the shackles of the old religion and old allegiances. The whole mood of fascism and Nazism is captured in the Nazi youth depicted in the movie *Cabaret* who sings not about a lost past but rather a "tomorrow" that "belongs to me." Fascism's appeal was, as both its critics and enthusiasts recognized at the time, more progressive and forward-looking than it was backward and reactionary.

Authoritarianism: This is a big one. "An American Authoritarian" reads a headline in the *Atlantic Monthly* linking Trump to Mussolini. After Trump's election, *New York* magazine fretted in a headline, "The Republic Repeals Itself." Two political scientists, Steven Levitsky and Daniel Ziblatt, write in the *New York Times* that Trump is not the "first American politician with authoritarian tendencies" but "he is the first in modern American history to be elected president." Invoking parallels to the authoritarian despots Hitler and Mussolini, historian Timothy Snyder notes that Trump "has said almost nothing in favor of democracy" and threatens the system of checks and balances by "denigrating judges."[17]

Hitler and Mussolini were indeed authoritarians, but it doesn't follow that authoritarianism equals fascism or Nazism. Lenin and Stalin were authoritarian, but neither was a fascist. Many dictators—Franco in Spain, Pinochet in Chile, Perón in Argentina, Amin in Uganda—were authoritarian without being fascists or Nazis. Trump admittedly has a bossy style that he gets from, well, being a boss. He has been a corporate boss all his life, and he also played a boss on TV. Republicans elected Trump because they needed a tough guy to take on Hillary; previously they tried bland, harmless candidates like Romney, and look where that got them.

That being said, Trump has done nothing to subvert the democratic process. While progressives continue to allege a plot between Trump and the Russians to rig the election, the only evidence for actual rigging comes from the Democratic National Committee's attempt to rig the 2016 primary in favor of Hillary over Bernie. This rigging evoked virtually no dissent from Democratic officials or from the media, suggesting the support, or at least acquiescence, of the whole progressive movement and most of the party itself.

Trump fired his FBI director, provoking dark ruminations in the *Washington Post* about Trump's "respect for the rule of law," yet Trump's action was entirely lawful.[18] He has criticized judges, sometimes in derisive terms, but contrary to Timothy Snyder there is nothing undemocratic about this. Lincoln blasted Justice Taney over the *Dred Scott* decision, and FDR was virtually apoplectic when the Supreme Court blocked his New Deal initiatives. Criticizing the media isn't undemocratic either. The First Amendment isn't just a press prerogative; the president too has the right to free speech.

Authoritarians undermine legitimate structures of authority; has Trump or the GOP done this? Some progressives accused the GOP Senate leadership of undermining checks and balances by invoking the "nuclear option" to shut down a Democratic filibuster and confirm Neil Gorsuch to the Supreme Court. Yet these progressives forgot to mention that it was former Democratic Senate leader Harry Reid who first invoked the "nuclear option" and thus Republicans were merely acting on his precedent.

Authoritarians typically try to run your private life. Think of the way that authoritarian regimes like the Nazis and the Soviets sought to regulate the way that people worshipped or what they read or how they conducted their everyday life, a mindset captured in the Nazi saying that "only sleep is a private matter." Do you think Trump remotely cares how you live your private life? Does it matter to him which deity you worship or what books you read? Of course not.

Authoritarians strike fear into their opponents. The very fact that Trump is flayed daily across countless media platforms shows that his opponents feel quite free to speak their minds. Consider a telling contrast. Hitler wiped out his opponents in the infamous Night of the Long Knives on June 30, 1934. Mussolini silenced his critics by taking over the presses and had one of his prominent opponents, Giacomo Matteotti, murdered. Consider what Trump did, by contrast, to the singer Cher who once said "some nasty shit" about him. "I knocked the shit out of her" on Twitter, Trump boasted, "and she never said a thing about me after that."[19] He let her have it on *Twitter*. This is hardly the mark of an authoritarian.

Nationalism: If there is one feature that progressives consider essential to fascism and Nazism, it's nationalism. This enables the Left to make an easy link between fascist nationalism and the patriotism of the American Right. One writer, Mark Rosenberg, spoke for many on the Left when he described Trump's inaugural speech as a "visceral, emotional appeal to re-establish some lost world of American greatness." Isn't this precisely what Hitler promised—to make Germany great again? Rosenberg concludes that Trump delivered "certainly the most fascistic inaugural address in American history."[20]

Clearly Trump is a nationalist, and the modern American Right is nationalist and comfortable with the symbols of traditional patriotism such as the waving of the flag or boisterous renditions of the national anthem and "God Bless America." By contrast, the modern Left is internationalist—it has little patience with displays of traditional patriotism—and this seems to distinguish the Left on the one hand from the Nazis, the fascists, and the American conservatives on the other.

Yet is nationalism or even ultra-nationalism sufficient to make one a fascist? Was Mussolini more of a nationalist than, say, Churchill or De Gaulle? George Washington and Abraham Lincoln were nationalists. The French revolutionaries were all nationalists. Nelson Mandela was a nationalist. Castro was a nationalist who coined the revolutionary slogan "The Fatherland or Death." Che Guevara was a nationalist, as was Pol Pot. Even when he lived in England and South Africa, Gandhi was a dedicated Indian nationalist. Obviously it makes no sense to call these men fascists. While Lenin professed to be a lifelong internationalist, awaiting a global communist revolution, Stalin modified Leninism to invoke what he called "Motherland Russia" and "socialism in one country." So does Stalin's nationalism make him a fascist? Obviously not.

It is also worth remarking that if Hitler and Mussolini were nationalists—as they unquestionably were—they were nationalists of a very different type than American conservatives. "Mussolini was not a traditional nationalist," historian Zeev Sternhell writes. Anthony James Gregor goes further: "Mussolini was opposed to traditional patriotism and conventional nationalist appeals." Early in his career Mussolini ridiculed the Italian flag and called the army "a criminal organization designed to protect capitalism and bourgeois society." Hitler called himself a nationalist, but he refused to call himself a patriot.[21]

Both sought a new type of nationalism which bred loyalty not to the nation as it was but to the new nation they sought to create. Fascist nationalism called upon citizens to subordinate their private concerns fully to the centralized state. This type of nationalism—let's call it statist or collectivist nationalism—more closely resembles the American Left than the American Right, since the American Right holds, with Reagan, that "government is not the solution. Government is the problem."

Militarism: Another characteristic regularly used by progressives to link Trump to fascism and Nazism is his alleged militarism. Even before Trump's election, the online magazine *Salon* alleged that Trump's candidacy represents an "embrace and glorification of militarism" of precisely the kind Hitler and Mussolini engaged in. According to a March 1, 2017, headline in the *Washington Post*, "The Trump Presidency Ushers in a New Age of Militarism." Invoking the fascist historical parallel, the article accuses Trump's military buildup of "casting a belligerent shadow across the world."[22]

Now fascism and Nazism were indeed militaristic. Hitler and Mussolini were both veterans of World War I, and of course they were, along with their Japanese allies, the joint perpetrators of World War II. Even so, historian Stanley Payne writes that "fascism is usually said to have been expansionist and imperialist by definition but this is not clear from a reading of diverse fascist programs." Indeed "several fascist movements had little interest in or even rejected new imperial ambitions" while others advocated war that was "generally defensive rather than aggressive."[23]

I mention this not to exonerate fascism and Nazism on this score, but to highlight that we should not confuse the incidental features of an ideology with its central characteristics. If the fascists advocated military expansionism when they flourished in the interregnum between two world wars, it doesn't follow that fascism is inherently militaristic or that militarism is one of its defining features. By analogy, if the American founders were farmers, it doesn't follow that farming was central to the American founding. Leftists seem to routinely attribute the accidental features of Nazism and fascism to the ideologies themselves.

Trump is not a militarist. He is, in fact, less militarist than his party. Of course Trump wants to defeat ISIS militarily, but this is because ISIS is a terrorist organization that seeks to destroy America. In early April 2017, Trump ordered a strike against a Syrian airfield. This seems to have been an outraged response to horrific pictures Trump saw showing the victims of a chemical gas attack by the Syrian despot Bashar Assad. Trump's action was a surprise to his critics and supporters alike, neither of who expected Trump to intervene in this way.

Trump's Syria action seems anomalous given his general semi-isolationist stance. While the GOP generally supported Bush's invasion of Iraq, for instance, Trump campaigned for the presidency on his opposition to the war. If Trump wanted to annex Mexico and make it part of a greater U.S. then he could be accused of imitating Hitler's *Lebensraum*. But nothing could be further from Trump's mind. He has outlined a vision of a less interventionist America that focuses on its own internal problems.

Capitalism: Finally, capitalism. I'll admit it takes a real dummy to make this charge. Still, here's leftist scholar-activist Cornel West claiming that Trump is a fascist and a Nazi because "in an emerging neofascist movement you have the rule of big business, which is big banks and big corporations."[24] West is mindlessly repeating a charge that was invented by the Soviet communist propaganda machine, that the fascists were brought to power by big business financing and that fascism is the last gasp of industrial capitalism.

The Soviet communists first came up with this line and then fed it to the Italian and German communists to attempt to stem the growth of fascism in those countries. Stalin used "fascism" to refer to any country that was ideologically opposed to the Soviet Union. When the Soviet-Sino split occurred, the Soviet communists called the Chinese communists "fascists" and the Chinese communists in turn called the Soviet communists "fascists." Clearly we are moving into la-la land here. Even though the old Soviet canard that fascism is a byproduct of capitalism has been fully discredited—even the progressive Robert Paxton will have nothing to do with it—others on the Left besides Cornel West still echo the accusation that Trump is a fascist because capitalism is a defining feature of fascism.

Yes, Trump is a capitalist but this is yet another example of what distinguishes him from the fascists and the Nazis. "It is unthinkable," Renzo De Felice says in his book *Fascism*, "that Italy's great economic forces wanted to bring fascism to power." Big business, it turns out, supported neither Mussolini's fascists nor Hitler's National Socialists. The Nazi Party, Stanley Payne points out, "was primarily financed by its own members."[25] Big business viewed the fascists and Nazis as dangerous radicals. But after the radicals came to power, German and Italian corporations, not surprisingly, opted to cooperate with them. This is true of big business generally: businessmen do business with whoever is in power. America's great economic forces worked with Obama and they would surely have worked with Hillary had she been elected.

The historian Anthony James Gregor points out that it makes no sense to describe Italian fascism as the product of late modern capitalism because "there was very little that was modern about the Italian economy at the time of the First World War."[26] As we will see in the next chapter, this was recognized clearly by Mussolini and the early fascists. Mussolini saw fascism as Hitler later saw Nazism: as a mechanism for rapid economic development operating through a framework that was not capitalist but rather collectivist, statist, and socialist. As we are about to discover—in the rest of this chapter and in the next one—collectivism, statism, and socialism are the essence of fascism and Nazism.

The Karl Marx of Fascism

For Fascism...the State and the individual are one.[27]
Giovanni Gentile, *Origins and Doctrine of Fascism*

Giovanni Gentile is not exactly a household name today. Even among educated people in America, he is an unknown figure. Yet Gentile was, in his day, which is the first half of the twentieth century, considered one of the leading philosophers alive. A student of Hegel and Bergson and director of the *Encyclopedia Italiana*, Gentile was not merely a widely published and widely influential thinker; he was also a political statesman who served in a variety of important government posts. Why, then, has Gentile vanished into the mist of history?

Let's consider some key aspects of Gentile's philosophy.[28] Following Aristotle and Marx, Gentile argues that man is a social animal. This means that we are not simply individuals in the world. Rather, our individuality is expressed through our relationships: we are students or workers, husbands or wives, parents and grandparents, members in this or that association or group, and also citizens of a community or nation. To speak of man alone in the state of nature is a complete fiction; man is naturally at home in community, in society.

Right away we see that Gentile is a communitarian as opposed to a radical individualist. This distinguishes him from some libertarians and classical liberals, who emphasize individuality in contradistinction to society. But Gentile so far has said nothing that conservatives—let's say Reaganite conservatives—would disagree with. Reagan in 1980 emphasized the importance of five themes: the individual, the family, the church, the community, and the country. He accused the centralized state—big government—of undermining not merely our individuality but also these other associations.

Gentile now contrasts two types of democracy, which he says are "diametrically opposed." The first is liberal democracy which envisions society made up of individuals who form communities to protect and advance their individual rights and interests, specifically their economic interests in property and trade. Gentile regards this as selfish or bourgeois democracy, by which he means capitalist democracy, the democracy of the American founding. In its place, Gentile recommends a different type of democracy, "true democracy," in which individuals willingly subordinate themselves to society and to the state.

Gentile recognizes that his critique of bourgeois democracy echoes that of Marx, and Marx is his takeoff point. Like Marx, Gentile wants a unified community, a community that resembles the family, a community where we're all in this together. I'm reminded here of New York Governor Mario Cuomo's keynote address at the 1984 Democratic Convention. Cuomo likened America to an extended family where, through the agency of government, we take care of each other in much the same manner that families look out for all their members.

While Marx and Cuomo seem to view political communities as natural, inevitable associations, Gentile emphasized that such communities must be created voluntarily, through human action, operating as a consequence of human will. They are, in Gentile's words, an idealistic or "spiritual creation." For Gentile people by themselves are too slothful and inert to form genuine communities by themselves; they have to be mobilized. Here, too, many modern progressives would agree. Speaking in terms that both Obama and Hillary would sympathize with, Gentile emphasized that leaders and organizers are needed to direct and channel the will of the people.

Despite Gentile's disagreement with Marx about historical inevitability, he has at this point clearly broken with modern conservatism and classical liberalism and revealed himself to be a man of the Left. Gentile was, in fact, a lifelong socialist. Like Marx, he viewed socialism as the sine qua non of social justice, the ultimate formula for everyone paying their "fair share." For Gentile, fascism is nothing more than a modified form of socialism, a socialism arising not merely from material deprivation but also from an aroused national consciousness, a socialism that unites rather than divides communities.

Gentile also perceived fascism emerging out of revolutionary struggle, what the media today terms "protest" or "activism." Unlike Marx, he conceived the struggle not between the working class and the capitalists, but between the selfish individual trying to live for himself and the fully actualized individual who willingly puts himself at the behest of society and the state. Gentile seems to be the unacknowledged ancestor of the street activism of Antifa and other leftist groups. "One of the major virtues of fascism," he writes, "is that it obliged those who watched from their windows to come down into the street."

For Gentile, private action should be mobilized to serve the public interest, and there is no distinction between the private interest and the public interest. Correctly understood, the two are identical and the enlightened citizen understands that and lives by it, treating society and the state as, in a sense, his larger self. Gentile argued that society represents "the very personality of the individual divested of accidental differences...where the individual feels the general interest as his own and wills therefore as might the general will." In the same vein, Gentile argued that corporations too should serve the public welfare and not just the welfare of their owners and shareholders.

Society and the state—for Gentile, the two were one and the same. Gentile saw the centralized state as the necessary administrative arm of society. Moreover the state is, as it were, unaccountable to citizens. "The authority of the State is not subject to negotiation," he writes. "It is entirely unconditioned. It could not depend on the people, in fact, the people depend on the State. Morality and religion...must be subordinated to the laws of the State." How familiar this all sounds to anyone acquainted with the ideology and rhetoric of the modern American Left.

Gentile urges that all citizens must submit to the authority of the state, not just in economic matters, but in all matters. Since everything is political, the state gets to tell everyone how to think and also what to do—there is no private sphere unregulated by the state. Fascism, according to Gentile, is a "total conception of life... One cannot be a Fascist in politics and not a Fascist in school, not a Fascist in one's family, not a Fascist in one's workplace." The state must work to bring about this generalized fascist consciousness.

To achieve it, Gentile advocated that all of society be brought into line with fascist ideology, what the Nazis would later call *Gleichschaltung*. While Gentile never condoned the brutal tactics of Nazi *Gleichschaltung*, he sought the same ideological conformity through law and education. The government, Gentile insisted should act not merely as a lawmaker but also a teacher, using schools to promulgate its values and priorities. Expressing a doctrine that most progressive faculty in America would most likely endorse, Gentile said, "Our work as teachers is considered to be at an end when our students speak our language."[29]

"All is in the state and nothing human exists or has value outside the state." Mussolini said that in *La Dottrina del Fascismo*, one of the doctrinal statements of early fascism, but Gentile wrote it or, as we may say today, ghost-wrote it. Gentile was, as you have probably figured by now, the leading philosopher of fascism. "It was Gentile," Mussolini confessed, "who prepared the road for those like me who wished to take it."[30] Gentile served as a member of the Fascist Grand Council, a senator in the Upper House of the Italian Parliament, and also as Mussolini's minister of education. Later, after Mussolini was deposed and established himself at Salo, Gentile became at *Il Duce*'s request the president of the Italian Academy.

He was not an evil man. He rejected anti-Semitism and worked with Jews even when this became controversial in Italy following Mussolini's alliance with Hitler. He rejected many of the strong-arm doctrines of fascism, arguing that the state, though all-powerful, should seek to persuade citizens rather than force them. This is what he called the "tutelary state." In 1944, Gentile was accosted in his apartment by members of a rival leftist faction who shot him at point-blank range. Mussolini promised to execute the killers, but Gentile's family urged that they be released, and somewhat surprisingly, Mussolini did so.

I think of Gentile in somewhat the same way I think of Robert E. Lee, General in Chief of the Confederate States Army. Lee was in general a good man, yet as Ulysses Grant said of him, never did a man fight "so long and so valiantly" and suffer "so much for a cause, though that cause was, I believe, one of the worst for which a people ever fought." And so it can be said of Gentile: never did a more decent man fight for a more horrendous movement. Yet although Gentile is forgotten, his philosophy could not be more relevant, because it closely parallels that of the modern American Left. In fact, the slogan unveiled by Obama at the 2012 Democratic Convention—"we belong to the government"—was not coined by Gentile but is utterly congruent with his core philosophy.

This then is the reason for Gentile's obscurity—not that his ideas are dead but that they are very much alive. Not one to dabble in incidentals, Gentile gets to the core of things. In many respects he provides a deeper and firmer grounding for modern American progressivism than anyone writing today. John Rawls, widely considered a philosophical guru of modern progressivism, seems like thin gruel compared to Gentile in offering an intellectual rationale for the strong centralized state. While Rawls feels abstract and dated today, Gentile seems to be speaking directly to leftist activists in the Democratic Party, in the media, and on campus.

One might naively expect the Left, then, to embrace and celebrate Gentile. This, of course, will never happen. The Left has the desperate need to conceal fascism's association with contemporary leftism. Even when the Left uses Gentilean rhetoric, its source can never be publicly acknowledged. And since the Left dominates academia and popular culture, it has the clout to perform this vanishing trick. That's why the progressives intend to keep Gentile where they've got him: dead, buried, and forgotten.

In Speech and in Deed

Fascism was not conservative at all in inspiration but was aimed at creating a new society with a new kind of human being.[31]
Walter Laqueur, *Fascism: Past, Present, Future*

In order to get the core of an ideology, we must always explore it in theory before exploring it in practice. That's why I began with Gentile: he spells out authoritatively the statism and collectivism that defines fascism and ultimately even Nazism. From Gentile we move to the doctrinal statements and political platform of Italian fascism and German National Socialism. These too represent utopian fascism, one might say "fascism in speech." Only then does it make sense to examine what Mussolini and Hitler actually did, because what they did is necessarily an application, with predictable adulteration and dilution, of what they originally intended to accomplish. Fascism in speech is necessarily compromised by fascism in deed.

I mention this distinction at the outset because it has become the basis for leftists to minimize the core principles of fascism, so as to camouflage their similarity—and in some cases identity—with modern progressivism. Once again I turn to progressive darling Robert Paxton, who in his public interviews emphasizes that while fascism "sounded quite radical, when it's in power it allies with banks, industrialists, the army, churches, and so forth." Paxton also points out that "when you read Hitler's program, his twenty-one points, and when you read Mussolini's first program in 1919, it had very little to do with what they eventually did."[32] Paxton's implication is that despite their professed goals, fascism and National Socialism cannot be equated with leftism and progressivism because Mussolini and Hitler did not actually implement the full scope of their ideology.

As a counterargument to my thesis, I have to say this is true but utterly unconvincing. Obviously all theories must accommodate the realities of the situation; this does not undermine the theory as a vision of the way things ought to be. Lincoln was anti-slavery but it was a political necessity for him to keep the border states in the union if he was going to win the war. Consequently, his Emancipation Proclamation applied only to areas in rebellion against the United States that were not already occupied by the Union Army. To point this out is hardly to prove that Lincoln was not in fact anti-slavery because he didn't outlaw it throughout the country.

For a second example, I cite Lenin. As a dedicated Marxist and communist, Lenin had pledged to outlaw capitalism throughout the Soviet Union, and he did. But the Soviet economy went into a nosedive, and in the early 1920s, by his own acknowledgement, Lenin embraced capitalist measures to solve the problem. He allowed private property, including private farms; he allowed businesses and farmers to keep some of their earnings; he even encouraged foreign businesses to invest in the Soviet Union. Lenin did not see his New Economic Policy as betraying communism but as stabilizing the economy as well as his political hold on the country so that he could truly institutionalize communism. Yet despite his temporary pivot away from socialism, can anyone seriously maintain that Lenin wasn't a socialist?

Now let's turn to Mussolini, who was in theory a complete statist. One of Mussolini's favorite phrases was "Everything in the state, nothing outside the state, nothing against the state."[33] We can see here the echoes of Gentile and also the echoes of a modern leftist progressivism carried to its end point. Mussolini, in other words, seems to say what modern progressives dream about but dare not publicly confess. Mussolini was such a thoroughgoing statist that I venture to say he was more statist than Barack Obama when Obama confessed to the *New York Times* that he envied the Chinese communist leaders the extent of their power.[34]

Mussolini was so statist that he considered the word "totalitarian" a positive term. For Mussolini it didn't mean what Orwell depicted in *1984*. Mussolini had no intention to smash a jackboot against every Italian face. Rather, totalitarianism for him meant the state totally took care of everything and looked after everyone. Mussolini sought an Italy in which the state—embodied in him—exercised full and complete control over every aspect of the lives of the citizens.

But Mussolini never had the heart to be a true totalitarian, in part because he was, well, Italian. His totalitarianism was always Italian, which is to say, half-assed. He sort of had his opponents arrested and he sort of controlled the media and he sort of had parliament under his thumb, but he lacked that punctiliousness that characterized his more grim totalitarian counterparts Stalin and Hitler. Throughout his twenty year reign, Mussolini killed very few of his own citizens and allowed people, including Jews, to leave Italy. Stalin and Hitler would never dream of allowing this. What kind of totalitarian control can you have over people if they are free to pack up and say *sayonara*?

While Mussolini's totalitarianism was somewhat anemic, however, his socialism was not. The original platform of the fascists, as outlined by the *Fasci di Combattimento* in Milan in 1919, included universal suffrage, lowering the voting age to eighteen, abolishing the elitist senate, mandating an eight-hour workday, a massive public works program, worker participation in industrial management, nationalization of defense-related industries, old age and sickness insurance for all citizens, state confiscation of uncultivated land, steeply progressive taxation, an 85 percent tax on war profits, and strong anti-clerical policies including no religious instruction in schools and government appropriation of the property of religious institutions.

Mussolini was able to get some of this agenda enacted, notably a public works program unrivalled in Europe at the time. The fascists built bridges, canals, roads, railway stations, schools, hospitals, and orphanages. They drained swamps, reclaimed land, planted forests, and endowed universities and research institutions. Mussolini also expanded social services in a program that he frankly confessed matched and exceeded Franklin D. Roosevelt's New Deal. (More on this in a later chapter.) Even so, much of Mussolini's original socialist program remained on his wish list.

The reason for this is that Mussolini, unlike Hitler and Stalin, never had absolute power. He was appointed by King Victor Emmanuel III, who also had the power to depose him, and eventually did. Even while Mussolini ruled, he had to work with the existing structures of power, including members of the traditional ruling class. Mussolini detested the Catholic Church, yet he realized that church opposition would make governing difficult for him, so in 1929 he entered into a concordat with the papacy that involved giving up his full control over the education system.

Mussolini's power also waxed and waned, depending on circumstances. He was not the absolute ruler of Italy when he first came to power, but after socialist politician Giacomo Matteotti was murdered by fascists, Mussolini made a risky yet successful bid to assume dictatorial control. Mussolini was clearly at the height of his power during the mid-1930s, and during this time he ensured that the state controlled all industrial activity and virtually all finance and credit. Once he allied with Germany, however, Mussolini again had to operate within the framework established by Hitler. During this period, as we'll see later, Mussolini partially embraced a racism and anti-Semitism that he did not really believe and that did not characterize his career when he himself was calling the shots.

In 1943, Allied forces landed in Italy. Through the action of the king and the Grand Council of Fascism, Mussolini was ousted from power. But Hitler rescued him from captivity and reestablished Mussolini as the ruler in Salo, in the northern territory of Italy under German control. Here, for a brief period, Mussolini could do what he wanted; he was his own man.

So what did Mussolini do? He founded, as he put it, the only genuinely socialist government in the world, with the possible exception of the Soviet Union.[35] Mussolini attempted to put into effect what he termed the "true socialism" that he said "plutocratic elements and sections of the clergy" had prevented him from implementing in Italy.

At Salo, Mussolini outlined a socialist program that went beyond anything he attempted in Italy. The new program of November 1943 called for the state to take over all the critical sections of the economy—energy, raw materials, all necessary social services—leaving only private savings and private homes and assets in the hands of the citizens. The public sector was to be run by management committees in which workers would have a key role. Unions would also be part of the fascist governing assembly.

The next step, declared Mussolini's adviser Ugo Spirito, would be to abolish all private property. Interestingly Mussolini's closest adviser in Salo was Nicola Bombacci, once a friend and disciple of Lenin who had in 1921 been a co-founder of the Italian Communist Party. Mussolini's Salo period, although short-lived, proves that he never abandoned his original leftist ideals; he remained to the last a dedicated statist, collectivist, and socialist.

The National Socialist Platform

With Hitler, too, we see a dedicated socialist who, shortly after assuming the leadership of the German Workers' Party, changed its name to the National Socialist German Workers' Party (NSDAP). In statement after statement, Hitler could not be clearer about his socialist commitments. He said, for example, in a 1927 speech, "We are socialists. We are the enemies of today's capitalist system of exploitation...and we are determined to destroy this system under all conditions."[36]

The Nazi Party at the outset offered a twenty-five point program that included nationalization of large corporations and trusts, government control of banking and credit, the seizure of land without compensation for public use, the splitting of large landholdings into smaller units, confiscation of war profits, prosecution of bankers and other lenders on grounds of usury, abolition of incomes unearned by work, profit sharing for workers in all large companies, a broader pension system paying higher benefits, and universal free health care and education.

If you read the Nazi platform without knowing its source, you could easily be forgiven for thinking you were reading the 2016 platform of the Democratic Party. Or at least a Democratic platform drafted jointly by Bernie Sanders and Elizabeth Warren. Sure, some of the language is out of date. The Democrats can't talk about "usury" these days; they'd have to substitute "Wall Street greed." But otherwise, it's all there. All you have to do is cross out the word "Nazi" and write in the word "Democrat."

Progressives like Paxton who recognize the leftist content of the Nazi platform attempt to distance it from Hitler by associating it with a supposed leftist faction in the Nazi Party that Hitler later eliminated. This faction was headed by the Strasser brothers, Otto and Gregor. Otto Strasser was expelled from the Nazi Party in 1930 and went into exile in Czechoslovakia. Gregor Strasser was killed on Hitler's orders on June 30, 1934, during the Night of the Long Knives.

Yet the Strassers wrote the original Nazi platform in conjunction with Hitler himself. The Strassers remained key figures in the Nazi Party throughout the 1920s. The party kicked Otto Strasser out because of his threats to found his own dissident party, which he eventually did. Gregor Strasser publicly repudiated his brother and stayed in the Nazi Party. Hitler appointed him head of the party in the northern and western regions of Germany; there he was second in authority only to Hitler himself. At no point did Hitler repudiate the principles that he and the Strassers advanced at the outset.

Why then did Hitler have Gregor Strasser killed? A clue can be found in the writings of Joseph Goebbels, Strasser's close ally who became Hitler's confidant and propaganda minister. In one of his diary entries Goebbels asked a simple question about National Socialism: "What has priority and what comes second?" And Goebbels answered, "First socialism and then national liberation."[37]

Hitler's answer was the opposite: first German liberation and then socialism. Goebbels, who fell under the personal magnetism of Hitler, succumbed to Hitler's priorities. Gregor Strasser did not. He blasted Hitler for betraying revolutionary socialism even though Hitler assured him that socialism would come after Germany consolidated its military power. Strasser was unpersuaded. Ultimately Hitler grew weary of Strasser's criticism and had him executed, eliminating a dangerous rival in the process.

Strasser believed Hitler could have both nationalism and socialism because, unlike Mussolini, Hitler enjoyed nearly absolute power to do what he wanted. Yet what Hitler wanted to do, before he did anything else, was to fight a war. His goal was essentially to first, bring Europe or at least most of Europe into subjugation; second, to expel or eliminate the Jews; and third, to implement socialism for Germany while institutionalizing subordination and slavery for everyone else. Hitler's view was that socialism is too good for anyone other than true Aryans, and consequently he was not about to institutionalize socialism before carrying out his first two assignments.

So Hitler, too, made a deal with the Vatican and attempted to appease Christians. He needed the support of Bavarian Catholics and Lutherans elsewhere in Germany. Hitler also needed big business, both to keep the German economy humming and to supply him with the vast supplies of war materials that he knew he would need for his invasions of eastern Europe, France, and Russia. Hitler did achieve his objective of bringing virtually all sectors of the economy under state control. He launched huge state-owned conglomerates such as the Hermann Goring Reichwerke. Yet he deferred several of the other objectives from the Nazi platform. This deferral, and his bargains with erstwhile foes, in no way proves that he ceased to be a socialist or a true Nazi. Like Lincoln, he needed the successful conclusion of a war to fully realize his original ambitions.

For Hitler, however, unlike for Lincoln, the war didn't end well. So fascism and Nazism, as early as 1945, ended up on the ash heap of history. It took Soviet communism a lot longer to fully collapse. One may see, in these two examples, a disheartening lesson for the modern American Left. It seems that collectivism was twice tried and proved to be a failure. But this is not quite true. Soviet communism was tried and failed of its own accord. Fascism and Nazism, however, were destroyed from the outside, by war.

Consequently, one might say that, as ideological blueprints for society, fascism and National Socialism have still not failed because they were never fully tried. In modern progressivism, then, we may be seeing an attempted revival and resurrection. Obviously the revival has to be under a different name, and the Left will surely need some anti-fascist camouflage. (Look, no fascists here! Can't you see we're fighting fascism?) Even so, for people who know how to recognize it, today's Left is still the party of fascism and National Socialism, old ideologies now marching on a different continent under new colors, a fascism for the twenty-first century.

Three

Mussolini's Journey

*The conflict between the Fascist or National Socialist
and the older socialist parties must be very largely
regarded as the kind of conflict which is bound to arise
between rival socialist factions.*[1]

Friedrich Hayek, *The Road to Serfdom*

On March 23, 1919, one of the most famous socialists in Italy
founded a new party, the *Fasci di Combattimento*, a term that
means "fascist combat squad." This was the first official fascist
party and thus its founding represents the true birth of fascism. By the
same token, this man was the first fascist. The term "fascism" can be
traced back to 1914, when he founded the *Fasci Rivoluzionari d'Azione
Internazionalista*, a political movement whose members called themselves *fascisti* or fascists.

In 1914, this founding father of fascism was, together with Vladimir
Lenin of Russia, Rosa Luxemburg of Germany, and Antonio Gramsci
of Italy, one of the best known Marxists in the world. His fellow Marxists and socialists recognized him as a great leader of socialism. His
decision to become a fascist was controversial, yet he received congratu-
lations from Lenin who continued to regard him as a faithful revolutionary socialist. And this is how he saw himself.

That same year, because of his support for Italian involvement in World War I, he would be expelled from the Italian Socialist Party for "heresy," but this does not mean he ceased to be a socialist. It was common practice for socialist parties to expel dissenting fellow socialists for breaking on some fine point with the party line. This party reject insisted that he had been kicked out for making "a revision of socialism from the revolutionary point of view."[2] For the rest of his life—right until his lifeless body was displayed in a town square in Milan—he upheld the central tenets of socialism which he saw as best reflected in fascism.

Who, then, was this man? He was the future leader of fascist Italy, the one whom Italians called *Il Duce*, Benito Mussolini.

Mussolini's socialist credentials were impeccable. He had been raised in a socialist family and made a public declaration in 1901, at the age of eighteen, of his convictions. By twenty-one, he was an orthodox Marxist familiar not only with the writings of Marx and Engels but also of many of the most influential German, Italian, and French Marxists of the fin de siècle period. Like other orthodox Marxists, Mussolini rejected religious faith and authored anti-Catholic pamphlets repudiating his native Catholicism.

Mussolini embarked on an active career as a writer, editor, and political organizer. Exiled to Switzerland between 1902 and 1904, he collaborated with the Italian Socialist Party weekly issued there and also wrote for *Il Proletario*, a socialist weekly published in New York. In 1909 Mussolini made another foreign sojourn to Trento—then part of Austria-Hungary—where he worked for the socialist party and edited its newspaper. Returning the next year to his hometown of Forli, he edited the weekly socialist publication *La Lotta di Classe* (The Class War). He wrote so widely on Marxism, socialist theory, and contemporary politics that his output now fills seven volumes.

Mussolini wasn't just an intellectual; he organized workers' strikes on behalf of the socialist movement both inside and outside of Italy and was twice jailed for his activism. In 1912, Mussolini was recognized as a socialist leader at the Socialist Congress at Reggio Emilia and was appointed to the Italian Socialist Party's board of directors. That same year, at the age of twenty-nine, he became editor of *Avanti!*, the official publication of the party.

From the point of view of the progressive narrative—a narrative I began to challenge in the previous chapter—Mussolini's shift from Marxian socialism to fascism must come as a huge surprise. In the progressive paradigm, Marxian socialism is the left end of the spectrum and fascism is the right end of the spectrum. Progressive incredulity becomes even greater when we see that Mussolini wasn't just any socialist; he was the recognized head of the socialist movement in Italy. Moreover, he didn't just climb aboard the fascist bandwagon; he created it.

Today we think of fascism's most famous representative as Adolf Hitler. Yet as I mentioned earlier, Hitler didn't consider himself a fascist. Rather, he saw himself as a National Socialist. The two ideologies are related in that they are both based on collectivism and centralized state power. They emerge, one might say, from a common point of origin. Yet they are also distinct; fascism, for instance, had no intrinsic connection with anti-Semitism in the way that National Socialism did.

In any event, Hitler was an obscure local organizer in Germany when Mussolini came to power and, following his famous March on Rome, established the world's first fascist regime in Italy in 1922. Hitler greatly admired Mussolini and aspired to become like him. Mussolini, Hitler said, was "the leading statesman in the world, to whom none may even remotely compare himself."[3] Hitler modeled his failed Munich Putsch in November 1923 on Mussolini's successful March on Rome.

When Hitler first came to power he kept a bust of Mussolini in his office and one German observer termed him "Germany's Mussolini."[4] Yet later, when the two men first met, Mussolini was not very impressed by Hitler. Mussolini became more respectful after 1939 when Hitler conquered Austria, Poland, Czechoslovakia, Belgium, Norway, and France. Hitler continued to uphold Mussolini as "that unparalleled statesman" and "one of the Caesars" and confessed that without Italian fascism there would not have been a German National Socialism: "The brown shirt would probably not have existed without the black shirt."[5]

Hitler was, like Mussolini, a man of the Left. Hitler too was a socialist and a labor leader who founded the German Socialist Workers' Party with a platform very similar to that of Mussolini's fascist party. Yet Hitler came to power in the 1930s while Mussolini ruled through most of the 1920s. Mussolini was, during those years, much more famous than Hitler. He was recognized as the founding father of fascism. So any account of the origin of fascism must focus not on Hitler but on Mussolini. Mussolini is the original and prototypical fascist.

From Socialism to Fascism

So how—to return to the progressive paradigm—do progressives account for Mussolini's conversion from socialism to fascism, or more precisely for Mussolini's simultaneous embrace of both? The problem is further deepened by the fact that Mussolini was not alone. Hundreds of leading socialists, initially in Italy but subsequently in Germany, France, and other countries, also became fascists. In fact, I will go further to say that all the leading figures in the founding of fascism were men of the Left. "The first fascists," Anthony James Gregor tells us, "were almost all Marxists."[6]

I will cite a few examples. Jean Allemane, famous for his role in the Dreyfus case, one of the great figures of French socialism, became a fascist later in life. So did the socialist Georges Valois. Marcel Deat, the founder of the *Parti Socialiste de France*, eventually quit and started a pro-fascist party in 1936. Later, he became a Nazi collaborator during the Vichy regime. Jacques Doriot, a French communist, moved his *Parti Populaire Français* into the fascist camp.

The Belgian socialist theoretician Henri de Man transitioned to becoming a fascist theoretician. In England, Oswald Mosley, a socialist and Labor Party Member of Parliament, eventually broke with the Labor Party because he found it insufficiently radical. He later founded the

British Union of Fascists and became the country's leading Nazi sympathizer. In Germany, the socialist playwright Gerhart Hauptmann embraced Hitler and produced plays during the Third Reich. After the war, he became a communist and staged his productions in Soviet-dominated East Berlin.

In Italy, philosopher Giovanni Gentile moved from Marxism to fascism, as did a host of Italian labor organizers: Ottavio Dinale, Tullio Masotti, Carlo Silvestri, and Umberto Pasella. The socialist writer Agostino Lanzillo joined Mussolini's parliament as a member of the fascist party. Nicola Bombacci, one of the founders of the Italian Communist Party, became Mussolini's top adviser in Salo. Gentile's disciple Ugo Spirito, who also served Mussolini at Salo, moved from Marxism to fascism and then back to Marxism. Like Hauptmann, Spirito became a communist sympathizer after World War II and called for a new "synthesis" between communism and fascism.

Others who made the same journey from socialism to fascism will be named in this chapter, and one thing that will become very clear is that these are not "conversion" stories. These men didn't "switch" from socialism to fascism. Rather, they became fascists in the same way that Russian socialists became Leninist Bolsheviks. Like their Russian counterparts, these socialists believed themselves to be growing into fascism, maturing into fascism, because they saw fascism as the most well thought out, practical form of socialism for the new century.

Progressivism simply cannot account for the easy traffic from socialism to fascism. Consequently, progressives typically maintain complete silence about this whole historical relationship which is deeply embarrassing to them. In all the articles comparing Trump to Mussolini I searched in vain for references to Mussolini's erstwhile Marxism and lifelong attachment to socialism. Either from ignorance or from design, these references are missing.

Progressive biographical accounts that cannot avoid Mussolini's socialist past nevertheless turn around and accuse Mussolini—as the Socialist Party of Italy did in 1914—of "selling out" to fascism for money and power. Other accounts contend that whatever Mussolini's original convictions, the very fact that his fascists later battled the Marxists and traditional socialists clearly shows that Mussolini did not remain a socialist or a man of the Left.

But these explanations make no sense. When Mussolini "sold out" he became an outcast. He had neither money nor power. Nor did any of the first fascists embrace fascism for this reason. Rather, they became fascists because they saw fascism as the only way to rescue socialism and make it viable. In other words, their defection was *within* socialism— they sought to create a new type of socialism that would actually draw a mass following and produce the workers' revolution that Marx anticipated and hoped for.

Vicious fights among socialist and leftist factions are a recognized feature of the history of socialism. In Russia, for example, there were bloody confrontations between the rival Bolsheviks and Mensheviks. Later the Bolsheviks split into Leninists and Trotskyites, and Trotsky ended up dead on Lenin's orders. These were all men of the Left. What these bloody rivalries prove is that the worst splits and conflicts sometimes arise among people who are ideologically very similar and differ on relatively small—though not small to them—points of doctrine.

In this chapter I will trace the development of fascism by showing precisely how it grew out of a doctrinal division within the community of Marxian socialists. In short, I will prove that fascism is exclusively a product of the Left. This is not a case of leftists who moved right. On the contrary, the fascists were on the left end of the socialist movement. They saw themselves not as jettisoning Marxism but as saving it from obsolescence. From their perspective, Marxism and socialism were too inert and needed to be adjusted leftward. In other words, they viewed fascism as more revolutionary than traditional socialism.

The story by itself is a largely untold chapter in the history of ideas. I have excavated it from the densely scholarly works of the leading historians of fascism in order to put it in the reach of a general audience. As these scholars emphasize, this is fascism not as it ended up but as it started. Today we think of fascism in terms of the extreme villainies of

World War II, but fascism would not have attracted many followers if it was originally viewed that way. It must have had a logical and emotional appeal that is invisible to us today.

Here I try to show the force of that original logic and appeal. My goal is to produce a genealogy in the sense of the term that Nietzsche wrote in his *Genealogy of Morals*. Nietzsche hopes, by giving an account of the origin of Christian morality, to discredit it by revealing its allegedly base roots. My goal is to show the base origins of fascism, not so much to discredit it—it should hardly be necessary in our time to do that—but to put to bed once and for all the big lie that makes fascism a phenomenon of the Right. Without this lie, the claim that Trump and the GOP are fascists simply crumbles.

Crisis of Marxism

Fascism arose out of the deep crisis faced by Marxism in the early part of the twentieth century. Therefore, we must begin with that crisis. Marx, let us recall, did not call for the workers of the world to rise up and revolt against the bourgeoisie or capitalist class. Rather, he predicted that they would. Marx saw himself as a kind of prophet, foretelling what was going to happen. For Marx it didn't matter whether you were for communism or against it; either way, communism was coming inevitably.

How did Marx know this? Marx was a historical materialist. He didn't get his prophecies from God; he got them from studying what he considered the material foundations of history. According to Marx, history is divided into two classes, the working class or proletariat and the capitalist class or bourgeoisie. Essentially, the capitalist class gets rich by continually exploiting the working class. Therefore, it is predictable, at some point, that this conflict becomes so bitter that a revolutionary overthrow of the capitalist class by the workers becomes unavoidable.

Marx considered his work "strictly scientific" and also "strictly realistic." His sidekick, Engels, spoke of the "general laws of motion." Marx and Engels even claimed to know the precise conditions under which this revolt would take place. First, it would take place in the most advanced capitalist countries. Specifically, Marx expected communism to first arrive in Germany or England. Then, he expected it to spread to other European countries and eventually throughout the world. Second, Marx insisted that the signs of the imminent revolution would be the increasing impoverishment of the working class and their mounting alienation from their employers and their society.

It seems almost comic in retrospect that highly intelligent people took all this Marxist rigmarole—the unsupported assumptions, the highfalutin nonsense—as gospel. But clearly they did. By the early twentieth century, however, it became obvious to most people—even to many Marxists—that none of what Marx predicted was actually occurring. Not only were there no signs of revolution in Germany or England but also the working classes in those nations seemed increasingly well off and notably well settled.

In Germany and England, for example, per capita income, adjusted for inflation, had roughly doubled in the half-century between Marx's predictions and the early twentieth century.[7] In short, the capitalist bargain seemed to be working; the proletariat and the bourgeoisie were getting along pretty well. Socialism seemed even less likely in America, the German economist Werner Sombart wrote, because everyone was just too comfortable. In Sombart's terms, all revolutionary utopias come to grief on roast beef and apple pie.

The crisis of Marxism can be seen in a single letter written by Eduard Bernstein, a German exile in England who had become Engels's closest protégé. As early as 1898 Bernstein wrote, "I have tried, by stretching Marxist teachings, to bring them into accord with practical realities.... But when I got through with my artistic performance, I said to myself—this cannot go on. It is idle to try to reconcile the irreconcilable. What is necessary is to become clear just where Marx is right and where he is wrong."[8]

The need for fundamental revisions in Marxism became even more obvious in the early decades of the twentieth century. In 1917 there was a communist revolution, but it occurred in Russia of all places, one of the least developed countries in Europe. This, for Marxists, came as a surprise. Marx had insisted that revolution in Russia, Asia, or Africa was impossible without those regions going through the stages of capitalist development. Marx's historical trajectory was from feudalism to capitalism to communism. In other words, you had to become capitalist before you could become communist.

As Marxists no less than others could see, the Russian revolution was not a revolt of the proletariat against a capitalist class but an organized military operation by professional revolutionaries against a czarist dictatorship. The revolutionaries were not from the labor class but mainly drawn from the intelligentsia—lawyers, journalists, social activists. This was not what Marx had foreseen at all. As for the kind of revolution Marx did predict, a revolt of the working class, no revolution has ever taken place that is proletarian in any intelligible sense of the term.

How did Marxists respond to these surprising and, to them, disturbing developments of history? Most of the official Marxist parties in Europe responded with bovine stupidity. Marxism fell into a kind of intellectual stupor. Many in the Marxist leadership basically ignored the world as it was and continued to wait for the world as it ought to be. Karl Kautsky and Rosa Luxemburg were two leading lights of the German Social Democratic Party, the leading socialist party in the world, and later of the Independent Social Democratic Party of Germany. Their position was that revolution would indeed come to Germany, just as soon as the conditions were ripe.

Like Eduard Bernstein, however, many of the most intelligent Marxists and socialists recognized that this was socialist daydreaming. Conditions across Europe were becoming less ripe. Each decade the living conditions of workers had gotten measurably better. And how to explain Russia? Marx would have had a fit over that one. A great debate erupted among Marxists, socialists, and leftists, and the result was the emergence of two new strains of Marxian socialism that would dominate the new century. The first was Bolshevism or Leninism. The other was fascism or National Socialism.

Let's begin with Lenin, the revolutionary leader of the Russian revolution. Lenin was, like Mussolini, both an intellectual and a practical

revolutionary. And like Mussolini he started out as an orthodox Marxian socialist. He would remain, to the end of his life, loyal to the bulk of
Marxist doctrine. Yet Lenin knew he also had to account for why communism came to Russia and not to advanced capitalist countries like
Germany or England.

His explanation, offered in a book called *Imperialism, the Highest
Stage of Capitalism*, was ingenious. Basically Lenin argued that capitalism had "exported" its crisis via colonialism and imperialism to the Third
World. In other words, capitalists in the West were buying off their
working classes by exploiting the poor in other countries. This, Lenin
argued, was not something that Marx foresaw. Consequently, Lenin
argued, we should expect revolution not in the central metropolis of
capitalism, western Europe, but rather on the periphery. Russia was
simply the first case of what Lenin predicted would be socialist revolutions breaking out throughout the underdeveloped world.

Lenin also knew that his Bolshevik revolution was not a working
class revolution. He saw there was no accounting for this except with a
revision of Marx. In his most famous book *What Is to Be Done?* Lenin
insisted that Marx had been too complacent in expecting his revolution
to occur by itself. In a way, Marx had placed too much confidence in
working people. Lenin viewed them as too ignorant and downtrodden
to initiate much of anything.

Future revolutions, Lenin said, would require a professional vanguard of militant fighters, led by people like him, to instigate class consciousness in society and actually overthrow the ruling class on behalf
of the working class. These militants did not have to be proletarians; they
could be intellectuals, artists, even members of the bourgeoisie. As
political scientist Joshua Muravchik puts it, from Lenin's point of view,
"The proletarian revolution did not need to be carried out by proletarians; it could be done for them."[9]

But in the end, Lenin expected things to turn out pretty much as
Marx had predicted. Lenin agreed with Marx that the communist revolution was an international event. Eventually it would be a worldwide
phenomenon. Moreover, it would be revolution driven by class differences,

which we see in all countries. Therefore, communism cannot be restricted to a single country; in fact, as Marx once put it, the working man has no country.

Lenin also expected that when the revolution is finally consummated, the state itself will wither away. This was the central theme of Lenin's *The State and Revolution* in which he predicted that the revolution of the proletariat would be followed by a dictatorship of the proletariat and that, in turn, would be followed by the complete disappearance of any kind of state. In other words, in the communist utopia everyone in society will jointly own the means of production and there is no need to have a state at all.

This little piece of Marxian ideological claptrap becomes especially risible when we ponder Lenin's Soviet Union with its militarized and overweening state, confiscating the people's wealth and ruling with an iron rod over their lives. Even as he ruthlessly exploited the Russian people in the name of socialist ideology, Lenin continued to fatuously predict the disappearance of the entire apparatus of the communist state.

It should be noted that Lenin's innovations in Marxism were not well received by the mainstream of European Marxists, such as Kautsky and Luxemburg, who accused Lenin of corrupting Marxist teachings and undermining the whole logic of Marxism. Lenin didn't care. He knew he was the wave of the future. Leninism would survive the "crisis of Marxism" and change the world. And what happened to Kautsky and Luxemburg? He disappeared into the musty archives of Marxist history, and she ended up as a footnote—executed by the Weimar regime in 1919 for her association with a failed armed uprising.

Over in Italy, a man very similar in temperament to Lenin, and no less ruthless and practical, was pondering the very same crisis as the Soviet despot. He was joined in this quest by a whole movement of revolutionary socialists, mostly in Italy but also in France and Germany. They would come to quite different conclusions than Lenin and envision a very different type of socialist future. Even so, together they launched a movement, fascism, that would rival Soviet communism in its ultimate global reach and tragic destructiveness.

A Myth of Revolutionary Violence

The fascist response to the "crisis of Marxism" took a different turn than Lenin's did, while maintaining some similarities with his approach. This turn is more interesting for our purpose because Mussolini's fascism has more relevance to American progressivism than Lenin's Bolshevism. Here, however, we must view Mussolini's trajectory along with that of others, because he didn't do it alone. Italian fascism—the first fascism—emerged as a synthesis of two socialist movements: the nationalist movement and the revolutionary syndicalist movement. Both were built on the foundation of one man, Georges Sorel.[10]

Sorel was a French Marxist who nevertheless started from the premise that Marx's predictions had failed: "We know that things do not happen as simply as Marx supposed in 1847." The problem for Sorel was Marx's historical determinism. He claimed, "We are promised science, but we are offered only words. We are not given any new means of acting in the world." In other words, for Sorel the revolution doesn't just happen to the working class, it has to be caused by the working class.

But how? Here Sorel goes beyond Marx and dives into the realm of psychology. Humans, he says, are motivated by powerful inner aspirations which are not entirely rational. Sorel calls these aspirations "myths" by which he means powerful ideas that rally large groups of people to action. The Crusades, he points out, were driven by the myth of the holy quest of recapturing Jerusalem. Myths are "not descriptions of things," Sorel insists, "but expressions of will."

Sorel, like Lenin, considered the working class to be inert, incapable of revolution by itself. What it needed was leaders who would infuse its class struggle with powerful myths, and these myths would unify the proletariat and move it to action. Sorel seems to call for something similar to Lenin's revolutionary vanguard, a leader or group of leaders who would awaken the consciousness of the working class.

Here we see the concept of "consciousness raising" that is common to Leninism and early fascism and also an important feature of modern American progressivism. Consciousness raising implies that the place that revolution occurs is in the human mind. Consciousness—not circumstance—determines if you are a true revolutionary. An intellectual who has his consciousness raised can count himself one of the proletariat. A working man who rejects revolution can be diagnosed as suffering from "false consciousness."

The New Left in the 1960s was obsessed with consciousness raising. Saul Alinsky, a mentor to Obama and Hillary, devoted a large part of his training seminars to consciousness raising. Today Black Lives Matter and other left-wing groups routinely conduct consciousness-raising workshops as part of their protest training. All of this is a replacement of Marx's notion of historical inevitability with the recognition that people don't agitate of their own accord; their grievances have to be created or at least interpreted for them, and they have to be stirred up to get off their butts and take action.

While he recognized that he was revising Marx, Sorel insisted that his revision was entirely in the spirit of Marx. Marxism wasn't wrong, it merely required a "work of completion" that would itself be carried out "by Marxist methods." The problem was that Marxism had been corrupted by Marxists who were too blind to see that revolution wasn't happening in the normal course of events and too inept and lazy themselves to move the proletariat to action.

Sorel agreed with Marx that the central division of society is a class division—a division between workers and capitalists. "Class struggle is the alpha and omega of socialism," he wrote. Class struggle was "what was really true in Marxism, what was powerfully original, superior to all formulas." And the early Marx, Sorel insisted, spoke less in terms of the inevitability of revolution and more in terms of motivating workers and galvanizing them to action. So in a sense Marx had gotten it right from the beginning.

The action that Sorel wanted to see was a general strike. This was the "myth" or cause that would stir the workers to decisive action. By a general strike, Sorel envisioned not a series of clashes between workers and capitalists in various industries but rather a single nationwide strike that would, in one blow, bring down the capitalist system. Sorel, like Lenin, realized that such a strike could hardly be peaceful for the simple reason that capitalists would never give up their power without a fight.

Sorel, therefore, welcomed the general strike as a means to violent revolution. He was by no means allergic to violence; in fact, his main work is called *Reflections on Violence*. Sorel spoke of violence as "beautiful" and "heroic." For him, violence was a kind of healthy cleansing—a removal of the social debris—and we see here in early fascism, Leninism, and later in American progressivism this same glorification of the violence that attends uprising and protest. For all these ideologies, beating people up is an important way to purge society of its longstanding evils.

Sorel remained all his life a Marxist. He dedicated *Reflections on Violence* to Lenin. He welcomed the Russian revolution. While he never called himself a fascist, he was aware that the fascists had been influenced by his work, and he never disavowed them. Sorel, like so many that would follow him, saw fascism as a continuation and fulfillment of socialism, a completion, as he termed it, of the "historical role" of the Left.

Mussolini was very impressed with Sorel. "The masses," he wrote, "cannot be the protagonists of history—they are its instrument."[11] Naturally he saw himself as the kind of leader who would invoke the collective myths that would move the proletariat to action. And Mussolini, like Sorel, affirmed the necessity and even beauty of violence as a consummation of revolution. In other words, the socialism of words had to eventually result in the socialism of deeds. The revolutionaries of the Left must actually take over the country, and to do so they would obviously have to break some heads.

It's the Nation, Stupid

In 1911, Italy invaded Tripoli and Cyrenaica to pluck the province of Libya from the Ottoman Empire. Observing the Italian campaign,

Mussolini made a startling discovery. He noticed that the Italian working class responded more powerfully to the appeal of the nation than they had ever responded to the appeal of class. This realization was fortified a few years later when Italy entered World War I on the side of Britain and France. Mussolini saw that Italian socialists fought for Italy, French socialists fought for France, and German socialists fought for Germany.

The importance of this discovery cannot be overstated. As a socialist deeply imbued with Marxian concepts of class, Mussolini believed that class association was the primary engine of history. He firmly believed that people were primarily attached to their class. They would die, if called upon to do so, for their class. This applied equally to working people and to the bourgeoisie. In the second decade of the twentieth century, Mussolini saw this was not true. People will not give their lives for their class, but they will give their lives for their country.

At first, Mussolini refused to believe this. Marx insisted that class alliances were fundamental and that nationalism was an invention of the bourgeoisie ruling class. In fact, Marx reviled the old patriotism with its display of flags and paraphernalia as a ruse by the bourgeoisie ruling class to keep the working class in line. Patriotism, he believed, was a strategy to repress class conflict. Mussolini agreed with this. He vigorously opposed the Libyan war and ridiculed displays of Italian patriotism. The Italian flag, he famously said, was a "rag" that deserved to be "planted on a dunghill."[12]

By 1914, the year of the Great War, Mussolini was starting to think differently. His change of heart came primarily from direct personal observation of what actually rallied the working class, namely, their attachment to Italy rather than their attachment to this group called the proletariat. In the trenches, Mussolini observed, "no one spoke any longer of returning to his village or region. One talked of returning to Italy."[13] Mussolini's shift, however, was also influenced by a group of revolutionary socialists who had long been championing nation over class. These were the nationalists whose most prominent figures were Roberto Michels, Enrico Corradini, and Alfredo Rocco.

Later, all of them became fascists. Michels was a German socialist before he moved to Italy and joined first the Italian Socialist Party and then Mussolini's fascist party. Corradini and Rocco were socialist activists; the former was the prime mover of the Italian Nationalist Association which Rocco later joined. Eventually this group was merged into the fascist party. Corradini was nominated by Mussolini to serve in the Italian Senate and joined Mussolini's government in 1928. Rocco was elected as a fascist to the Chamber of Deputies and later, as Mussolini's minister of justice, became a major architect of the criminal code of the fascist state.

A former student of Max Weber in Germany, Michels made the case for nationalism through a sociological examination of what made groups cohere. He agreed with Marx that man is not a solitary creature and that man has, since earliest history, coalesced into social groups. Even so, Michels argued that the strongest human association, outside of the family, was not social class but rather tribe. Tribes, he said, are the ancestors of modern nations and nations, built upon shared mores and shared history. They are what command people's deepest allegiances. Michels called nations "communities of will."

Corradini and Rocco went further, arguing that it made no sense to talk about class differences in an undeveloped, agricultural country like Italy. Here, they said, there are no sharp differences between the working class and the capitalist class. Here the whole country is poor and pretty much everyone has to work with their hands. In a sense, all Italians belong to a single struggling class.

Their allegiances, then, arose not from class but from a common attachment to shared memories and shared participation in the Italian way of life. What Italians had in common, in other words, was their ethnicity. Here we see the basis of the nationalism that is an important feature of fascism. But it should be recognized at the outset that this is ethnic nationalism—a nationalism of ethnic identity. As such it is at the root not only of fascism but also of modern progressivism, with its affirmation and celebration of ethnic identity as the basis for political motivation and participation.

From their reflection on ethnicity as the shared identity of Italian workers, Corradini and Rocco drew the conclusion that ethnic nationalism was the galvanizing myth of working people. Only a sacrificial dedication to the Italian nation, they argued, would enable Italy to go beyond the fragile unification of the *Risorgimento* and achieve a "second *Risorgimento*" that would truly make Italy into a mature, developed country.

Corradini also pointed out that destitute Italians often had to go abroad to seek work, where they ended up being exploited for their labor by rich countries like England, France, and Germany. Given this, Corradini proposed a revision of the Marxist concept of class division. The real division, he said, was between rich nations and poor nations. Germany, England, and France were plutocratic countries—nations of capitalists—and Italy itself, the whole country, could be considered a "proletarian nation," a nation of exploited workers.[14]

Ultimately the revolutionary nationalists proposed that Italy itself would have to unify and revolt against the global capitalist exploitation of the rich European countries which had grown fat not only on Italian labor but also on foreign colonies and conquests that had extended their living space. This was called *spazio vitale* in Italy; the Germans called it *Lebensraum*. The nationalists advocated *spazio vitale* for Italy because they believed that that was the only way for Italy to rise up from its status as a proletarian nation.

In the view of the socialist nationalists who ultimately became fascists, Italy, too, needed its own living space, and this might require either overseas colonial campaigns or war within Europe itself to extend Italy's influence and power and enable its people to join the community of rich nations. Unlike Mussolini, the nationalists supported Italian intervention in Libya in 1911 and they also supported Italian participation in World War I. Mussolini avidly read these nationalists and—at first reluctantly, but eventually enthusiastically—came to agree with them.

The Fascist Synthesis

While the nationalists pressed their case in Italy for socialist allegiance on the basis of ethnicity, another group in Germany called for socialist unity on the basis of race. A good representative of this group was the Marxist Ludwig Woltmann, who sought to integrate Marx's scientific materialism with the evolutionary science of Darwin.[15] Basically Woltmann argued that the Darwinian struggle for survival didn't take place among individual creatures but—within human communities—between races. This *Rassenkampf* or racial struggle, as he put it, would naturally result in the triumph of superior races and the elimination of inferior races.

Woltmann was one of the original inspirations for Hitler's National Socialism. Notice that from the outset German National Socialism differs from Italian fascism in making race—as opposed to national allegiance—primary. Interestingly modern American progressivism also developed an obsession with race. Today if you propose removing racial categories from the census, the strongest opposition is likely to come from the progressives who believe, as one of their number, Cornel West, put it in the title of a book, *Race Matters*. Mussolini would not have agreed, but Woltmann would have, as would any dedicated member of the Nazi Party.

Mussolini didn't believe in race, and he wasn't initially a nationalist; rather, he was a revolutionary syndicalist. The term syndicalism refers to the associations or syndicates to which workers belonged. These were autonomous workers organizations that resembled unions, but they were not unions because the syndicates were organized regionally rather than by corporation or occupation. As dedicated Marxists, the revolutionary syndicalists agreed with Marx that class associations were primary, and that they must be the organizing principle of socialist revolution.

Very much in keeping with this class emphasis that was so central to Marx, the syndicalists, strongly influenced by Sorel, sought to rally the labor syndicates through a general strike that would overthrow the ruling class and establish socialism in Italy. This is what made them "revolutionary." They intended to foment revolution, not wait for it to happen. They were considered the smartest, most dedicated people in the Italian Socialist Party and they occupied the left wing of the party.

The big names in revolutionary syndicalism were Giuseppe Prezzolini, Angelo O. Olivetti, Arturo Labriola, Filippo Corridoni, Paolo Orano, Michele Bianchi, and Sergio Panunzio. Most of them were writers or labor organizers. All of them were socialists, and shortly all of them would become fascists, even though Labriola opposed Mussolini's regime when it came to power and Corridoni, who was killed in World War I, didn't live to see it.

Mussolini was their acknowledged leader. He knew them well and conspired with them at meetings and rallies. He read their books and articles and published in their magazines like the *Avanguardia Socialista*, founded by Laboriola, which was the leading journal of syndicalist thought. Mussolini also reviewed and published the leading syndicalists in his own socialist publications.

Like all revolutionary socialists, the syndicalists had little faith in democratic parliamentary procedures and, consistent with Sorel and Lenin, they sought a charismatic leader who would inspire the workers to action. Mussolini, more than anyone else, fit their prescription. Mussolini was the one who led the syndicalists into a union with the nationalists in order to form the new socialist hybrid called fascism in Italy and (with some modifications) National Socialism in Germany.

The syndicalists organized three general strikes in Italy in 1904, 1911, and 1913. Mussolini supported the strikes. The 1904 strike began in Milan and spread across the country. Five million workers walked off their jobs. The nation was paralyzed: there was no public transportation, and no one could buy anything. Even so, the strike ended without causing either the fall of the government or the installation of socialism.

Mussolini himself organized the second general strike in 1911, mainly as a protest against Italy's Libyan war. The strike failed and Mussolini was arrested and imprisoned for five months. The following year, Mussolini's compatriot Filippo Corridoni tried again with a general strike, which was another flop. These failures of action caused Mussolini and his fellow syndicalists to give up on the class basis of socialism and the general strike concept and to look to nationalists like Corradini, Rocco, and Michels for a better approach.

From the collaboration of the syndicalists and the nationalists came the new fascist synthesis. This synthesis replaced the traditional Marxist category of class with the new category of the nation. Revolutionary struggle would henceforth not be class war but a national struggle. Revolutionary war would not be a fight between classes—rich and poor—but a fight between rich nations and poor nations in which the proletarian nations would overthrow the hegemony of the plutocratic ones. In effect, the myth of the general strike was replaced by the myth of revolutionary war, a war that the fascists conceived as a "war of redistribution."[16]

It may seem, at first glance, that the concept of colonial or even global war runs directly counter to Marx. But as Angelo O. Olivetti—a syndicalist turned fascist and, interestingly enough, Jewish—pointed out, Marx himself had supported colonialism as a necessary mechanism for the development of backward countries. Moreover, both Marx and Engels did not hesitate to promote German interests—they supported Bismarck's nationalist war against France and his irredentist claims against czarist Russia. After Marx's death, Engels backed the German annexation of Schleswig, which was part of Denmark. Fascists emphasized all this as a way of stressing that their nationalism was consistent with Marxism and that they remained, in the end, good socialists.

The fascist synthesis did not view Italy as a society divided by class but rather as a unified country in which all sectors of society could come together. The fascists replaced the old Marxist divide between unproductive capitalists and productive labor with the single category of the productive nation. Mussolini called this a *Fascio nazionale*, a national union. "We have become," Mussolini said, "and will remain, a nation of producers."[17] We can already see, here in Italy, the fusion that would later give Hitler's fascism its distinctive name. When you fuse the two ideas of "nation" and "socialism," what you get is National Socialism.

Mussolini never used the term "national socialism" and indignantly repudiated it when it became associated with Hitler and Nazi Germany.

Even so, Mussolini created the first National Socialism, stripped of its German racial connotations. His was a vision of a nation organized along socialist lines in which everyone would share in the benefits and all would contribute their due portion. This language of course has Obama overtones, and we see an obvious congruence between the fascist unification and the modern progressive insistence that America is a single community and that everyone should come together and each one contribute his "fair share."

Finally, the fascist synthesis added the new element of the state as the executive arm charged with defining and carrying out the overall good of the nation. This is the point at which Giovanni Gentile, discussed in the previous chapter, emerged as the leading philosopher of fascism. Gentile was the great apostle of the centralized state. For him, the state was the nation and the nation was the state. Our identities and welfare are all subsumed not merely under the nation but also under the rod of the all-powerful centralized state. One can see why Mussolini loved all this; he saw it as the intellectual basis for, well, himself.

Marx, let's recall, had predicted the withering away of the state. So, oddly enough, did Lenin. Far from withering away, the state greatly expanded under Lenin into a totalitarian monster. Even so, Lenin's theory continued to invoke the disappearing state. In this sense fascism is the first left-wing ideology of the twentieth century to explicitly affirm the need for a powerful centralized state. Around the same time, however, and beaten by the fascists by only a hair, a closely related ideology developed in America that also called for a powerful centralized state. That ideology was, of course, progressivism.

The fascists, like the progressives, sought a radical transformation of society that is the very antithesis of classical liberalism or modern American conservatism. The only revolution that American conservatives ally themselves with is the American revolution, the revolution that established the bourgeois capitalism that fascists and progressives seek to transform and overthrow. The roots of fascism fully expose the connection between fascism and America's political Left, and the antithesis between fascism and America's political Right.

Both the fascists and the progressives viewed the centralized state as the logical outgrowth of everything they stood for. It's all very well to talk about the nation of producers and the interests of the nation, but who decides what its true interests are? Socialists claim to be in favor of equitable redistribution of income and wealth, but who determines what is equitable and does the actual redistribution? To these questions, the fascists answered: we do, through the instrument of the powerful centralized state. And this is also, in America, the answer that today's progressives give.

In addition, the fascists adopted an economic policy that is closely parallel to, and in many respects identical with, today's progressivism. Mussolini called this policy "corporatism," but a more descriptive term would be state-run capitalism. Mussolini envisioned a powerful centralized state directing the institutions of the private sector, forcing their private welfare into line with the national welfare. Isn't this precisely how progressives view the federal government's control of banks, finance companies, insurance companies, health care, energy, and education? Although today's American Left dares not invoke Mussolini's name, the honest among them will have to admit that it was he and his fellow fascists who were their pioneers and paved their way.

four

A Democratic Party Secret

*As Hitler imagined the future, Germany would deal with
the Slavs much as the North Americans had dealt with the
Indians. The Volga River in Russia, he once proclaimed,
will be Germany's Mississippi.*[1]

Timothy Snyder, *Bloodlands: Europe Between Hitler and Stalin*

itting in Landsberg Prison in 1924, Adolf Hitler had a big idea.
We know that it occurred to him there because that's where he
did most of the strategic thinking that guided his later actions.
Hitler outlined the fruits of his reflections in his autobiography, *Mein
Kampf*, and also in subsequent speeches and recordings that are now
available. *Hitler's Table Talk*, for example, is an extensive archive of
Hitler's private statements during World War II recorded by an aide
Heinrich Heim, acting on the orders of Hitler's secretary, Martin
Bormann.

Before we examine Hitler's idea, let's review the background. Hitler,
a veteran of World War I, was like many Germans smarting under his
country's defeat and the humiliating terms imposed by the Treaty of
Versailles, including the confiscation of Germany's few colonies and her
forced return of Alsace and Lorraine to France. Hitler also knew that
Britain and France were global powers with colonies all over the world.

There was little further territory for Germany, a latecomer to colonialism, to conquer and occupy.

Hitler also had a domestic problem, the Jews. Yet Hitler's "final solution," involving the extermination of the Jews, would come much later through Nazi coordination initiatives like the notorious Wannsee Conference on January 20, 1942. At this point Hitler simply sought a way to deal with the roughly three quarters of a million Jews who lived in Germany at the time.

One idea was to ghettoize the Jews and force them to live in segregated communities as second class citizens. Another was to expel the Jews, to relocate them to the French colony of Madagascar in the Indian Ocean off the coast of Africa, or just force them to go to some other country. Eventually some 500,000 Jews would leave Germany in the period between Hitler's ascent to power in 1933 and the beginning of World War II in 1939.[2]

As he thought about these problems, Hitler's attention was turned to America. Hitler didn't know a lot about America. He had never been to America. And he despised America. "My feelings against Americanism," he later said in 1942, "are feelings of hatred and deep repugnance." Why? He claimed, "Everything about the behavior of American society reveals that it's half Judaised and the other half negrified." Moreover, America is "a country where everything is built on the dollar." For Hitler, America represented the worst case of unrestricted Jewish capitalism.[3]

Even so, Hitler had a genuine interest in certain aspects of American history. As a boy, he had been captivated by a series of cowboy novels set in the American West written by the German novelist Karl May. Hitler wasn't May's only fan; the novels were beloved by Albert Einstein, Albert Schweitzer, and millions of other Germans. May was the J. K. Rowling of his day, penning widely popular stories of two Wild West buddies, a German surveyor named Old Shatterhand and his Apache sidekick Winnetou. The general theme of the novels was the tragic disappearance of the Indians from the continent, Indian heroism giving way to the inevitability of white settlement and progress.[4]

Hitler was also interested in the lessons of the American Civil War. Again, his knowledge was derived largely from impressionistic and novelistic sources, yet the paucity of his knowledge did not stop Hitler from drawing very firm conclusions. Historian Ira Katznelson tells us, "Hitler denigrated blacks, admired American racism, and regretted the South's defeat in 1865.... Like other Nazi leaders, Hitler was fascinated in 1937 by *Vom Winde verweht*, the German edition of *Gone With the Wind*. This melodramatic epic of the Civil War and Reconstruction was a bestseller. The film, not surprisingly, proved a big hit. Nervous as he awaited the dawn invasion of the USSR, a move that would start Operation Barbarossa, Joseph Goebbels spent the hours after midnight on June 22, 1941, watching a pre-release German version with a group of invited friends."[5]

All this, of course, came much later. Let's go back to Landsberg Prison and Hitler's big idea. It occurred to him, Hitler writes in *Mein Kampf,* that Germany did not need to imitate the British and the French in their quest for overseas colonies in Asia, Africa, and South America. Who wants to rule a bunch of brown and black people? Besides, Hitler says, the climate in those places is not suited to settlement by Nordic Germans. Let the British and the French have Asia and Africa. "For Germany," Hitler writes, "the only possibility of carrying out a healthy territorial policy lay in the acquisition of new land in Europe itself...land on the home continent."[6]

Hitler called his plan *Lebensraum* and he found an important historical precedent for it in the United States of America. In the nineteenth century, Hitler knew, the white man basically cleared most of the North American continent of its original inhabitants, the Native Americans. This was done through merciless policies of treaty breaking, waging war against the Indians, wiping out resistance, forcibly displacing and relocating them, and seizing their land for white settlement. Basically, Hitler decided to adopt this precise plan for settling Germans on large parts of the European continent.

As Hitler himself put it in a 1928 speech, Americans had "gunned down the millions of Redskins to a few hundred thousand, and now

keep the modest remnant under observation in a cage." Far from object-
ing to this precedent, Hitler intended to emulate it. As historian Norman
Rich put it, "The United States policy of westward expansion in the
course of which the white men ruthlessly thrust aside the 'inferior'
indigenous populations served as the model for Hitler's entire conception
of *Lebensraum*."[7]

Hitler knew, of course, that the land he had in mind—Poland, much
of eastern Europe, and a large part of the European section of Russia—
was occupied respectively by Poles, Slavs and other eastern Europeans,
and Russians. These, for Hitler, were his "Indians." He resolved for them
the same fate as the Native Americans: wage war against them, murder
the resistance, forcibly displace and relocate them, and seize their land.
For those who remained, Hitler had another plan also derived from
American history: enslave and enroll them in forced labor for the benefit
of the white Aryan citizens of Greater Germany.

Lebensraum, Hitler confessed, was the concept that would "dominate my entire existence." I'm not suggesting he got the idea solely from
America; there were German writers calling for *lebensraum* going back
to the turn of the previous century. In 1900, for example, the German
anthropologist Ludwig Woltmann argued on racial grounds for *lebensraum*. The "German race," he said, "has been selected to dominate the
earth." Woltmann got his idea not from German overcrowding—Germany was not overcrowded—but from a concept of territoriality derived
from the animal kingdom and applied to human society.[8] Woltmann
was a progressive social Darwinist, and progressive social Darwinism,
as we'll see later in this book, was an important progenitor of fascism
and Nazism.

Hitler's specific program of *Lebensraum*, however, appears to have
been inspired by the nineteenth-century policies and practices of the
Democratic Party in America. The analogy doesn't end there. Here is a
telling passage from historian John Toland's book *Adolf Hitler: The
Definitive Biography*: "Hitler's concept of concentration camps as well
as the practicality of genocide owed much, so he claimed, to his studies
of English and United States history. He admired the camps for Boer

prisoners in South Africa and for the Indians in the Wild West, and often praised to his inner circle the efficiency of America's extermination—by starvation and uneven combat—of the red savages who could not be tamed by captivity."[9]

The same theme is stressed even more forcefully in Timothy Snyder's book *Bloodlands: Europe Between Hitler and Stalin.* Snyder discloses that under the scheme called Generalplan Ost, Hitler sought to "deport, kill, assimilate or enslave" some thirty to forty-five million Poles, Ukrainians, and Slavs. The Nazis intended to create, on their land, German farming communities of 15,000–20,000 people. Snyder writes, "Colonization would make of Germany a continental empire fit to rival the United States, another hardy frontier state based on exterminatory colonialism and slave labor.... In Hitler's view, 'In the East, a similar process will repeat itself for a second time as in the conquest of America.'"[10]

A Pre-History of Nazism

Let's draw out the implications of this. First, the Left loves to portray Hitler as a right-winger but notice here how he allies himself completely with the pro-slavery and Indian removal policies of the Democratic Party. Clearly Hitler would be far more at home with Democratic President Andrew Jackson or Democratic Senator John C. Calhoun than he would be with, say, Abraham Lincoln. Notice, also, that part of the reason Hitler hates America so much is that it is so capitalist. Hitler identifies America with capitalism and capitalist corruption with the Jews. More on this later.

A second implication is that here in America we tend to be very provincial about our history. We cannot imagine how events in America like Indian removal and slavery could possibly influence goings-on across the Atlantic, just as we don't recognize how European happenings have an impact here. This book is intended as a corrective to this provincialism. This is not to say that, without American influence, Hitler would not have invaded Poland and Russia or that he would not have had concentration camps. It is to say that the American example played a role in showing him how it could be done and in giving him confidence, based on history, that something like this had been done already.

This chapter, on slavery and Indian removal, and the next one, on racism, segregation, and racial terrorism, are intended to provide a pre-history of Nazism and the Holocaust. I use the term "pre-history" in precisely the same sense as historian Gotz Aly who, in a recent book, provides what he terms "the pre-history of the Holocaust."[11] Racial anti-Semitism in Germany in the late nineteenth and early twentieth centuries, Aly shows, precedes and paves the way for the Holocaust. Obviously the late nineteenth-century and early twentieth-century anti-Semites didn't themselves kill six million Jews, yet they did lead pogroms against Jews and adopted discriminatory laws that offered a ghastly preview of things to come. Hitler later drew on that anti-Semitic culture to recruit Germans to participate in the Final Solution.

So, too, my pre-history is intended not merely as a foreshadowing of the horrors of German fascism but also to show the historical susceptibility of the Democratic Party in America to fascist appeals and fascist practices. Long before the rise of fascism itself, they invented some of those practices here. No wonder that when fascism actually arrived, as I show later in the book, the Democrats were completely on board. So, to put it in the strongest way possible, one may say that Nazi DNA was in the Democratic Party from the very beginning. The Democrats—not the Nazis—are the originators of the politics of hate.

In this chapter, I take some of the "signature" concepts of Nazism—*Lebensraum*, concentration camps, genocide—and show that they had an application in the United States long before they were applied in Nazi Germany, through the Democratic Party's support for Indian removal and plantation slavery. I realize that in making these comparisons, I risk stirring the indignation even of some conservatives who will say, in their ritual fashion, "Are you comparing the United States to Nazi Germany?" Actually no. I am merely comparing the practices of the Democratic Party to those of the German Workers' National Socialist Party. The idea that "America" is responsible for Democratic Party atrocities is part of the big lie I am trying to expose in this book.

Second, I risk offending the sensibilities of Jews and others who believe in the singularity of the Holocaust. According to this view, the Holocaust is unique and nothing can be compared to it. I largely agree with this. But while the Holocaust is singular, not everything that Hitler and the Nazis did was singular. Even genocide is not singular. The United Nations has published a working definition of "genocide" which is admittedly drawn from the example of the Nazis. Even so, the point of the definition is to help identify other cases of genocide that might occur around the world.

But wait a minute, you say. How can you even compare, for example, slavery in the Democratic South with German concentration camps? The former existed for forced labor, while the latter were built for mass extermination. Actually, the concentration camps were forced labor camps. One scholar, Marc Buggeln, titles a recent study *Slave Labor in the Nazi Concentration Camps*. Another recently published work, edited by Alexander Von Plato and others, is called *Hitler's Slaves*.[12] The depiction of the camps in these studies is chillingly similar to the depiction of the vast network of Stalinist labor camps given in Alexander Solzhenitsyn's *Gulag Archipelago*.

Scholars of Nazi Germany distinguish between concentration camps that existed for detention and forced labor and extermination or death camps that were designed solely for the purpose of killing people. Dachau, Buchenwald, Mauthausen, Flossenberg, Bergen-Belsen, and Ravensbruck were forced-labor concentration camps, all of them were located in Germany. (Ravensbruck was a women's camp with female prisoners and female guards.) Treblinka, Sobibor, Belzec, and Chelmno—all established in German-occupied Poland—were extermination camps. Auschwitz and Majdanek were both; they had a labor-camp section and an extermination section.

Some scholars have argued that even labor camps were extermination camps since death rates were high and the Nazis had an implicit policy of "slow extermination" or "extermination through labor." Admittedly the guards in labor camps routinely killed people, notably the old, the sick, and "troublemakers." Sometimes labor-camp inmates slotted for execution were transported to extermination camps to be killed there. Buggeln calculated the mortality rate in labor camps and found it to be consistently high, although mortality rates were significantly lower for Jewish prisoners in the women's camps.

Even so, most scholars agree the distinction between death camps and labor camps is important. Prisoners were routinely designated to go to one or the other; the former was a death sentence, while the latter was a *possible* death sentence. Of course in the case of the Nazi camps, as with the Soviet camps, neither Hitler nor Stalin personally cared how many laborers died. Nevertheless, the Soviet camps, like the Nazi camps, are rightly called slave labor camps, as opposed to extermination camps, because they existed for the purpose of extracting work out of inmates, even at the risk of working them to death.

In Hitler's case, the work was deemed necessary to feed the German war machine. Forced laborers in the camps worked mainly for the defense industry, for the Luftwaffe, and for the state-owned conglomerate Hermann Goring Reichwerke. Some worked for private companies contracted to the German state, such as the electrical giant Siemens, the armaments company Bussing, and the aircraft and auto manufacturer Volkswagen. According to Rudolf Hoss, commandant of Auschwitz, his boss Heinrich Himmler's motto for the camps became "Armaments! Prisoners! Armaments!"[13]

Nazi reliance on forced labor became even greater as the war proceeded, and the nation's labor supply became more and more scarce. At this point, remarkably, the Nazis ordered concentration camp officials to reduce mortality rates so that more work could be gotten out of the prisoners. Himmler actually authorized family members to send food parcels to relatives in concentration camps and ordered the death penalty for SS members who stole from those food parcels.[14] Buggeln notes that mortality rates actually went down in 1943 and stayed down until the end of the war when, in a burst of nihilistic rage, the Nazis went on a killing spree even in the labor camps in order to get rid of captives before the Allies got there.

Between 1943 and 1945, the Nazis forced camp inmates to clear rubble and rebuild roads and tracks that had been bombed by American and British planes and to dig anti-tank ditches to slow the advance of Allied troops. So the labor camps were humming with activity in the last phase of World War II. By contrast with labor camps, extermination or death camps from the outset had no work facilities. They were modern industrial execution centers; their sole objective was to kill people through gassing or shooting.

Overall there were between 15,000 and 20,000 concentration camps and sub-camps in Germany and German-occupied Europe. There was a much smaller number of death camps, none of them in Germany, since the regime wanted to hide their existence from the German people. Most of the death camps were constructed in the later phase of the war, since 1942, while concentration camps had been in operation since 1933 when the Nazis first came to power.

Recall the emaciated images of survivors following the liberation of camps like Dachau and Auschwitz in 1945. One hundred thousand people survived Auschwitz; had Auschwitz been solely a death camp, that number would be close to zero. Moreover, most of the survivors at Dachau and Auschwitz weren't Jews; they were non-Jewish Germans and eastern Europeans. That's because the Jews typically were killed in the death camps.

Most of these Jews, by the way, were not German Jews. Only a quarter of a million Jews remained in Germany in 1939. So there is no way Hitler could have killed anywhere near six million German Jews because there weren't that many German Jews to kill. But the population of Jews under Hitler's control expanded greatly with his conquests in Poland, eastern Europe, and Russia. So most of the Jews killed in the death camps were from those places.

As Timothy Snyder puts it in *Bloodlands: Europe between Hitler and Stalin,* "The vast majority of Jews killed in the Holocaust never saw a concentration camp.... People spend the night in camps.... Most of the people who entered German concentration camps survived. The fate of concentration camp inmates, horrible though it was, is distinct from that of those many millions who were gassed, shot or starved."[15]

So it's not unreasonable to make a comparison between two types of forced-labor systems, one in America and the other in Germany. Indeed, the notion of viewing the slave plantation as a type of concentration camp is quite familiar to American scholars, at least since the publication of slavery scholar Stanley Elkins's book *Slavery* which is the single most provocative treatment of the subject. Elkins knows as well as anyone the truth of the academic saying that no analogy travels on all fours. This means that no two things are exactly alike; therefore, when making fruitful comparisons, we have to note the differences no less than the similarities. But when we do, the result can be a better understanding of the phenomena on both sides of the comparison.

Once again, I'm not claiming that Andrew Jackson's *lebensraum* was identical to Hitler's, only that the one was a foreshadowing and a partial inspiration for the other. I'm not saying that slave camps in the Democratic South were identical to German concentration camps, only that Democrats are capable of atrocities that bear a resemblance to Nazi atrocities not so much against the Jews as against the Poles, the Slavs, and the Russians. I know the Nazis killed far more people than the Democrats did. It is also true that Nazi atrocities lasted for a dozen years while Democratic atrocities have been going on since the party was founded in 1828.

The Fake Genocide and the Real One

Inmates in Nazi concentration camps noticed that among their number there was a strange and particular type, which they called the *Muselmann.* No one knows how the term originated, since literally it means "Muslim." Even so, *Muselmann* in this context refers to an inmate emotionally destroyed by his camp experience, a person that historian Wolfgang Sofsky terms "between life and death."[16] *Muselmanner* walked around as if in a daze; they did not respond to conversation, orders, or even blows. They had difficulty even seeing beyond what was immediately in front of them. These inmates had quite literally lost the will to live and merely existed like the zombie characters in *The Walking Dead*.

To me, the *Muselmann* is a tragic metaphor for what has happened here in America to the native Indians. Obviously I don't mean that native Indians are literally human zombies. Some of them are quite successful and fully assimilated into American life. What I mean, rather, is that as a community, the Indians seem to be an American version of *Muselmanner*. They have lost their original moral personality and are still having difficulty replacing it with something else.

I am referring not merely to the pathetic conditions of the American Indian reservation—the poverty, the crime, high rates of alcoholism and suicide, the reduction of a proud people into casino operators and makers of turquoise trinkets. Think about this: while black culture is a vibrant presence in America today, Indian culture is ignored, forgotten, virtually nonexistent. Even after the Holocaust, Jewish culture thrives, in Israel, America, and around the world. By contrast, American Indians seem still to bear the original shock of their displacement and virtual obliteration as a people.

The left-wing historian David Stannard titles his history of the Indians *American Holocaust*. From the title, we can see clearly that Stannard is not into the idea of the Holocaust as a singularity. In fact, he claims, "The destruction of the Indians of the Americas was, far and away, the most massive act of genocide in the history of the world." Stannard considers the whole history of the native people to be a continuing holocaust, what he terms "an unbroken string of genocide campaigns" that begin with the arrival of Columbus in 1492.[17]

We have to watch Stannard carefully, because he is onto something, but we have to be clear about what. He claims a holocaust occurred, but there was no holocaust for the Indians comparable to the Shoah of the Jews. He claims that Indians were victims of genocide—and in the end, we'll see, he's right to claim genocide. The genocide he points to, however, is emphatically not the real genocide.

He invents a fake genocide in order to avoid blaming Andrew Jackson and the Democratic Party for the real one.

Stannard begins with a stunning statistic: of the ten to twelve million native Indians who once populated the American continent, between 90 and 95 percent perished as a consequence of exposure to the white man. This is a catastrophic event, by any measure, but even so Stannard admits that most of these deaths were due to plagues and epidemics unwittingly transmitted from Europeans to the Indians. Whatever we call this, we cannot call it genocide because genocide involves the *intent* to exterminate a population.

Columbus had no intention to do this and neither did the American founders. Yet Stannard concentrates a good deal of his fire on them, because it's ideologically important for him to place the blame for Indian genocide on "the West" and on "America." Therefore, Stannard recalcitrantly refuses to distinguish between Indian deaths caused by epidemic and Indian deaths caused by deliberate massacre or relocation. Both, he insists, count toward genocide.

This is Stannard's fake genocide, and I believe it is this kind of shoddy refusal to make distinctions that provokes the kind of conservative response we see in Guenter Lewy's essay, "Were American Indians the Victims of Genocide?"[18] This essay, first published in *Commentary* but now available online, rushes to the defense of Columbus and the founders. Taking on Stannard directly, Lewy makes many valid points, such as pointing out that the Indians themselves were just as merciless as Andrew Jackson's troops in the Indian wars. He claims Jackson's men simply had better training and better ammunition.

Even so, Lewy has fallen here for a progressive trap, one into which I too fell in my earlier career. Basically in order to defend "the West" and "America," Lewy engages in what may be termed the genocide minimization strategy. Actually, there is no need for such a strategy because neither "the West" nor "America" is guilty of genocide; rather, Andrew Jackson and the Democratic Party are. Unfortunately, Lewy, in his defend-America stance, ends up minimizing even what Jackson and the

Democrats did. Yes, he admits, the Indians were largely wiped out, but no one's really to blame. And besides, it wasn't really genocide. Let's come up with some other, more benign term.

Yet wasn't it genocide? Let's begin with United Nations Resolution 96 (I) which places the term "genocide" into international law. It reads, "In the present Convention, genocide means any of the following acts committed with intent to destroy, in whole or in part, a national, ethnic, racial or religious group: a) killing members of the group, b) causing serious bodily or mental harm; c) deliberately inflicting on the group conditions of life calculated to bring about its physical destruction in whole or in part; d) imposing measures intended to prevent births within the group; e) forcibly transferring children of the group to another group."[19]

Notice that the definition does not require a group to be reduced to extinction. (Even the Jews are not extinct.) Nor does genocide require deaths of the magnitude of the Holocaust. Genocide means an attempt to destroy a group as a whole *or in part*. Moreover, genocide does not require the satisfaction of all the specific measures named; any one of them is sufficient. Taking this definition into account, let's turn to the actions of Andrew Jackson and the Democratic Party in the period from 1828 to 1860.

Dark When He Finished Killing Them

Andrew Jackson had an Indian problem. The Indians, as far as Jackson was concerned, were a "nation within a nation." They were aliens who were occupying American land—a land fated for white occupation and white settlement. Thus their very presence constituted a malignancy and a threat. Never mind that all of America, North and South America, was originally their land. The United States was growing. Growth required expansion. Expansion required the natives to get up and leave. In short, from Jackson's point of view, they had to be cajoled to abandon their ancestral land, or be forcibly evacuated or killed. This was *lebensraum*, Democratic Party style.

The ground for Jackson was laid by his Democratic allies like Democratic governor Lewis Cass of Michigan. "We speak of them as they are," Cass said of the Indians. He continued, "Government is unknown among them. They have no criminal code, no courts, no officers, no punishments. Reckless of consequences, the Indian is a child of impulse. Unrestrained by moral considerations, whatever his passions prompt, he does. To roam the forests at will, to pursue their game, to attack their enemies, to spend the rest of their lives in listless indolence, and to be ready at all times to die—these are the principal occupations of an Indian."[20]

So here we have the first criterion of genocide, the targeting of a specific racial and ethnic group. Cass denounces the Indians in racial terms quite similar to Nazi denunciations of Jews, gypsies, and other eastern European populations deemed inferior. Here we also see transference and blaming the victim—an attempt by Cass to fault the Indians for their own imminent removal. See, these people are unworthy of civilization; they are the ones who are making us throw them off their land.

Jackson himself didn't go this route. He professed to be a friend of the Indians, insisting that he was forcing them off their land to keep them "free from the mercenary influence of white men, and undisturbed by the local authority of the states." They could live elsewhere, on lands far away, where Jackson's federal government could "exercise a parental control over their interests."[21] Jackson routinely signed his letters to the Indians "Your Father," implying that he had a paternal devotion to their welfare. He did, in fact, adopt an Indian orphan as his son.

Jackson declared himself a partisan of the Indians in much the same manner that he and his fellow Democratic slave-owners professed to be concerned, first and foremost, with the welfare of their slaves. But professions of paternalism from those days to the present, we should by now be able to see, are a ploy aimed at ruthlessly exploiting people while insisting that Democrats are doing them endless favors. All we can say about these transparent pretenses is that with friends like the Democrats, who needs enemies?

For a friend of the Indians, Jackson seemed remarkably adept at killing them. In fact, his nickname was "Indian killer" and he took it as a compliment. At Horseshoe Bend in the Mississippi Territory (now southern Alabama), Jackson and his troops cornered a group of several hundred Creek refugees, who were seeking shelter from the military conflict between Jackson's militia and a breakaway group of Creek fighters called the Red Sticks.

Jackson's forces wiped out the refugees. As Jackson put it in a letter to his wife Rachel, "It was dark before we finished killing them." Jackson estimated that in addition to the 557 corpses he found 300 Indians "buried in their watry grave." Jackson's men cut off the noses of dead Indians as they counted the bodies. Afterwards there were few regrets; one of Jackson's soldiers chuckled that he had killed a boy "five or six years of age" for the reason that "he would have become an Indian someday."[22] Here we have a distinct criterion for genocide: the wanton killing of members of a distinct racial group, in order to wipe out the group in whole or in part.

Jackson's Indian Removal Act—his chief priority upon assuming the presidency in 1829—later became the basis for the infamous Trail of Tears. His December 1830 speech to Congress on the implementation of the act presented it as of benefit to the Indians, claiming that it would "enable them to pursue happiness in their own way and under their own rude institutions" and spare them the fate of the "tribes which occupied the countries now constituting the Eastern States [who] were annihilated or have melted away to make room for the whites."[23] But throughout his career Jackson had used a combination of trickery, threats, and murder to evict native Indians from Florida, Alabama, Mississippi, and Tennessee. Several tribes—the Chickasaw, the Choctaw, the Creek, and the Seminole—were forced to evacuate. The Cherokee, however, held out. Jackson declared, "The whole Cherokee nation ought to be scourged."

He arrested the elected Cherokee leader John Ross and burned down the tribe's newspaper *The Cherokee Phoenix*. He found a rival group of Cherokee—unrepresentative of the tribe—and bribed them to approve a bogus treaty in which the Cherokees agreed to give up their land and relocate west of the Mississippi. Yet when the relocation deadline arrived, the vast majority of Cherokee had not relinquished their homes. Only 4,000 Cherokee had departed for designated Indian territory farther west, a thousand were in hiding, and 17,000 stayed. Consequently, the Democrats in Congress and the White House resolved to drive them out. Essentially they forced an entire nation to move at gunpoint.

The forced relocation of these 17,000 Cherokee became, in Stannard's words, a "death march" comparable to the Bataan Death March of 1942—one of the Japanese atrocities of World War II. The Democrats sent troops to raid Cherokee homes, seizing the occupants as prisoners and herding them into detention camps. Cabins were set on fire, cattle stolen or shot, and men, women, and children brutalized. A Georgia volunteer who later served in the Confederate army commented, "I fought in the civil war and have seen men shot to pieces and slaughtered by thousands, but the Cherokee removal was the cruelest work I ever knew."

The camps themselves were miserable holding pens, where starvation and disease ran rampant. This disease cannot be compared to the plagues that earlier haunted the Indian populations of the Americas, because those were accidental—the white man had no idea he had brought with him diseases to which the Indians had no immunities—while these were the product of official Democratic government policy and action. Because of the paucity of records, scholars don't know how many Cherokee died. Estimates range from 2,000 to as high as 8,000—which is Stannard's estimate. If Stannard is right, that amounts to nearly one-half of the 17,000 Cherokee that remained on their land and more than one-third of what then remained of the Cherokee nation.[24]

Meanwhile, in California, the Democratic-controlled legislature and executive mounted a war against the native Indian population. Democratic Governor Peter Burnett did not hesitate to call it a "war of extermination" that "must continue to be waged between the races until the Indian becomes extinct." Here again we have a clear expression of genocidal intent. The clear goal was to kill the Indians through militia expeditions and the unleashing of Democratic vigilante mobs and drive the remaining ones into the mountains so their land could be taken from them. It worked—the Indian population of the state was largely wiped out.

More recently, scholars have found evidence that the Indian Health Service (IHS) carried out a longtime strategy of sterilizing native Indian women and, in some cases, took from them their children and put them up for adoption in white homes. Recall that this is one of the specific criteria of genocide in the UN definition. One might expect that this was done before the UN issued its genocide rule, perhaps before the Nazi era, but in fact it continued through the 1970s. In a recent study, Jane Lawrence estimates that 25 percent of all Native American women between the ages of fifteen and forty-four were sterilized by the IHS in the 1970s. These women were conned into signing consent forms by progressive administrators who insisted their goal was to reduce the incidence of American Indian poverty by keeping the Indian population in check.[25]

This, then, is the genocide perpetrated by Andrew Jackson and his progressive Democratic successors. Jackson biographers on the Left like Sean Wilentz seek to minimize Jackson's atrocities. Their point seems to be that, comparatively speaking, the genocide of Jackson and his Democratic successors was a small genocide, but a small genocide is still genocide. Notice that these designations are not merely matters of numbers. Many dictators have killed large numbers of their own people but those incidents don't count as genocide because they did not specifically target a separate and distinct population. Moreover, Stalin and Mao seem to have killed more of their own people than Hitler killed Jews. Even so, Hitler's atrocity is generally agreed to be greater because of his willed intent to wipe out a whole ethnic population.

Recently, progressives—breaking with Democratic historians who lionize Andrew Jackson—have demanded that Jackson's face be removed from the twenty-dollar bill. As we will see throughout this book, normally progressives are the perpetrators, not the critics, of mass killing. More controversial—given that Jackson has been on the twenty-dollar bill since 1928, when Calvin Coolidge was president—is that President Trump has a portrait of Jackson in the Oval Office as well as a miniature reproduction on his desk of Jackson's equestrian statue in Lafayette Park. Trump visited Jackson's plantation and afterward spoke admiringly of the founder of the Democratic Party. Nor is he the only Republican president to have done so. Theodore Roosevelt did, and my former boss Ronald Reagan also visited Jackson's plantation and hung Jackson's portrait in the Oval Office.

Here, I have to admit, I side with the progressives. And I am glad that the horrid Democrat, Jackson, will be replaced with a Republican heroine, Harriet Tubman, on the twenty-dollar bill in 2020. Trump, like Reagan, is a former Democrat, and I imagine his enthusiasm for Jackson is partly driven by the Democratic Party's earlier hagiography of Jackson and partly by Jackson's current vilification at the hands of many left-wing progressives. Yet even progressives can occasionally be correct, and in this case I think they are.

Slave Camps and Nazi Camps

Now we turn from Indian removal to slavery. At first glance, it seems hard to compare the nineteenth-century American plantations to twentieth-century German concentration camps. The latter were modern industrial creations while the former seem antiquated echoes of a bygone era. Yet in 1959 the historian Stanley Elkins revolutionized the comparative history of these two institutions. In the same manner Marc Buggeln used the concept of slave labor to illuminate the concentration camp system, Elkins used the concept of the concentration camp to illuminate the study of the slave plantation.

Elkins began with a startling insight. He realized that even today we notice that stereotypical portraits of Southern slavery not only endure in the literature but also endure in contemporary experience. We can see, in other words, the subservient "house Negroes" and the rebellious "field Negroes" that the slaves and slave-owners talked about. In other words, the stereotypes were not racist fictions. They would not be so persistent, Elkins says, unless they contained at least a kernel of truth.

Elkins found one stereotype particularly arresting: that of the whimsical, happy-go-lucky, semi-idiotic Sambo. Elkins notes, "His behavior was full of infantile silliness and his talk inflated with childish exaggeration." Sambo, in other words, is a childish creature who never grew up to be a man. Sambo is a persistent character in the literature of the period, as well as in early twentieth-century vaudeville. Where, Elkins wonders, did Sambo come from? Elkins here isn't referring to the literary or artistic Sambo, but the real Sambo, the actual black personality corresponding to this strange, ridiculous character.

In thinking about this, Elkins had a flashing epiphany. He recalled that in the German concentration camps, inmates found, after the initial shock of displacement, that the rules of the outside world did not apply. Looking around them, they saw that the prisoners who survived completely gave up their normal dignity and responsibility. They became infantile, almost childlike, in their dependency and conformity to authority. "Their humor was shot with silliness and they giggled like children when one of them would expel wind."[26] In short, here, in a setting so distant and unfamiliar, emerged something like the Sambo character so vividly identified as an inhabitant of the Democratic slave plantation.

In addition, Elkins notes, there were Jews and other inmates in the camps who had been appointed as Kapos. These were prisoner functionaries who supervised work squads called Kommandos and were also scribes or record-keepers who organized everyday routines under the oversight of German SS personnel. Survivors of the camps said in interviews that these Kapos basically took over the roles of the Nazis. They were as harsh or even harsher than the Nazis, and some of them even began to dress and talk like Nazis. In sum, they assumed the roles of their oppressors. So here was a second type, not Sambo, but no less disfigured and strange than Sambo.

How could this happen? Elkins realized that Democratic slave plantations in America and Nazi concentration camps had something in common. Both were closed systems in which inmates lived in a separate world, sealed off to a large degree from the outside world. Consequently,

Elkins theorized, the normal rhythm of the plantation slaves and camp inmates was disrupted and overturned to such a degree that they developed new personalities—abnormal, twisted personalities with no equivalent in the normal world.

In Sambo's case, Elkins pointed out that this particular character simply did not exist in South America. South America had slavery, but no Sambo. Why not? Because, Elkins answered, South American slavery was not a closed system. Even plantation slaves lived in a wider world with protections from their masters that came from the Spanish Crown and from the Catholic Church. On the Democratic plantations of the American South, by contrast, the adult male slave was stripped of his usual male responsibilities—full-grown males were typically called "boy"—and the result was the infantilized creature called Sambo, whom Elkins terms the "perpetual child."[27]

As the entire community of slavery scholars immediately realized, Elkins's book had taken the whole debate to a new level. Nearly two decades after its publication the University of Illinois Press released *The Debate Over Slavery: Stanley Elkins and His Critics*, in which leading scholars responded to Elkins' thesis and then he responded to them. The late Eugene Genovese, perhaps America's most distinguished scholar of slavery, terms Elkins's book "one of the most influential historical essays of our generation."[28]

I will return to Elkins's thesis. But first I want to take up a subject that Elkins sidestepped. Elkins insisted that he had no intention of comparing the actual institutions of plantation slavery and Nazi concentration camps. He didn't go into the work schedules, the diet, the administration, the attitude toward the captive slaves and inmates, or the underlying ideologies that sustained the two systems. He implied that the two systems were so different that they were in most respects incomparable.

I don't agree with this. I suspect that Elkins didn't venture here because of his lack of knowledge of Nazi concentration camps. (He certainly didn't lack knowledge of the slave plantations.) Much of Elkins's knowledge of the Nazi camps seems to be derived from the work of sociologist Bruno Bettelheim, himself a survivor of Buchenwald and

Dachau and author of a path-breaking study, "Individual and Mass Behavior in Extreme Situations." Yet Bettelheim did not attempt a comprehensive survey of the camps; he merely highlighted the transformation of human behavior under conditions of extreme survival. My purpose in going where Elkins feared to tread is not to undermine Elkins but to further advance his thesis, to show that he actually understated the parallels.

Accommodations and food: The physical layout of Nazi concentration camps resembled a prison system more than it did a slave plantation. The typical concentration camp had a barracks, a workshop, an administrative office, an infirmary, a jail, and a crematorium. (The commandant and SS personnel lived outside the facility.) Slave plantations were constructed somewhat differently. They generally consisted of the master's mansion—the so-called Big House—ramshackle slave quarters, possibly a workshop, and fields for the planting of rice or cotton.

The Nazi camps were also segregated by sex, while slave quarters were family dwellings containing men, women, and children. Yet the actual physical contents of each compartment or cabin were quite similar: nothing more than a bed and blanket, a toilet or a bedpan, and maybe a chair. At the Ravensbruck camp, historian Sarah Helm reports, the only provisions were a plate, a cup, utensils, a toothbrush, a nugget of soap, and a small towel.[29]

In terms of food, the slaves were much better off since they received regular portions of meat and vegetables, while Nazi inmates got little more than thin gruel, bread, and water. Elie Wiesel, who was at Auschwitz and then at Buchenwald, describes his daily intake as a "bowl of soup" and a "crust of stale bread." At Ravensbruck the women seem to have had it a little better; on Sundays, they got a "dollop of jam, a square of margarine and a sausage" and they were also permitted to get money from home and to buy wafers and cookies at the camp shop.[30] Malnutrition was an episodic problem on the Democratic plantation, but it was a chronic problem in the Nazi concentration camps.

Both the Democratic plantation and the Nazi camps were sealed from the outside world, marked off in some cases by a tall fence, or barbed wire, and policed by prison camp guards or plantation overseers sometimes assisted by trained dogs. In both cases, captives were there for life; those who checked into the two systems were never supposed to come out again. So Elkins could not be more right that these were both closed systems, worlds unto themselves and largely detached from the outside world.

Work routines: Here the term "slave labor" applies equally to the Democratic plantation system and to the concentration camps. The daily work was from sunrise to nightfall, and it was continuous, backbreaking, and unremitting. While most slaves worked on cotton plantations, most concentration camp captives worked on construction sites and stone quarries. During most of the time he spent in Auschwitz, Elie Wiesel worked construction "where twelve hours a day I hauled heavy slabs of stone."[31] In the cases of plantations and Nazi camps, the work was mostly manual, unskilled or very lightly skilled, although in both systems there were skilled tasks such as welding, carpentry, masonry, and electrical work assigned to a small subset of qualified captives.

Slaves and prisoners were forced to work. Slaves typically worked six days a week, except in planting season, and had Christmas off as a holiday, which was usually celebrated with music and a feast. Nazi captives worked every single day, no holidays, no feasts. If a slave stopped work, he was likely to be whipped; if a Nazi inmate stopped, he was likely to be beaten or shot. Obviously in neither case were the laborers paid, although slave-owners and overseers sometimes offered slaves incentives to work, including keeping part of their produce. The only payment Nazi slaves received was the chance to live and work another day.

The limits of absolute power: Democratic slave-owners did not have absolute de jure power over slaves. In every Southern state, the murder of a slave was outlawed. In most states, extreme forms of mutilation and wounding were also prohibited. But slave-owners did have de facto power because they could always claim the slave resisted authority or make up some other excuse, and courts could be counted on to take their word for it.

With whippings and other punishments, Democratic masters had virtually unchecked authority. In the 1829 case of *State v. Mann*, judge Thomas Ruffin decided a case in which a master was accused of gravely wounding his slave. Ruffin was a Democrat but a relatively humane one. He said his conscience revolted against allowing the battery to go unpunished. Even so, he said, he had to side with the master because the "end of the slavery is the profit of the master" and the task of the slave is "to toil that another may reap the fruits."[32] Such a system could only survive if the will of the master was, practically speaking, absolute.

Ironically what protected slaves the most, if their Democratic masters were inclined to be vicious or murderous, was their very status as chattel or property. Wolfgang Sofsky makes this point in his book *The Order of Terror*, a study of concentration camp life. Sofsky notes that unlike slaves, concentration camp victims "were not the personal property of masters but inmates of an institution. They belonged to no one." Consequently, "the prisoners had neither a value nor a price."

By contrast, "The slave has a value and going market price. The master does not acquire slaves in order to kill them but to put them to work for the master's benefit."[33] Slaves cost between $1,200 and $1,500 in the period between 1830 and 1860, and this meant that Democratic masters had a big investment in their slaves. They didn't want to damage their slaves for the reason that that would depreciate their value, in other words, for the same reason that you wouldn't want to damage your car.

However marginal the slave's protection from his Democratic master, the Nazi camp inmates had no protection from their captors, who had full discretion to brutalize and kill them. Consequently, there is simply no comparing the level of danger felt by concentration camp inmates to that of slaves. Slaves feared their masters and overseers but they were not in constant danger of their lives; Nazi captives were. This level of danger was greatest, of course, for Jews, but all captives felt it to a high degree.

Just as with slavery, the very thin margin of protection that Nazi inmates got was because of their usefulness to the Nazi regime. When camp conditions improved, Buggeln tells us, "this had little to do with humanity" and was rather "a reflection of the workforce requirements" of the regime. Remarkably, Buggeln tells us that toward the end of the war the Nazis asked SS officials to feed camp laborers better, give them appropriate winter clothing, and allow them eight hours of undisturbed sleep. These rules even applied to Jews, suggesting the Nazis were so desperate for workers near the end that they were "prepared to temporarily rescind one of their core ideological demands—to make the Third Reich free of Jews."[34]

Revolts and runaways: Andrew Jackson once offered a fifty-dollar reward for the capture of a runaway on his slave plantation "and ten dollars extra for every hundred lashes any person will give him to the amount of three hundred."[35] Runaways were a regular feature of life on the Democratic plantation. Planters pursued laws—the Fugitive Slave Act— to compel free states to return runaways. They employed slave patrols to deter slaves from attempting escape and hired slave-catchers to retrieve them when they did. Democratic newspapers contained ads for "Negro dogs" to sniff out escapees hiding in the woods or the swamps. Slave revolts were less common, which is why we know about the few that occurred, such as the Nat Turner and Denmark Vesey revolts. Yet even these failed and the perpetrators were caught and executed.

"Very few prisoners escaped from the camps," Sofsky reports in his study *The Order of Terror*.[36] Sofsky counts a few hundred escapees and this in itself is a minor miracle, since the camps were such fortresses. Sofsky points out that smaller satellite camps offered better chances for escape, although even here extensive planning was required and there was always the risk that civilians in the local population would turn you back in.

As for camp revolts, Sofsky counts only three: one in Treblinka, another at Sobibor in 1943, and another in 1944 at Auschwitz. The Treblinka revolt involved a storming of the perimeter fences, and some 200 prisoners got out, pursued by SS guards in trucks and on horseback. Sofsky estimates that "it is unlikely that more than 50 or 60 of these escaped prisoners survived to see the end of the war." The Sobibor revolt was a failure and resulted in a hundred or so inmates being summarily executed. Similarly, at Auschwitz, all the escapees were hunted down and killed, although not before they killed three SS officers and wounded a dozen others.[37]

The basic message here is that with deeply oppressive closed regimes, such as those of the Nazi camps and the Democratic plantations, the oppressed, however motivated to revolt and overthrow the system, simply cannot do this. They may have the desire, but they do not have the power. Ultimately both plantation slavery and the Nazi concentration camp regime had to be overthrown from the outside, by external military invasion. The Allies in the one case and the United States Army in the other were the liberators of the captive and the enslaved captives.

Ideologies of inferiority: The term "slave" is actually derived from the term "Slav," and sure enough, the Nazi slaves were to a large degree Slavs and, racially speaking, they were white. Even so, the Nazis considered the Slavs—just as they considered the Jews and the Russians—to be *Untermenschen* or subhumans. Within the Nazi camps, there was a hierarchy of inferiority that determined the treatment of captives: the German captives were considered the highest and treated the best while the Jews—especially the non-German Jews—were regarded as the lowest and treated the worst.

So the Nazis didn't just draw a simple demarcation between captors and captives; they also had sub-categories which established a hierarchy or gradation among the captive populations. Among the Democratic slave-owners, by contrast, there was a single racial line. Not all the slave-owners were white—there were also a substantial, though proportionately small, number of black slave-owners. But all the slaves were black. The Nazis and the Democrats both enforced a racial code in their systems of enslavement, but the Nazi code was more varied and multifaceted than that of the Democrats.

Interestingly the Nazis didn't have to defend their ideology, since they faced no internal questioning of it. The Democrats, however, faced opposition first from the Whigs and then from the Republican Party and most vociferously from the small group of Republicans known as the abolitionists. Consequently, the Democrats developed a comprehensive pro-slavery ideology in which they asserted with a straight face that slavery was good not merely for the slave-owner but also for the slave.

Democratic writer George Fitzhugh argued that slaves were like animals, born to be ridden by their masters "and the riding does them good." Other Democrats like Senator John C. Calhoun insisted slavery was a "school of civilization" although it was apparently not a school from which anyone was intended to graduate.[38] Here we must compare the Democrats unfavorably with the Nazis. Even the Nazis didn't have the chutzpah and intellectual dishonesty to suggest that what they were doing to the *Untermenschen* and the Jews was somehow good for the *Untermenschen* and the Jews.

A Lasting Legacy

I return to Elkins now, to make a summary point and a single closing observation. The summary point is that even as a closed system, slavery, simply because of its long duration, produced over time a distinctive African American culture. This is a point stressed in Eugene Genovese's *Roll, Jordan, Roll* and in his mostly sympathetic critique of Elkins. Slaves, for instance, developed a repertoire of songs and stories and relationships—sometimes lifelong relationships—that ultimately helped to form a black identity in the United States.

There is no analog for this in the concentration camps, partly because of the nature of the camps and partly because they lasted for just a dozen years from 1933 to 1945. In general, camp prisoners did not form close relationships, partly because this was discouraged by the guards and partly because prisoners realized that the very person you befriended last week could be summarily executed this week. So the only behavioral changes that concentration camps produced were in the nature of short-term adaptations to camp life itself.

It follows from this that the cultural legacy of slavery long outlasted slavery while the cultural legacy of the camps—including the peculiar disfigurations of personality that Elkins detected—proved to be a temporary phenomenon. The phenomena of the zombie-like *Muselmanner,* the ersatz Nazism of the Kapos—all of this is now gone. It makes no sense to say that Jews or eastern Europeans today display any of the characteristics that developed within that temporary closed system.

With American blacks, however, the situation is quite different. Although slavery ended in 1865, it lasted more than 200 years, and it had its widest scope during the era of Democratic supremacy in the South from the 1820s through the 1860s. Many of the features of the old slave plantation—dilapidated housing, broken families, a high degree of violence required to keep the place together, a paucity of opportunity and advancement prospects, a widespread sense of nihilism and despair—are evident in Democrat-run inner cities like Oakland, Detroit, Baltimore, and Chicago.

"There was a distinct underclass of slaves," political scientist Orlando Patterson writes, "who lived fecklessly or dangerously. They were the incorrigible blacks of whom the slave-owner class was forever complaining. They ran away. They were idle. They were compulsive liars. They seemed immune to punishment." And then comes Patterson's punch line: "We can trace the underclass, as a persisting social phenomenon, to this group."[39] The Left doesn't like Patterson because he's a black scholar of West Indian origin with a penchant for uttering politically incorrect truths.

Big lie people don't like that. But how many lies can you tell? Who can deny that blacks are still living with the effects of what the Democrats did to them? Today blacks have an illegitimacy rate approaching 80 percent. I am not saying it's all due to slavery, but who can say that it's not partly due to the legacy of slavery? Black crime rates are vastly higher, with high rates of black-on-black homicide. Who can say that this is not at least partly the consequence of the Democratic planters' devaluation of black life? The progressive scholar W. E. B. Du Bois certainly did.

I offer these as questions, not answers, although I think Du Bois had it right on these points. If so, it means that the progress we have made in eradicating concentration camps and slavery is hardly complete. Certainly both institutions have been defeated in war and permanently shut down. Even so, the legacy of one of them lives on. While the Nazi legacy in Germany is largely a matter of memory, the Democratic slave-owners legacy in America still leaves its ugly scars on the lives of many African Americans.

five

The Original Racists

*It was with the passage of the Nuremberg Laws in 1935
that Germany became a full-fledged racist regime. American
laws were the main foreign precedents for such legislation.[1]*

George Fredrickson, *Racism: A Short History*

On June 5, 1934, shortly after Hitler's ascent to power, the leading
figures behind the Nuremberg Laws gathered at a meeting to deter-
mine what those laws should actually say. Among those present
were Bernhard Losener, principal drafter of the Nuremberg legislation;
Franz Gurtner, the Reich minister of justice; Roland Freisler, state secretary of the Justice Ministry and later president of the Nazi People's
Court; and Karl Klee, a presiding criminal court judge. One of the most
knowledgeable sources for the Nazis was a young lawyer named Heinrich Krieger, who had studied at the University of Arkansas and whose
research into U.S. race law formed the basis of the work of the Nazi
Ministry of Justice.

The mood was one of seriousness, even gravity, and a stenographer
was present to make a transcript. The meeting was significant because
the Nazis knew even then that they were constructing, for the first time
anywhere, a racist state. They were determined to do this with German

precision, which is to say, they were determined to do it right. As Michael Burleigh put it in *The Racial State*, "The Third Reich became the first state in world history whose dogma and practice was racism."[2]

Recently, legal scholar James Whitman studied that transcript and was astounded at what he found. As Whitman wrote in his book *Hitler's American Model*, "The meeting involved lengthy discussions of the law of the United States of America." The meeting opened with Gurtner presenting a memorandum on U.S. race law, and as it progressed, Whitman notes, "the participants turned to the U.S. example repeatedly."

Basically the Nazis were interested in three things from America: laws on interracial marriage, laws restricting immigration on the basis of race, and the Jim Crow laws. The Nazis recognized that U.S. segregation and miscegenation laws applied to blacks and U.S. immigration laws applied to other ethnic groups that were minorities in the United States. But the laws did not—Krieger optimistically noted "as yet"—apply to Jews. Nevertheless, the Nazis were convinced that they could apply these same laws with appropriate modification to their own situation. They were specifically formulating laws to deal with Jews, but they were also thinking of the gypsies and other "undesirable" populations.

The Nazis present at the meeting were divided into two camps, which Whitman calls the "moderates" and the "radicals." The moderates insisted it was impractical and absurd to have laws forbidding intermarriage between, say, Nordic or "Aryan" Germans and Jews. Such laws, they said, scarcely existed anywhere in the world. Moreover, new laws should be based on some German precedent and the only precedent they could find was that of laws against bigamy and polygamy. Rather than try and apply those laws, which dealt with the separate issue of multiple wives, this group proposed simply using "a campaign of public education and enlightenment" to discourage Nordic Germans from marrying or cohabiting with Jews.

To this, the radicals responded that there was no need for alarm because there actually was precedent for laws forbidding interracial marriage. That precedent came from the United States; some thirty American states prohibited interracial marriage. Freisler conceded that America was unique in passing this type of a law forbidding "mongrelization" but nevertheless insisted that the example of American racial jurisprudence "would suit us perfectly."

In addition, there was the U.S. Immigration Act of 1924 which established quotas for immigration based on race, extending preferential treatment to whites and discriminating against brown and black people who wanted to move to America and become citizens. There was also a whole network of segregation laws which separated whites and blacks—separate schools, separate hotel accommodations, separate drinking fountains, and so on. The Nazis put these laws into the category of "subjects without citizenship rights." In other words, the Nazis were excited about America having created the basis for two categories of citizenship: first-class citizens and second-class citizens. This, they knew, had direct applicability to the task of drafting their own Nuremberg Laws.

The moderates then raised a question: why single out the Jews? Perhaps, they said, the Nuremberg Laws should simply prohibit intermarriage between people of different races. Erich Mobius, a Nazi doctor affiliated with the Interior Ministry, pointed out that avoiding specific references to Jews would improve Germany's international reputation.

To this the radicals countered that Germany should take courage from the American example. Klee said that just as American race and immigration law specifically recognized the inferiority of certain races, notably blacks, so too should German law specifically recognize the inferiority of the Jew. In both cases, Klee said, the simple issue was "race protection," saving the white native majority from the menace and contamination posed by inferior races.

Then the meeting turned to a sticky question: who is a Jew? The moderates insisted it was not easy to identify a person's ethnicity, given the reality of mixed races. Does someone have to be 100 percent Jewish, or is being half-Jewish sufficient to count? Here the radicals pointed out that Southern segregation laws were based on the so-called "one drop rule." In other words, having any discernible black ancestry—theoretically even a single drop of black blood—made one count as black.

But, says Whitman, even the Nazi radicals thought this was too much. One confessed to the "human hardness" of the American rules. How could anyone, he asked, count someone "of predominantly white appearance" as black? The radicals were forced to back down from proposing anything so extreme for Jews. "To them," Whitman sardonically observes, "American racism was sometimes simply too inhumane."[3]

Eventually, and not surprisingly, the radicals prevailed, and the infamous Nuremberg Laws of 1935 reflected their triumph. These laws—officially termed the Law for the Protection of German Blood and the Reich Citizenship Law—were in fact modeled on the U.S. anti-miscegenation laws, immigration laws, and Jim Crow laws. The laws prohibited marriage and sexual relations between Jews and "citizens of German or kindred blood." And Jews were denied German citizenship; they were now considered resident aliens, stripped not of all rights but certainly of all political rights. As Burleigh notes, "The Nuremberg Laws officially rendered the Jews second-class citizens," just the way most blacks were in the United States.[4]

Remarkably the Nazi radicals rejected the "one drop rule" and determined that in order to be deemed Jewish you had to have three Jewish grandparents. Those who were one-fourth or even one-half Jewish would be counted only if they practiced Judaism or married other Jews, otherwise they would count as Germans. So the Nazis took a softer line in defining racial identity than their U.S. precedents. "To this limited extent," historian George Fredrickson writes, "German anti-Semitism was less rigorous in its attitude toward racial purity than was American white supremacy."[5]

Shifting the Blame

My original plan for this chapter was to show the parallel development of racism in the Democratic Party in America and racism of that special sort, anti-Semitism, in Nazi Germany. I had no idea that the racism of the Democrats actually shaped and influenced the policies of

Nazi Germany. I knew that the one preceded the other, but I didn't know it helped cause the other. I'm grateful, therefore, to Whitman and others for showing me the causal relationships between the two types of bigotry.

My gratitude is qualified, however, by a recognition that these scholars are virtually all practitioners of the big lie. Whitman consistently points his finger of blame at "America." He writes, "American law remained a regular Nazi point of reference." The Nazis "repeatedly turned to the American example." His conclusion is that "American white supremacy provided, to our collective shame, some of the working materials for the Nazism of the 1930s." Whitman wants for America a secure "place in the world history of racism."[6]

Another practitioner of the big lie, historian Ira Katznelson, takes a different tack in his book *Fear Itself*. Like Whitman, Katznelson has revealing things to say about how the Nazis looked favorably on the racism of the Democrats. He writes:

> When Americans complained about Nazi anti-Semitism, party officials rejoined by citing southern racial prejudices, claiming a kinship. The *Volkischer Beobachter*, the oldest Nazi Party newspaper, routinely disparaged Africans and African Americans. Like much of the German press, it frequently printed antiblack cartoons, reminded its readers that southern public accommodations were segregated and delighted in reporting how blacks, like German Jews, could not sleep in Pullman cars and could not exercise the right to vote.
>
> When the Nazi Party began mobilizing...*Der Weltkampf*, its ideological journal, reprinted speeches by the Imperial Wizard of the Ku Klux Klan about mongrelization. Lynching was a favorite subject. *Neues Volk* celebrated southern lynching for protecting white women from unrestrained black desire. The *Volkischer Beobachter* published many graphic stories that were intended to support lynching as a tool to shield white sexual purity. The SS journal *Schwarze Korps*

exclaimed that if lynching occurred in Germany as it did in the American South, the whole world would complain loudly.[7]

Now all of this is absorbingly interesting. Katznelson shows how the Nazis were aware of, and excited about, bigotry across the Atlantic that they believed paralleled and reinforced their own bigotry. Even so, notice how just as Whitman blames "America," Katznelson blames "the South." Never does either of them once say, "the Democrats." No fingers of blame ever identify "the progressives." Never do they point to "the Left."

This is significant because every segregation law in the South was passed by a Democratic legislature, signed into power by a Democratic governor, and enforced by Democratic sheriffs and Democratic city and state officials. Most anti-miscegenation laws were passed in Democratic states. Progressives passed the racist Immigration Law of 1924 and celebrated it as a victory of progressive science and progressive planning. The Ku Klux Klan was a creation of the Democrats and served for thirty years, in the words of progressive scholar Eric Foner, as "the domestic terrorist arm of the Democratic Party."

What might Whitman say in response to this? He could claim that his reason for blaming "America" is that the Nazis themselves cited American laws and American precedents. Certainly the Nazis, viewing America from thousands of miles away, might have thought that racist policies in the country were somehow the result of a national consensus. Such a consensus did at some point exist in Nazi Germany. But not in America, as Whitman and Katznelson undoubtedly know. They understand that racist policies in this country emerged out of a big fight between two rival parties and two rival ideologies going all the way back to slavery and the Civil War.

So the big lie here involves Whitman and Katznelson shifting the blame from the real culprits—the progressives and the Democrats—to a generic "South" and an even more generic "America." In doing this, they hope for two outcomes. First, they hope that conservatives will fall for this ploy and rush to the defense of the South and America. This would then make conservatives the apologists for racism, segregation, and racial terrorism.

Sure enough, my former AEI colleague Josh Muravchik deplores Whitman's attempt to trace Nazi policies to American policies. Muravchik doesn't deny the Nazis appealed to American examples. Rather, he asks, what's the big deal? In other words, what difference did it make? He writes, "Suppose for a moment the Nazis found no inspiration in American examples. Would there have been no Nuremberg laws? Had there been no American model, would one fewer Jew have died at Hitler's hand?"[8]

Muravchik makes a good point. My answer to his questions is that the Nuremberg Laws may have looked somewhat different, but the venom against the Jews and other target populations would have continued unabated. No one is saying the Nazis learned how to hate Jews from American examples of racism, or that America motivated the Nazis to kill more Jews. The point, rather, is that the Nazis figured out a way to institutionalize their anti-Semitism using a legal precedent that already existed across the Atlantic. In this respect, established racism in this country helped to establish racism in that one.

Alas, for all Muravchik's ingenuity, he has been trapped into a minimization of racism in a vain attempt to exonerate America. He is going just where Whitman and Katznelson hoped he would go. What he should be doing, instead, is showing that "America" didn't do any of this—the Democrats did. Unwittingly Muravchik ends up covering up for the racism of the Democratic Party, and letting the Left off the hook.

Practitioners of the big lie, like Whitman and Nelson, have a second objective. Incredibly, this is the objective of turning the villains of their story into its heroes. By clearing the Democrats and the progressives of blame, they intend to pave the way for these same Democrats to offer themselves as the solution for racism. As the big lie unfolds, somehow the very people who have poisoned the water reappear dressed as the water commissioner. It's an unbelievable scam.

Let's watch how Whitman, in a recent article, attempts to foist the Democratic atrocities praised by the Nazis onto Trump and the GOP: "Eighty years later, there is once again an American political movement dedicated to the proposition that America should return to its white nationalist roots. There are new laws in many former Jim Crow states that limit access to the polls. And bans have been put in place that once again seem to deem some would-be immigrants as 'undesirables.' There are powerful figures in Washington who seem willing to return us to what did happen here. It is a moment to remember the past and to stay vigilant."[9]

Utterly shameful tripe from an otherwise responsible scholar! To see just how deceitful this rhetoric is, let's undertake a searching examination of the profound relationship between Nazi racism and Democratic racism. We will see, first, how Nazi anti-Semitism, which seems on the surface to be dramatically different from Democratic bigotry, actually springs from the same source, what I call *herrenvolk* socialism. Second, we will see how the racial terrorism of the Ku Klux Klan anticipates and even supplies the operational template for the fascist cult of violence, witnessed in the 1930s during the murderous rampage of *Kristallnacht*— the Night of Broken Glass—and the other depredations of the Nazi Stormtroopers.

Finally, we will see how both Hitler and the Democratic governing class of the South both came to deplore the random, chaotic violence against targeted minorities. Having once approved it, Hitler subsequently railed against what he called the "emotional anti-Semitism" of the brownshirts and called for it to be replaced by the "rational anti-Semitism" of government policy.[10] Southern Democrats struck exactly the same note, deploring lynching and the Klan and institutionalizing instead, just as the Nazis did, the organized repression of state-sponsored segregation and discrimination.

Fascism as a Non-Racist Concept

I start with the phenomenon of fascist racism, and here I confront a paradox. There appears to be no such thing. "Fascist racism" seems to be an oxymoron. Despite the near-infinity of progressive humbug presuming fascism to be racist, there is nothing intrinsically racist about fascism. We can see this through the example of Mussolini and Italian fascism, which as we have seen is the original and most authentic fascism.

Mussolini had very little against blacks and absolutely nothing against Jews. Certainly he shared the generic European prejudice against Africa as primitive and uncivilized, and this carried over into a view of black civilizational inferiority. But there were hardly any blacks in Italy. As for Jews, Mussolini seemed to like them. Mussolini's mistress and biographer, Margherita Sarfatti, who accompanied him on his journey from socialism to fascism, was Jewish. There were Jews in the early fascist movement whom Mussolini worked and fraternized with, notably Angelo O. Olivetti. "Before the late 1930s," historian Anthony James Gregor writes, "Mussolini had never betrayed any evidence of anti-Semitism."

As was customary at the time, Mussolini did speak of nations in terms of race. Like many of his contemporaries, he used terms like "the Italian race." In 1923 Mussolini said, "Before I love the French, the English, the Hottentots, I love Italians. That is to say, I love those of my own race, those that speak my language, that share my customs, that share with me the same history."

In this context, Gregor emphasizes, race is not a matter of skin color but of a shared way of life. Race pride refers to "a new national consciousness." Italians of all ethnic backgrounds, Christians and Jews alike, can share in this "race pride." Mussolini places his affection for Italians above not just the black "Hottentots" but also the white French and English. Here, I think, we see the kind of national pride that Donald Trump reflects and promotes, and it resembles Mussolini, curiously, in its absence of racial bigotry.

Mussolini did, however, succumb to anti-Semitism after he entered into an alliance with Hitler. Scholars agree this was strategic anti-Semitism, not an anti-Semitism of the heart but anti-Semitism for the sake of demonstrating political solidarity. In 1938, Mussolini's government issued a *Manifesto of Fascist Racism*. The document, promulgated to show fascism's proximity with Nazism, actually reveals the distance between the two.

The document declared Jews unassimilable, outlawed intermarriage with Jews, and sanctioned discriminatory laws against them. This was the part that shamefully yielded to Nazi racism. "Many fascist intellectuals," Gregor writes, "represented at their best by Giovanni Gentile, found the legislation morally objectionable." Mussolini, however, felt he had to do it.

Still, Mussolini didn't follow Hitler all the way. He knew that Hitler's doctrine of Nordic superiority held other groups, including Italians, to be racially inferior. Not surprisingly, Mussolini found that doctrine completely abhorrent. Even during his alliance with Hitler, he never publicly endorsed it, and earlier, he flatly dismissed it. Despite its concessions to anti-Semitism, the *Manifesto of Fascist Racism* rejects the biological doctrine of Nordic superiority—indeed rejects all biological doctrines of superiority—instead affirming the unity and solidarity of Italians as a single race.

The paradox, of course, is that if being "Italian" is a race, then Italian Jews would be part of that race. Mussolini seems to have privately held this view. Gregor tells us that during Mussolini's twenty-year reign "there is scant, if any, evidence that any Jews died at the hands of fascists simply for having been Jewish." On the contrary, in Gregor's words, "thousands of Jews with fascist assistance, escaped destruction at the hands of National Socialists." Mussolini was exemplary among European leaders in rendering aid to Jews and helping them get away from Hitler. Hitler wanted Mussolini to turn over Jews from Italian-occupied France, Croatia, Yugoslavia, Greece, Albania, and North Africa to the Nazis. Mussolini communicated to his diplomatic and military authorities that no Jews should be turned over. And not one was.[11]

My purpose in showing this is not to vindicate fascism from the charge of racism—although in the interests of historical accuracy I'm glad to have done so—but rather to show that Mussolini's fascists were much less racist than both Hitler's National Socialists and the

Democratic Party in America. Those two groups reflected the deep and abiding racism that is the emphasis of this chapter.

The Jew as A Greedy Capitalist

Now we turn to Nazi racism, and here I raise two questions. First, was Nazi racism, in its characteristic form of anti-Semitism, right-wing or left-wing? Second, what was the cause of it? By this I don't mean what was it about the Jews that stirred so much hate in Hitler and the Nazis, but what was it about Hitler and the Nazis that made them hate Jews so much? The point of this is to get to the psychological root of anti-Semitism and examine its similarities and differences with Democratic racism in the United States.

The true source of Nazi hatred for the Jews is taken up in an important, recent book by the German historian Gotz Aly. Aly emphasizes the secular and racial aspect of anti-Semitism, distinguishing it from the old religious animus against Jews for rejecting the messiah and their role in his crucifixion. The old anti-Semitism, he points out, always had an escape hatch: Jews could escape it by converting to Christianity.

Modern anti-Semitism, however, defines Jews not as a religious but as a racial group and—since their faults are biological rather than confessional—contains no escape hatch. So what is to be done about the Jews? This was *Judenfrage*—the Jewish question—and since the middle of the nineteenth century, it was treated as a legitimate and important question. Something apparently had to be "done" about the Jews, and anti-Semites presented themselves as the ones with ready solutions.

Aly reaches a surprising conclusion: modern anti-Semitism is rooted not in a perception of Jewish inferiority but in a perception of Jewish success. The Jews are hated because they are more hardworking, more creative, better educated, and richer than other Germans. In other words, anti-Semitism is anchored in the worst of the seven deadly sins, namely envy.

Normally racism involves looking down on people who are seen as inferior, but Aly shows that anti-Semitism involves looking up at the Jews and despising them for their achievements. In the end, anti-Semitism joins with typical racism in declaring these achievements themselves to be the result of wickedness. Anti-Semites portray Jews as sly, cunning, money-minded, "usurpers," and "swindlers." In sum, Jewish success is portrayed not as the consequence of entrepreneurship or effort but as the consequence of Jewish moral depravity.

Aly mobilizes a plethora of evidence for this argument, of which I offer only a couple of examples. Wilhelm Marr, a leftist agitator who founded the German League of Anti-Semites in 1879 and coined the term anti-Semitism, described his motivation as "a cry of pain from someone kept down" and faulted the Jews for outperforming ordinary Germans. He railed, "We are no longer equal to the challenge of this foreign tribe."

Historian Heinrich von Trietschke, another nineteenth-century anti-Semite, described Jewish immigrants to Germany from eastern Europe as "an invasion of young, ambitious trouser salesmen" seeking to have their "children and grandchildren dominate Germany's financial markets." Trietschke contrasts the honest labor and "old-fashioned love of work" of Germans with slick profiteering of the Jewish fat cats. There is more, much more, in this vein that Aly culls from anti-Semitic sources from the 1880s through the 1930s.[12]

I'd like to focus here on a source that Aly does not use very much: Hitler. Early in his career Hitler attended a lecture by the German leftist economist Gottfried Feder, who later became a National Socialist. Feder's lecture was titled, "How and by What Means is Capitalism to be Eliminated?" Hitler was struck by Feder's distinction between "productive capitalism" and "finance capitalism." Feder argued that this distinction eluded Marx, who was simply not radical enough. Feder saw himself as mounting a critique of Marx from the Left.

Feder argued that productive capitalism is based on making things that have actual value while finance capitalism is based on usury, which is to say, on fraud. To Hitler's added enthusiasm, Feder associated productive capitalism with honest Germans and finance capitalism with nefarious Jews. Hitler writes in *Mein Kampf*, "Right after listening to Feder's first lecture, the thought ran through my head that I had now found the way to one of the most essential premises for the foundation of a new party."[13]

Hitler put Feder's distinction to use in his infamous August 20, 1920, lecture, "Why We Are Anti-Semites." Here Hitler identifies Jews with two abhorrent characteristics: money and materialism. Hitler argues that Jews accumulate wealth "without putting in the sweat and effort required of all other mortals." Jewish domination of international finance, Hitler alleges, "corrupts all honest work." National Socialism, Hitler declares, has arrived on the scene to "awaken, augment and incite the instinctual antipathy of our people for Jewry."[14]

Notice here that the distinction that Feder and Hitler make between two types of capitalism—productive capitalism and finance capitalism—is precisely the distinction made by the Democratic Left in America today. Democrats rarely rail against "productive capitalism." When have you heard them denounce General Mills or Procter and Gamble? Instead they focus their bile on "finance capitalism," on the alleged crimes of banks and Wall Street. The only word missing from this invective that Hitler would have added is "Jews."

The following passages are from *Hitler's Table Talk*, reflecting Hitler's private statements made during World War II and transcribed by a Nazi top aide. Hitler predictably rails against Jews, but let's pay attention to what he rails against them for. "The Jew totally lacks an interest in things of the spirit...Previously words were used to express thoughts; he used words to invent the art of disguising thoughts. The Jew is said to be gifted. His only gift is that of juggling with other people's property and swindling each and everyone. Suppose I find by chance a picture that I believe to be a Titian. I tell the owner what I think of it, and I offer him a price. In a similar case, the Jew begins by declaring that the picture is valueless, he buys it for a song and sells it at a profit of 5,000 percent."

In a dinner speech on March 29, 1942, Hitler praises the Hanseatic League of the Middle Ages for keeping prices fixed despite the vicissitudes of supply and demand: "That's how the price of bread could be kept the same for four hundred years, that of barley—and consequently that of beer—for more than five hundred years, and all this despite all the changes of money." By contrast, in Hitler's words, "As soon as the Jews were allowed to stick their noses out of the ghetto, the sense of honor and loyalty in trade began to melt away. In fact, Judaism…has made the fixing of prices depend on the laws of supply and demand—factors, that is to say, which have nothing to do with the intrinsic value of an article."[15]

It should be obvious from the argument above that, for Hitler as for others, anti-Semitism is to a large extent rooted in anticapitalism. The Jews are the capitalists par excellence. "From its very inception," Aly writes, "anti-Semitism was directed against liberal economic policies and capitalism in general, and against finance capital and stock exchanges in particular."[16] Aly shows that anti-Semitism springs from the same source as leftism and socialism. The leftist antagonism to entrepreneurship as a form of unfair "profiteering" and finance as a form of "greed" and "swindling" morphs into the anti-Semitic depiction of the Jew as an unfair profiteer and greedy swindler.

Do leftists and socialists actually think this way? Here is a passage from Marx's 1844 essay *On the Jewish Question*: "Let us consider the actual, worldly Jew—not the Sabbath Jew, as Bauer does, but the everyday Jew. Let us not look for the secret of the Jew in his religion. What is the secular basis of Judaism? Practical need, self-interest. What is the worldly religion of the Jew? Huckstering. What is his worldly god? Money. Very well then! Emancipation from huckstering and money, consequently from practical real Jewry, would be the self-emancipation of our time."

So leftists and socialists can and do think this way. For Marx, socialism represents the emancipation of mankind from Jewish capitalism. Jewish capitalism is the real enemy. Aly shows this is the central thrust of anti-Semitism, not just the anti-Semitism of the Nazis but the anti-Semitism that preceded and laid the ground for Nazism in Germany over the previous half-century.

So what do the anti-Semites get out of it? By demonizing capitalism and its representative, the Jew, they get to restrict and outlaw capitalism and also to restrict and outlaw Jews from participating fully in the economy. By removing the threat of Jewish success, they get to eliminate the Jews as competitors and improve the prospects of their own success. By confiscating the fruits of Jewish success, they can now distribute those among themselves.

Quite apart from these material benefits, there is also a psychological benefit that we must not lose sight of here. Anti-Semitism offers to under-performing people a solution to their own inner sense of inferiority. They can now persuade themselves that even if they're not as smart or as indus-trious as Jews, they are in fact morally superior to them, and that Jews only beat them at the game of life because Jews are so low and wicked. Anti-Semitism is a source of self-esteem for the unintelligent and the lazy.

It is also a source, strangely enough, of equality and solidarity. Aly recognizes this. "The desire for social equality is at the heart of the Ger-man brand of anti-Semitism."[17] How is this possible? Instead of the old division between those who succeed and those who fail—in other words, between winners and losers—anti-Semitism creates a new division: between Jews at the bottom and whites or Nordics at the top. Every white or Nordic German, however uneducated and incompetent, is now ele-vated above every Jew. And since all Jews equally belong to the bottom group, all whites or Nordics equally belong to the upper group. So anti-Semitism promises a kind of equality among whites or Nordics. Anti-Semitism is, in this respect, a white or Nordic type of socialism, a socialism that especially appeals to losers in the race of life. In this sense, as we will see, it closely mirrors the racism of the Democrats.

The Hidden Appeal of Racism

Now we turn to the racism of the Democrats and progressives from the 1860s through the 1930s. This racism was, of course, primarily directed against blacks. I have to say from the outset that, in its sheer volume and vehemence, the racism of the Democrats and progressives outdistances not only Italian fascist racism, which was marginal, but also German anti-Semitism. Only the anti-Semitism of the Nazi era matches the racism of the Democrats. The vile invective in *Der Sturmer*, the anti-Semitic newspaper of Hitler's early associate Julius Streicher, is very much in the same vein as the vile invective of the racist Democrats.

Consider how Democrats routinely talked about blacks prior to World War II. Here's Democratic Senator James Vardaman responding to Republican President Theodore Roosevelt's 1901 dinner meeting with America's foremost black leader Booker T. Washington: "I'm just as opposed to Booker T. Washington with all his Anglo-Saxon reinforcements as I am to the coconut-headed, chocolate-colored typical little coon Andy Dotson who blacks my shoes every morning." Democratic Senator Benjamin Tillman added, "Now that Roosevelt has eaten with that nigger in Washington, we shall have to kill a thousand niggers to get them back to their place."[18]

Here's Senator Theodore Bilbo, a close ally of Democratic President Franklin D. Roosevelt, during one of his reelection campaigns, advocating violence on the part of his white supporters to stop blacks from casting ballots: "White people will be justified in going to any extreme to keep the nigger from voting. You and I know what's the best way to keep the nigger from voting. You do it the night before the election. I don't have to tell you any more than that. Red-blooded men know what I mean."[19]

Here is Democrat Robert Byrd, "conscience of the Senate," lionized by Obama, Hillary, and Bill when he died in 2010, speaking during the war about his reluctance to fight in a racially integrated military: "I am loyal to my country and know but reverence to her flag BUT I shall never submit to fight beneath that banner with a negro by my side. Rather I should die a thousand times, and see this old glory trampled in the dirt never to rise again, than to see this beloved land of ours become degraded by race mongrels, a throwback to the blackest specimens from the wilds."[20]

And here are simply the titles of a few books published by progressive Democrats in the early twentieth century: Charles Carroll's *The Negro a Beast* (1900), Robert Shufeldt's *The Negro: A Menace to American Civilization* (1907), Charles McCord's *The American Negro as a Dependent, Defective and Delinquent* (1914), and again Shufeldt's *America's Greatest Problem: The Negro* (1915).

As part of their big lie, progressives like to convey the impression that this racism is somehow an intrinsic feature of American history, that it's somehow part of the American psyche, and that it goes all the way back to the American founding. The leftist legal scholar Derrick Bell claimed that "racism is an integral, permanent and indestructible component of this society." In *White Racism*, Joel Kovel contends that "racism is ultimately indivisible from the rest of American life." Leftist scholar-activist Cornel West insists that America is "chronically racist."[21]

Yet we can search the founding period in vain for the kind of bigoted extremism that defines Democratic rhetoric and practice in the nineteenth and early twentieth centuries. Consider the proof that progressives typically give to prove Thomas Jefferson's racism. Here is the smoking gun from Jefferson's *Notes on the State of Virginia*: "I advance it therefore as a suspicion only that the blacks, whether originally a distinct race, or made distinct by time and circumstance, are inferior to the whites in the endowments of body and mind."[22]

Jefferson isn't even sure that blacks originally constituted a race. He has a "suspicion," but only a suspicion, that blacks may be less intelligent than whites. None of the other founders agreed with him. Hamilton, for example, was convinced that black inferiority was the result of the conditions under which blacks lived and that better circumstances would remedy the problem. Moreover, neither the founders nor their successors implemented racist schemes like comprehensive state-sponsored segregation or created institutions like the Ku Klux Klan for the purpose of terrorizing and exterminating blacks. These were inventions of a later era and of a new party founded in the 1820s, the Democratic Party.

Of Democratic racism, as we did with German anti-Semitism, we must ask: what did they get out of it? How did racism help to maintain the Democratic Party's hegemony in the South for nearly three generations after the Civil War? These questions establish the political purpose of racism. Contrary to the progressive big lie, racism doesn't just exist as some inexplicable feature of American society from the beginning; rather, it is manufactured, encouraged, and used for partisan purposes by the very party that perpetuates the big lie.

Racism, of course, preceded the Democratic Party but the Democrats, in a sense, invented political racism in the early nineteenth century in order to defend slavery against Republican and abolitionist attack. The attack went like this: all men are created equal, blacks are men, therefore, blacks should not be enslaved. Republicans like Lincoln admitted that the founders had temporarily permitted slavery because there was no other way to have a union. Even so, Lincoln said of the right to life and liberty listed in the Declaration of Independence that the founders "meant simply to declare the right so that the enforcement of it might follow as fast as circumstances should permit."[23]

Progressive Democrats in the twentieth century would in fact attack the founding fathers as misguided or their ideas as out of date. But in the nineteenth century, Democrats took a different line. They denied that blacks were men, which is to say, they denied the full humanity of black people. So the Democratic defense went like this: all men are created equal, blacks are subhuman, which is to say, not fully men, therefore, we are justified in enslaving them.

So racism emerged within the Democratic Party as a rationalization for slavery. Nowhere was that racism more clearly expressed than in the words of that Jacksonian Democrat Roger Taney, chief justice of the Supreme Court, in his notorious *Dred Scott* decision. Taney infamously stated that blacks "have no rights which the white man was bound to respect."[24] This same racist doctrine was the basis for the Northern Democrat Stephen Douglas's advocacy of popular sovereignty—let each state and territory decide for itself whether it wants slavery—as well as the Southern Democrat John C. Calhoun's advocacy of slavery as a positive good.

Even after slavery ended, Democrats found racism to be very useful for them. In fact, they relied on it more than ever. They constructed a whole ideology and structure of white supremacy in order to establish their political domination in the South. We'll shortly see how they did this. But here I ask: how did they make it work for them? What does white supremacy offer that might convince white Southern voters to keep reelecting the Democrats?

We can answer this question by turning momentarily back to slavery itself and answering a question that historians have raised about the Civil War. Why did poor whites, the vast majority of whom didn't own slaves, fight on the Confederate side? Of course we know why slave-owners fought, to protect their "property." But how did they convince non-slaveholding whites to join them?

A clue to this question is provided in an address delivered in 1860 by a Democratic planter, John Townsend. Speaking on behalf of secession to a group called the 1860 Association, Townsend directly addressed the question of how the plantation system benefited whites who didn't own slaves. He insisted that "the color of the white man is now in the South a title of nobility in his relations with the Negro." While an individual black man "may be immensely superior in wealth, yet the poorest non-slave-holder, being a white man, is his superior in the eyes of the law, may serve and command in the militia, may sit upon juries, to decide upon the rights of the wealthiest in the land, may give his testimony in court, and may cast his vote, equally with the largest slaveholder, in the choice of his rulers."[25]

There we have it. What the Democratic slave-owner offered the poor white is precisely what the Democratic Party offered the white Southern voter, namely, the opportunity to belong to an aristocracy of color. By drawing a sharp line between white and black, and placing every white above the line, and every black below it, the Democrats could assure the poorest, laziest, stupidest white man that he was still above the richest, most industrious, and most intelligent black man.

Moreover, as Townsend stresses, there is a presumed equality of pride among members of the upper class, just as there is a presumed equality of degradation among members of the lower one. So racism, we can now see, performs exactly the same psychological function as anti-Semitism. Both reinforce what may be called *herrenvolk* social-ism—the social equality of the master class. And this is how racism paid off in self-esteem for the white man, strongly fortifying the Dem-ocratic Party's political stranglehold on the South from the Civil War through the 1960s.

Racial Terrorism There and Here

In this concluding section I intend to show how the Democrats and the Nazis unleashed orgies of terrorist violence on blacks and Jews respectively, and then moved from chaotic mob violence to establishing and enforcing systematic institutions of racism. I begin by noting a close similarity between the Ku Klux Klan and the Nazi brownshirts. Inter-estingly, during their height in the 1920s and 1930s, the two organiza-tions were roughly the same size, with memberships in the range of three to five million.

The Klan and the brownshirts also targeted the same types of people. Both, for instance, aimed their violence not merely at racial minorities but also at political opponents. The early Klan, for instance, killed just as many white Republicans as it did blacks. Moreover, even though the Klan's main minority target was blacks, it was also anti-Catholic and anti-Semitic—as evidenced by its 1915 lynching of Leo Frank. While the brownshirts focused their racial hatred toward Jews, they were also rac-ist toward the gypsies—the Roma and Sinti people whose origins trace back to India—and blacks, as seen in the anti-black invective in brown-shirt pamphlets and publications.

Americans who visited Germany in the 1930s often remarked on the similarity between the KKK and the brownshirts. And Germans famil-iar with America made precisely the same comparison. Here's a sample from *Neues Volk*, a propaganda newsletter from the National Socialist

Office on Racial Policy: "What is lynch justice if not the natural resistance of the *Volk* to an alien race that is attempting to gain the upper hand?"[26] The article compares anti-Jewish pogroms with the lynchings carried out by groups like the Ku Klux Klan. The article concludes that the two are basically aiming at the same goal.

But then, again in both countries, comes a turn, and once again the Democrats and the Nazis are in complete lockstep. Starting in the 1890s, the ruling powers in the Democratic Party seek to replace KKK racial terrorism with state-sponsored discrimination, reflected in a comprehensive structure of segregation laws. These laws disenfranchise blacks and force them to the very bottom of Southern society. Along precisely the same lines, some three decades later, the Nazis move from brownshirt racial terrorism to the Nuremberg Laws and other measures to dispossess and disenfranchise Jews and force them to the very bottom of society.

Let's probe the similarities between the Ku Klux Klan and the Nazi brownshirts. The original Klan started as a kind of hazing society. White Klansmen raided black homes at night with the objective of scaring the poor blacks half to death. Sometimes Klansmen surrounded a black man on the street and forcibly took down his pants. Similarly, the brownshirts bullied Jews by making them perform various acts of abasement and humiliation; one favored tactic was to strip off their clothes or shave off half their beards.

Both the Klan and the brownshirts wore outfits and developed styles that reflect, at least to the modern eye, the style of high "camp." Part of the attraction of the Klan was to ride horses clad in elaborate costumes, to call yourself "Kleagle" or "grand dragon," to attend top-secret "klonciliums," and to participate in nocturnal cross burnings. Similarly, the brownshirts wore distinctive brown shirts and breeches, jackboots, and caps. Their uniforms displayed swastikas and other insignia and they marched in high-step, and used the raised-arm salute. Both groups had elaborate hierarchies of organization and authority. Brownshirts cultivated the same aura of cultic secrecy as the Klan.

Both were paramilitary groups that believed in the efficacy of violence. When the Klan conducted a lynching, Klan members and their families typically showed up to watch. Klansmen burned crosses to enhance public excitement, and sometimes provided food and drink so that everyone could be entertained. Brownshirts, too, viewed violence not as a regrettable necessity in the mode of the character Sollorzo in *The Godfather*—"blood is a big expense"—but rather as beautifully cleansing, a social reform measure to be regularly performed and enjoyed.

The brownshirts, like the Klan, portrayed themselves as champions of social justice. While the Klan performed extrajudicial murders, these were viewed by Klansmen as meting out justice to black offenders who didn't even need to go to trial. So, too, the Nazi brownshirts viewed themselves as punishing Jews for crimes that had been committed but either weren't on the books or had gone undetected. Brownshirts, like Klansmen, considered themselves vigilantes or "political soldiers" charged with overriding the dysfunctional justice system and acting decisively to set things right.

On *Kristallnacht*—the Night of Broken Glass—in November 1938, Nazi brownshirts torched synagogues, vandalized Jewish homes and schools and businesses, killed approximately one hundred Jews, and hauled many others to concentration camps. This horrific incident, which Goebbels said was provoked by the atrocities committed by the Jews themselves, seemed like an eerie reenactment of Ku Klux Klan-instigated Tulsa race riot of 1921. In that incident, supposedly in retaliation for an atrocious rape of a white woman by a black man, thousands of racist Democrats rampaged through black neighborhoods, burning homes, looting businesses, killing dozens of people, detaining hundreds, and leaving thousands of blacks homeless.

In the end, however, both the Democrats and the Nazis came out against the type of random street violence represented by the Klan and the brownshirts. Let's see how this unfolded, first in the case of the Democrats, then in the case of the Nazis. Historian Joel Williamson tells us the Democrats used the Klan to help consolidate the party's power in the South, but once this was accomplished, the ruling powers of the Democratic Party decided to deemphasize the Klan and implement instead a formal system of segregation and state-sponsored discrimination that would institutionalize white supremacy. Terrorism would now, in a sense, not be so important because it would be built into the law.[27]

Thus the Democrats institutionalized a comprehensive system of state-sponsored discrimination against blacks throughout the South. This was far more invidious than the de facto discrimination against blacks in other parts of the country because it was backed up by the force of law. Blacks were systematically excluded from virtually all government positions except the most lowly and menial. This state-sponsored discrimination persisted for three quarters of a century, from the 1880s through the 1960s.

Democratic segregation in the South was so thoroughgoing that it was premised on the "one drop rule" which basically meant that any black heritage whatsoever classified someone as black. Some historians trace the one-drop rule back to slavery but this is not correct. During slavery, a different rule was in place: slave status passed through the mother.[28] This meant that if a Democratic slave-master had sex with a female slave and produced a child, that child would be a slave because its mother was a slave. Quite a convenient rule, if you think about it, from the point of view of the Democratic planters. Yet under the rule of slavery if a black slave produced a child with a free white woman— admittedly this was extremely rare—this child would be free.

By the one-drop rule however, the offspring of all these liaisons would be counted as black. In practice, of course, there were light-skinned blacks who managed to evade the rule and "pass" for white. But the rule itself required 100 percent whiteness in order to qualify for attending a white school, or drinking from a white water fountain, or frequenting the white section of a public beach. This as we saw earlier is the rule that even the Nazis found a bit too extreme and repellent.

Interestingly while the Nuremberg Laws are now history, the "one drop rule" is very much with us, not only as a matter of law but also as a matter of personal identity. Think about Obama: he's half white and half black, yet he identifies as black. Many African Americans have white ancestry, yet they consider themselves black. Why? Because of the one-drop rule. If any of these people tried to self-identify as white—or refuse to racially classify themselves at all—left-wing groups like the Black Caucus and the Southern Poverty Law Center would condemn them for it. The Census Bureau, even today, counts blacks and whites according to the one-drop rule and uses it to implement a host of affirmative action and other race-based programs.

From Brownshirt Riots to Nuremberg Law

Remarkably, the Nazis followed in the precise historical tracks of the Democrats with regard to handling their street violence. In the late 1920s and early 1930s, Hitler's brownshirts—led by flamboyant homosexual Ernst Röhm—ruled the streets in much the same manner that an inner-city gang might rule a neighborhood. Hitler encouraged the violence of the brownshirts, and he and Röhm were closely allied.

Yet once he came to power in 1933, Hitler viewed Röhm as a threat. Röhm had his brownshirts, but Hitler now had the military as well as the SS under the supervision of Heinrich Himmler. Hitler wanted military force to be concentrated within the government, under his full control. So Hitler dispatched Theodor Eicke, the commandant at Dachau, and another officer at the camp to execute Röhm. The suggestion by some progressive pundits that Hitler had Röhm killed because he was a homosexual is pure nonsense. Hitler did not want a rival gang leader organizing random street violence. He wanted to be the sole gang leader organizing violence through the operations of the state itself.

Earlier, Hitler had spoken of "rational anti-Semitism" replacing "emotional anti-Semitism." Goebbels now invoked this distinction to call upon all Germans to "strictly desist from all further demonstrations and acts of retribution in any form against Jewry." Here is an incredible instance of a top Nazi leader urging restraint in expressions of public anti-Semitism. Yet of course Goebbels intended something even more insidious in its place. He pledged, "Jewry will be given the ultimate answer in the form of legislation and ordinances."[29]

In 1935, seven years before the Nazis fully implemented the Final Solution, Hitler advocated emigration and ghettoization as interim solutions to the Jewish problem. The Jews, Hitler said, must be "removed from all professions, ghettoized, restricted to a particular territory, where they can wander about, in accordance with their character, while the German people looks in, as one looks at animals in the wild."[30]

Starting in 1933, the first year of the Third Reich, the Nazis also began the systematic exclusion of Jews from public office. Hitler added an "Aryan clause" to the civil service law which effectively banned Jews from government employment. Soon Jews were also removed and excluded from journalism, farming, teaching, and the theater. By 1938, Jews could not practice investment banking or the professions of law and medicine. This combination of segregation and state-sponsored discrimination against Jews mirrors what the Democrats did to African Americans.

As should be obvious by now, the Nazi race laws were the precise equivalent of the Democratic Party's race laws. It isn't merely that the former provided a precedent for the latter; the two sets of laws also had the same functional purpose. Just as the segregation and discrimination laws were intended to supplement, and in some respects replace, the random violence of the Ku Klux Klan, so too the Nuremberg Laws and Nazi discrimination laws were intended to supplement, and in some respects replace, the random violence of the brownshirts. In this respect, as in so many others, the Nazis and the Democrats draw so close that it becomes increasingly difficult to tell one from the other.

Six

Disposable People

More children from the fit; less from the unfit—that is the chief issue of birth control.[1]

From *Birth Control Review*, edited by Margaret Sanger

ow does highly abnormal and pathological behavior on the part of some people come to seem normal to them? Behavior that is monstrous or bestial for humans is, of course, quite customary in the animal kingdom. It's normal, for instance, for a gorilla to enter a cave, seize a female, stupefy her with blows, drag her bleeding to his lair, and then mate with her. With animals, this elicits no moral condemnation; this is just the Nature Channel. For a human to act in such a way, however, the person would have to be sick, morally anesthetized, deeply messed up.

So how do humans cross over into the domain of the unconscionable? History shows they sometimes do it without any awareness of the horror of what they are doing. Hannah Arendt termed this the "banality of evil," evil that seems to its perpetrators, and even to many observers, as utterly ordinary. And this raises a frightening possibility: is it possible that we, here in America, are doing or putting up with things that are completely base and horrific? What guarantee do we have that they would not seem normal to us just as they seemed to those who did monstrous things in the past?

Josef Mengele—like so many of the other Nazis—didn't appear abnormal when he came to Auschwitz in the spring of 1943 as a physician and research scientist. He was a workaholic, a stickler, and somewhat anal retentive, but those are traits common to many Germans. As a medical student, Mengele regularly attended the lectures of Ernst Rudin, a leading eugenic scholar who inspired Mengele with the Nazi doctrine of social progress, fostered through the creation of a new type of human being.[2] Yet Mengele never saw himself as a political activist. Rather, he was a scientific investigator with a special interest in twin research.

He had previously worked under the direction of Otmar von Verschuer, a respected geneticist who headed the Kaiser Wilhelm Institute of Anthropology, Human Heredity, and Eugenics. The Kaiser Wilhelm Institute was well known in Germany and around the world as doing pioneering work in the field of heredity and genetics. Verschuer wrote a letter of recommendation for Mengele that helped him secure his Auschwitz appointment.

Mengele's interest was heredity: he hoped that by studying the anatomy of twins—both identical twins who share the same genes, and fraternal twins who share half their genes—he could disentangle the relative importance of nature and nurture in human development. Mengele also wanted to study dwarves, mutants, and other abnormalities in order to see to what degree their traits were passed on to the next generation. At Auschwitz, Mengele found a ready supply of lab specimens for his experiments, especially children. These were Jewish children, gypsy children, the children of Slavs and Russians captured in the war.

Since Mengele viewed these captives as the lowest of the low, the debris of war, disposable people, he decided that they could be put to use by experimenting on them. Thus began his macabre regimen of torture and testing, electroshock treatment, chest injections, and eye injections. Mengele extracted eyeballs and mailed them in military cartons marked "War Materials—Urgent" to the Kaiser Wilhelm Institute for further study. He also mailed body parts to Verschuer and to fellow Nazi brain researcher Julius Hallervorden at the Max Planck Institute of Psychiatry in Munich.

Mengele was determined to break new ground in twin research. To this end, he once sewed a pair of gypsy twins together to see if he could create Siamese twins. He performed autopsies on fraternal and identical twins. But for his data to be useful, he needed the twins to die at the same time. Only simultaneous deaths allowed for a meaningful comparison of corpses. Thus Mengele paid careful attention to the various twin pairs in captivity; if one died of hunger or illness, Mengele did not hesitate to administer a lethal injection to the other one. Basically, he was a serial killer in a laboratory coat.

Throughout all this, Mengele never displayed the slightest awareness that he was doing anything wrong. Later, in the 1970s, he would tell his son Rolf that the inmates at Auschwitz were going to die anyway, and that his role was merely to separate the fit from the sick, and to advance the cause of science by experimenting on useful human specimens.[3] Mengele's research was legal, it was sanctioned by the state, and it was for a progressive cause, so from his point of view, what was there to be ashamed of?

The Left's Own Mengele

Today we consider Mengele's crimes as unthinkable, unconscionable. We readily assent to the slogan of the Holocaust, "Never Again." And we're convinced that it can't happen again and isn't happening again because we expect that, if it did, it would happen in the same way as before. We're looking for another guy today who executes twins and performs hideous eye injections. Since we don't find him, we complacently convince ourselves that Mengele and the Nazis were a historical aberration.

Yet Nazism was a product of a time and a place, and we are in a different time and a different place. As Robert Paxton observed earlier, an American fascism, if it arises, is not likely to involve jackboots, raised-arm salutes, and chants of Heil Hitler. It might not even target Jews but rather some other group. An American fascism would be a fascism in American accouterment, a fascism devised by our progressives and leftists instead of their progressives and leftists. Our Mengele would do things no less horrific than Mengele, but his cause would be protected by a new and fashionable ideology of science and progress.

Actually, we do have our Mengele, and his name is Kermit Gosnell. Since 1979, Gosnell ran an abortion clinic called the Women's Medical Society in West Philadelphia. There he performed late-term abortions and partial-birth abortions, mostly on poor women. If by some mistake children were born alive, Gosnell killed them in a process he termed "ensuring fetal demise." Gosnell's preferred technique for abortion was to heavily drug the premature infants and then stick scissors into their necks and cut the spinal cord. Over a period of three decades, Gosnell killed hundreds if not thousands of children in this way, far more than Mengele killed during his two-year stint at Auschwitz.[4]

If Gosnell is our Mengele, we also have our Kaiser Wilhelm Institute, and its name is Planned Parenthood. Gosnell didn't work for Planned Parenthood, but neither did Mengele work for the Kaiser Wilhelm Institute. Yet both men had institutional legitimacy for their work that came from the longtime support and advocacy of organizations like Planned Parenthood and the Kaiser Wilhelm Institute. Both men saw themselves as pioneers working on the scientific and progressive frontier; Gosnell carried forward the Planned Parenthood vision in precisely the same way that Mengele viewed himself carrying forward the vision of the Kaiser Wilhelm Institute.

Does it seem far-fetched, and wrong, to compare the core institution of Nazi eugenics to Planned Parenthood? Not at all. In some respects, Planned Parenthood's conduct is worse. While the organization poses as a benign promoter of "birth control," its modus operandi was confirmed by a series of undercover videos showing officials willing to sell fetal body parts resulting from the organization's nationwide abortion industry. The officials represented in the videos showed no moral revulsion or compunction about the practice.

In May 2017, the undercover group released a new video featuring ghoulish admissions by Planned-Parenthood-affiliated abortion providers. One spoke of ensuring death by using "a second set of forceps to hold the body at the cervix and pull off a leg or two." Another confessed, to laughter from the crowd, that during a recent abortion procedure "an eyeball just fell into my lap, and that is gross." A third confessed that when stem cell companies want to purchase brains, "we'll leave the calvarium in till last, and then try to basically take it, or actually, you know, catch everything and keep it separate from the tissue so it doesn't get lost."[5] The Kaiser Wilhelm Institute, which regarded itself as a top-notch research organization, never did anything remotely like this.

Progressives are keen to distance themselves from Gosnell even as they fiercely defend Planned Parenthood. In a sense, the Left is giving up one of its pioneers while attempting to save the premier institution that will carry on his type of work. Bye, bye, Gosnell; keep going, Planned Parenthood. And if you're wondering whether the eugenic project of the Kaiser Wilhelm Institute persists today, it does. As we'll see, in suitably modified fashion, it continues now under the banner of International Planned Parenthood.

Back to Gosnell and Mengele. In the progressive narrative, Gosnell "went too far," but this is like saying Mengele went too far. Would Mengele be acceptable to these people if he had merely held back a little? In truth, as the Left knows, both Mengele and Gosnell simply travelled down a path that the progressives in their respective countries had prepared for them. Both thought they were getting rid of disposable people to advance the cause of progress. Mengele's cause was "in" among leftists and progressives in Germany then; Gosnell's cause is "in" among American leftists and progressives now.

Writing in *Slate*, the progressive columnist William Saletan raised the question: what precisely was Gosnell's crime? What did he actually do that was so bad? From the Left's point of view, it couldn't just be late-term abortion because many leftists and Planned Parenthood enthusiasts support late-term abortions. Saletan cites reproductive rights activists Steph Herold and Susan Yanow, arguing that "women have no obligation to make a decision as soon as they possibly can" and should be allowed to choose abortion even in the eighth or ninth month of pregnancy. In the same vein, Marge Berer, editor of *Reproductive Health Matters*, insists that regardless of time limits "anyone who thinks they have the right to refuse even one woman an abortion can't continue to claim they are pro-choice."[6] Here, then, is the Planned Parenthood ideology that helped produce Gosnell just as surely as the Nazi eugenic ideology helped produce Mengele.

Gosnell was tried and convicted on three charges of murdering infants at his clinic. These were merely the most clear-cut cases that the state decided to prosecute. Gosnell is currently serving a life sentence for first-degree murder. In my view he deserved the death penalty to pay for all the infants he murdered. Had Mengele been captured after the war, he would surely have been executed. But Mengele evaded capture by fleeing to Argentina where he became, interestingly enough, an abortionist.[7] In 1979, he died of a stroke at the age of sixty-seven in San Paulo, Brazil.

The First Death Camps

So far we've examined the connections between Nazis and Democrats on issues like slavery, Indian removal, and racism that are, to some extent, issues of the past. Of course, the past is still with us but not in the same form. Racism, for example, is not the same today as it was half a century or a century ago. The Democrats admittedly have replaced their old rural plantations with new urban plantations called ghettos for blacks, barrios for Latinos, and reservations for American Indians. They have turned millions of minorities into disposable people, whose lives don't matter to them and whose primarily utility is their fruitful dependency on the Democrats. As long as the Democrats get their votes, they are happy with them and done with them.

Even so, there are important differences between the new Democratic plantations and the old ones. The slaves had to work while today's minority populations don't have to; in fact, the Democrats would prefer they didn't. The Democrats want voters who rely on them for the basic necessities of life. Moreover, even though these dependents are, in a sense, captive to the Faustian bargain offered by the Democrats, they can choose to leave the plantation. If slaves ever attempted this, they were hunted down and returned to captivity. Consequently, urban plantations are not slavery in the traditional sense, and while the old plantation slavery can be meaningfully compared to a concentration camp, as I did earlier, today's Democratic urban plantations cannot.

But in this chapter and in subsequent chapters we examine parallels and connections between Nazis and the Democratic Left that are not "ancient history" but rather apply to the Left's actions today. This, by itself, is a conundrum. How is it possible for leftist Democrats to continue now with practices that trace back to the Nazis? These practices are presumably discredited because of their Nazi association. So how can the Left, which now purports to be the anti-fascist and anti-Nazi party, get away with fascist and Nazi-style policies and practices? Such a move would seem to require not just chutzpah but also extreme resourcefulness.

Such resourcefulness, to be sure, would require some big lies. The Left needs a way to take its own shared associations with the Nazis and blame them on the Right. But even this is insufficient because the Left wants to continue doing the things it used to do when it was in close alliance with the Nazis. To get away with this, leftists need a new name for their practices to camouflage the link with the past. The Left also needs a new strategy and a new program that will somehow still achieve the old objective, or as much of the old objective as is achievable now. This, then, is a story about how the Left learned to become so crafty.

Let's begin by examining the crime that connects the Nazis to the Democrats—or in this case, more precisely, the progressives—before we see how the Left figured out how to avoid blame and indeed move ahead with its crime spree, despite the stench and odor that attended the discovery of the crimes in question. I begin not with the Holocaust, which came later, but with the crime that initiated the Holocaust, what scholars sometimes refer to as the "dress rehearsal" for the Holocaust.

In 1933, the year the Nazis took power, they issued the Law for the Prevention of Offspring with Hereditary Diseases. The law mandated the forcible sterilization of people deemed "unfit," including imbeciles, schizophrenics, manic-depressives, the blind and the deaf, people diagnosed with physical or mental deformities, and drug and alcohol addicts. Around 350,000 Germans were sterilized under these laws between 1933 and 1939.

In 1939, upon the onset of World War II, the sterilization law was supplemented and to some degree supplanted by a new euthanasia law. By this time the Nazis had an operational network of concentration camps, including death camps where extermination could be carried out by shooting or lethal gas. Under a program called T4, the Nazis between 1939 and 1941 rounded up 200,000 Germans who had been diagnosed as insane or incurably ill. Those people were then euthanized in gas chambers.[8]

These were the first gas chambers, used not to kill Jews per se but to kill the physically and mentally ill. They were the original disposable people. "The gas chambers were not developed for concentration camps," historian Timothy Snyder writes, "but for the medical killing facilities of the euthanasia program." These early gas chambers were smaller and more basic—less industrial—than the subsequent ones constructed and used for the murder of Jews, gypsies, and others on a much greater scale. Yet the procedures proved quite similar. The victims were medically examined and gold fillings were removed from their teeth. They were then euthanized with poison gas, typically carbon monoxide pumped out of mobile trucks.

In reference to four of the most notorious death camps, Snyder notes, "The 1.6 million or so Jews killed at Treblinka, Chelmni, Belzec and Sobibor were asphyxiated by carbon monoxide." At Auschwitz, the Nazis used Zyklon B hydrogen cyanide gas to kill an additional one million Jews. Snyder tells us that the men who oversaw the operations at Treblinka, Belzec, and Sobibor were all veterans of the Nazi euthanasia program.[9] Thus the Nazi euthanasia program and the Nazi final solution are indissolubly linked.

Notice that already our ordinary language is being twisted and manipulated. In this respect, a big lie is already at work with the Nazis. The word "euthanasia" means mercy killing. The term refers to people who are very old or sick and in such pain that they welcome death as a relief. In these circumstances, and with their consent, or if they are unable to give it, with their family's consent, they are euthanized as an act of mercy or compassion. But as historian Michael Burleigh points out, mercy killing had nothing to do with the Nazi program and euthanasia was simply "a cosmetic term for murder."[10]

Learning from the Progressives

Who, then, is responsible for these horrific crimes, the crimes that opened the door to the even greater horrors of the Holocaust? The Nazis are, of course. But where did they get the idea to do this? The answer is that they got it from American progressives. Not "Democrats" this time, but specifically "progressives." By progressivism, I refer to the early twentieth-century, left-wing movement that sought to reform labor laws and working conditions but was also obsessively concerned with social improvement through race-based immigration restriction and the elimination of so-called inferior, unfit, and disposable people.

Yes, some Republicans were also progressives, but they were moderate progressives. A typical example is Theodore Roosevelt who, it should be noted, only became an ardent progressive when he quit the Republican Party, after two terms as president. Then he ran again on the "Bull Moose" ticket. Even then, Roosevelt's soft progressivism stood in contrast with Democrat Woodrow Wilson's hard progressivism rooted in a racist eugenicist philosophy. While it is conceivable that Wilson, had he lived, would have embraced the Nazi forced sterilization laws, it is inconceivable that Roosevelt would have. So I am not indicting all progressives, only left-wing progressives who are the political and spiritual ancestors of the ones we have now.

America's left-wing progressives not only outpaced the Nazis in initiating mass programs of forced incarceration and forced sterilization, but they also showed the Nazis how to implement such programs. The Nazis acknowledged the pioneering role of the American Left in shaping their own life-preventing and killing schemes. Progressives for their part congratulated each other on their influence on the Nazis. All of this has been swept under the rug by a subsequent generation of progressives in order to hide left-wing culpability and enable current-day eugenic schemes to continue uncontaminated by any association with Nazism.

"America led the way in legalizing and promoting coerced eugenic sterilizations," historian Angela Franks writes.[11] Progressives had their first success in 1907 when Indiana passed a law requiring sterilization of "confirmed criminals, idiots, imbeciles and rapists." Over the next thirty years, twenty-six other states passed similar laws. In the early 1930s, when the Nazis came to power, American states were sterilizing 2,000 to 4,000 people a year. In all, around 65,000 people were sterilized against their will as a consequence of progressive eugenic legislation in the United States.

Around the same time, progressives persuaded states across the country to pass marriage restriction laws that prohibited whites and blacks from intermarrying. These laws were based on an acknowledged principle of black inferiority. They were supported by social pressures that discouraged all minorities, including Native Americans and Hispanics, from marrying whites. For progressives, these anti-miscegenation laws and customs had the same purpose as forced sterilization laws: to protect the racial stock from being swamped and contaminated by "useless" and "unfit" people.

The third prong of this same project was immigration restriction. Progressives understood that if you kept these supposedly degraded people out in the first place, it would not be necessary to segregate them, sterilize them or restrict their marriage prospects. In 1924, progressives won a huge victory with the passage of the Immigration Act that sharply curtailed immigration by preferring northern Europeans or "Nordics" and discriminating against immigrants from Asia, Africa, South America, and even southern and central Europe. Progressives today charge Trump with supporting racist immigration policies while they are the ones who actually implemented such policies and to this date have never acknowledged or apologized for this record.

The centerpiece of the progressive enterprise in America, however, was eugenics. It was originally conceived in England by Charles Darwin's cousin, Francis Galton. Attempting to apply Darwin's theory of survival of the fittest to the human species, Galton coined the term "eugenics" to describe a project for improving humanity through genetic selection. "Although conceived in England," Angela Franks writes, "eugenics was really born in America where a highly successful political and legal program was developed" to improve what progressives termed the American genetic stock.[12] This, let's note, goes well beyond survival of the fittest.

Progressives in America founded a plethora of eugenic organizations, among them were the Eugenics Record Office at Cold Spring Harbor in Long Island, the National Conference on Race Betterment, and the American Breeders Association. Leading eugenicists included Charles Davenport, founder of the Eugenics Record Office; Harry Laughlin, first superintendent of the Eugenics Record Office; Leon Whitney, executive secretary of the American Eugenics Society; Madison Grant, president of the New York Zoological Society and trustee of the American Museum of Natural History; Paul Popenoe, editor of the *Journal of Heredity*; Eugene Gosney, director of the Human Betterment Foundation; and the progressive philanthropist Clarence Gamble.

Laughlin, perhaps the most influential eugenicist in America, developed a scheme for mass sterilization that envisioned, as a first step, covering 10 percent of the population. In short, Laughlin sought to sterilize eleven million people. Laughlin intended to compensate for these reductions in the population by, in his words, "encouraging high fecundity among the more gifted." Nothing so ambitious as Laughlin's 10 percent scheme was ever carried out, but what was implemented was his strategy of getting women to go along with state-sponsored sterilization.

Basically, progressive educators and health officials would begin by classifying uneducated, lower-class women—the majority of them black, Hispanic, or American Indian—as congenitally "imbecilic" or "unfit."

The police were then called, and these women were imprisoned or seg-regated from the general population, ostensibly to avoid them contaminating others. In some cases, women were held indefinitely, with the goal of preventing them from breeding throughout their reproductive years.

After a period of incarceration or forced confinement, the women would be given the option of being sterilized and returning to normal life. Faced with the choice of segregation or imprisonment on the one hand, or sterilization on the other, many women consented to being sterilized. Consequently, progressive social service officials listed the sterilizations as "voluntary" rather than coerced.

Progressive eugenicists in America also introduced the idea of euthanasia as an alternative to incarceration and forced sterilization. The leading advocate for killing off undesirables was the California geneticist Paul Popenoe, who argued in his textbook *Applied Eugenics* that, when it came to the congenitally feebleminded or the habitually criminal, "the first method which presents itself is execution."[13] Popenoe proposed "lethal chambers" to carry out these executions.

Popenoe's suggestion was controversial from the outset. Ultimately progressives rejected euthanasia as a viable program for getting rid of disposable people, while affirming the principle that such people ought to be eliminated in other ways. Where American progressives drew the line, however, the Nazis pushed forward with their own euthanasia program largely drawn along the lines Popenoe originally proposed.

Progressive eugenicists in America connected with their European counterparts via international conferences. Here we see how eugenics attracted the political Left not only in America but also in England and Germany. In England, for example, champions of eugenics included the Fabian socialist George Bernard Shaw, the utopian leftist novelist H. G. Wells, and the progressive economist John Maynard Keynes. In Germany, the leading Marxist theorist Karl Kautsky promoted eugenics, as did fellow his fellow socialist Eduard David.

Another noted socialist, the German physician Alfred Ploetz, championed eugenics going back to the 1880s and lived long enough to see his eugenic dream realized in Nazi Germany. Ploetz and his fellow socialist Ernst Rudin founded the Society for Racial Hygiene. Rudin later became a chief architect of the Nazi eugenic program and a participant in Nazi health courts set up to decide who should be forcibly sterilized. The leading Nazi eugenicists of the 1930s—Rudin, Fritz Lens, and Eugen Fischer—were all men of the Left who interacted closely with progressives in the United States.

At international eugenics conferences, the Germans were typically considered the second most advanced eugenic community in the world, and the Americans the most advanced. Perhaps the most significant of these was the Third International Congress of Eugenics, hosted in 1932 at New York's Museum of Natural History. One year before the Nazis came to power, the German press enthusiastically reported on the "progress" of America's eugenic policies.

"Germany had certainly developed its own body of eugenic knowledge," Edwin Black writes in *The War Against the Weak*. "Yet German readers still closely followed American eugenic accomplishments as the model—biological courts, forced sterilization, detention for the socially inadequate, debates on euthanasia." For American progressives, even before the Nazis, "a superior race of Nordics was increasingly seen as the final solution to the globe's eugenic problems." And when the Nazis implemented their eugenic policies, American progressives were openly envious, with one of them protesting that "the Germans are beating us at our own game."[14]

Controlling "Human Weeds"

One shady figure closely connected with the eugenic movement is Planned Parenthood founder Margaret Sanger. Actually the leading eugenicists shunned Sanger, whom they viewed as lacking academic credentials and something of a crackpot. Despite Sanger's regular appeals, they refused to speak at her conferences or invite her to join their boards. Among themselves, they exchanged communications warning that Sanger would bring the eugenic cause into disrepute. Even so, throughout her life Sanger shamelessly championed eugenics and desperately sought the approbation of eugenicist leaders.

An example of Sanger's persistent courtship with the eugenic heavyweights was her annual invitations to Charles Davenport to speak at her various conferences. Davenport consistently refused. Desperate to "get" Davenport, Sanger urged her coworker, Edward East, a friend of Davenport, to persuade Davenport to join the board of the Birth Control League of Massachusetts. Davenport again said no. Finally, after multiple entreaties, Davenport agreed to serve on a round-table panel on eugenics and birth control at the 1925 International Neo-Malthusian and Birth Control Conference. This was Davenport's sole nod to Sanger. It was less of an effort to ally with her than to resist her dogged pursuit.

To highlight Sanger's avid eugenic advocacy, consider two telling documents, her January 1932 article "My Way to Peace" and her March 27, 1934, article "America Needs a Code for Babies." In the latter, Sanger calls for the government to establish a code "for the better distribution of babies…to protect society against the propagation and increase of the unfit." This code should declare, she proposes, that "no woman shall have the legal right to bear a child, and no man shall have the right to become a father, without a permit for fatherhood." Moreover, "No permit for parenthood shall be valid for more than one birth."

As for the unfit, Sanger urges that "Many groups of the socially unfit, as for example the feeble-minded and the criminal, are not sufficiently susceptible to education or the moral pressure of the community." Sanger identifies five million Americans as meeting her criteria for "mental or moral degenerates." She grimly declares, "For such people sterilization is indicated" but "in cases of doubt" they should be "so isolated as to prevent the perpetuation of their afflictions by breeding." In her 1932 article, Sanger calls for the establishment of "farmlands and homesteads where these segregated persons would be taught to work under competent instructors" and prevented from reproducing "for the period of their entire lives."[15]

Sanger was, like many progressives of her time, a blatant racist who saw blacks as low, uneducated people deserving of segregation and forced sterilization. Sanger accepted an invitation to speak to the women's chapter of the Ku Klux Klan in New Jersey, and she established a special Negro Project to pressure poor blacks to enroll in birth control and sterilization programs. In a letter to her friend and associate Clarence Gamble, Sanger explained why she hired black ministers to be her ambassadors to the black community. "We do not want word to go out that we want to exterminate the Negro population and the minister is the man who can straighten out that idea if it ever occurs to any of their more rebellious members."[16]

Sanger's militancy is so flagrant and persistent that one can clearly see the dishonest attempts of her progressive biographers to deny the centrality of eugenics in her core ideology. In Linda Gordon's book *Woman's Body, Woman's Right*, a history of the birth control movement in America, the author attempts to distinguish Sanger's supposedly moderate, benign, left-wing eugenics from supposedly extreme, malign, right-wing eugenics that emerged with Nazism.[17] This distinction is pure fiction and relies entirely on the supposition that Nazism was somehow right-wing. As we know by now, this is part of the big lie. In reality, Sanger's eugenics and Nazi eugenics were cut from the same cloth, as Sanger herself realized.

We can see this from two of Sanger's close associates, Clarence Gamble, who funded Sanger's projects and spoke at her conferences, and Lothrop Stoddard, who published in Sanger's magazines and served on the board of the American Birth Control League—the forerunner of Planned Parenthood. Stoddard was the bestselling author of a notorious tract, *The Rising Tide of Color Against White World Supremacy*, that portrayed the pristine Nordic race being swamped through immigration and interracial marriage by degenerate hordes from other lesser races. Both Lothrop and Gamble became avid Nazi sympathizers who sought to import Nazi sterilization programs in their full magnitude to America.

Gamble proclaimed that the Nazi program "will secure Germany a place in the history of races" and insisted that it "sets the pattern which other nations and other racial groups must follow."[18] Stoddard traveled to Germany where he met with top Nazi racial eugenicists Eugen Fischer and Fritz Lenz. He also met with top Nazi officials Heinrich Himmler and Joachim von Ribbentrop, and even secured a coveted audience with Hitler. Stoddard's 1940 book *Into the Darkness* is a paean to Hitler and Nazi eugenics. These were the circles in which Sanger moved and the kind of people with whom she associated.

Now we turn to Sanger herself. In April 1933, Sanger's magazine *Birth Control Review* published an article "Eugenic Sterilization, an Urgent Need" authored by Ernst Rudin, chief architect of the Nazi sterilization program and mentor of Joseph Mengele, and also reprinted a pamphlet he had prepared for British eugenicists. Writing in 1938, while Nazi sterilization was in full swing, Sanger urged America to do as the Nazis were doing. "In animal industry, the poor stock is not allowed to breed," Sanger said. "In gardens, the weeds are kept down." America, Sanger concluded, should learn from the Germans and carry out nature's own mandate of getting rid of "human weeds."[19]

Hitler's American Example

Adolf Hitler seems never to have heard of Margaret Sanger. By the time he entered Landsberg Prison, however, Hitler was already a social Darwinist. Hitler's Social Darwinism shaped not only his social philosophy but also his foreign policy. He saw nations, for example, engaged in a Darwinian struggle for survival with only the strongest or fittest of them destined for survival. Historian Richard Weikart writes in *From Darwin to Hitler* that "Hitler drew upon a bountiful fund of social Darwinist thought to construct his own racist philosophy."[20]

While in prison, Hitler commented about how progressives in America had passed race-based immigration laws that gave preferential treatment to whites while discriminating against black, yellow, and brown people. Even among whites, the laws preferred immigrants from northern Europe—the Nordic countries—over those from eastern and southern Europe whom progressives deemed inferior. Hitler entirely approved of the premises behind this progressive legislation.

"The Germanic inhabitant of the American continent," Hitler wrote in *Mein Kampf*, "who has remained racially pure and unmixed, rose to be master of the continent; he will remain the master as long as he does not fall a victim to the defilement of the blood." One way to preserve the purity of the Nordics in America was, of course, to restrict entry to others. Hitler invoked the American example in order to explain why he favored laws against racial mixing in Germany.

Hitler also intended, upon taking power, to purge Germany of what he considered to be lesser races, and he invoked America's progressive immigration laws to show how America had already adopted, via its immigration laws, the same general principle. Hitler didn't like to concede American leadership—he wanted Germany to lead on all fronts—but even so, he grudgingly conceded that immigration was one area where the Nazis would have to play catch up to American progressives.

In *Mein Kampf*, Hitler writes, "There is today one state in which at least weak beginnings toward a better conception are noticeable. Of course it is not our model German Republic but the American union, in which an effort is made to consult reason at least partially. By refusing immigration on principle to elements in poor health, by simply excluding certain races from naturalization, it professes in slow beginnings a view which is peculiar to the *Volkish* state concept."

If Hitler saw immigration policy as a mechanism to keep disposable people out, he saw eugenics as a mechanism to prevent them from reproducing and from being born in the first place. "The demand that defective people be prevented from propagating equally defective offspring," Hitler wrote, "is a demand of clearest reason. If systematically executed, it represents the most humane act of mankind." [21] Notice how Hitler, in classic progressive fashion, presents his ideas not as an assault on humanitarianism but as its best fulfillment.

Hitler conveyed his familiarity with progressive eugenic laws in the United States. Again, Hitler recognized with some irritation that here too progressives and socialists in Germany would have to follow their counterparts in the United States. "I have studied with great interest the laws of several American states concerning prevention of reproduction by people whose progeny would in all probability be of no value or be injurious to the racial stock."

Remarkably, Hitler knew there were religious conservatives in America who opposed such laws as draconian and excessive. He scorned these people whom he called "liars" and "hypocrites." And he moved quickly to rebut such objections. "The possibility of excess," Hitler said, "is still no proof of the incorrectness of these laws. It only exhorts us to the greatest possible conscientiousness."[22]

Hitler is sometimes characterized by the Left as a social conservative dedicated to marriage and the traditional family. Let's listen to what Hitler actually says in *Mein Kampf* about the purpose of marriage: "Marriage cannot be an end in itself, but must serve the one higher goal, the increase and preservation of the species and the race. This alone is its meaning and its task."[23] So marriage is not primarily for uniting people who love each other nor is it for giving them the joys of parenthood; rather, marriage exists largely to serve the collective goals of the state and the species. No traditionalist will agree with this, but many progressives did and still do.

Where did Hitler get his familiarity with American sources? While in prison, Hitler avidly read eugenic tracts and textbooks that extensively quoted Davenport, Popenoe, and other progressive eugenicists. Hitler shared his ideas with his cellmate Rudolf Hess, later a prominent figure in the Third Reich who popularized the slogan "National Socialism is nothing but applied biology."[24]

Hitler himself was especially taken by the writings of Leon Whitney of the American Eugenics Society, and Madison Grant, author of several books extolling Nordic racial superiority and bewailing its corruption by lesser breeds. To his delight, Hitler observed that these Americans did not merely champion European or white racial superiority but specifically Germanic or Nordic superiority.

During the 1930s, Whitney on one occasion visited Grant who was at the time chairman of a eugenic immigration committee. Whitney came to show Grant a letter he had just received from Hitler requesting a copy of Whitney's book *The Case for Sterilization*. Not to be outdone, Grant pulled out his own letter from Hitler, which praised Grant for writing *The Passing of the Great Race*, a book Hitler called his eugenic "Bible."[25] What this shows is that progressive eugenicists in America were not only aware of Hitler but also proud of their association with him.

Shortly after the Nazis implemented their sterilization and euthanasia programs, Paul Popenoe praised Hitler for basing "his hopes for biological regeneration solidly on the application of biological principles of human society." Harry Laughlin and Charles Davenport's *Eugenic News* termed the Nazi program "a milestone which marks the control by the most advanced nations of the world of a major aspect of controlling human reproduction." If such comments seem virtually incomprehensible today, historian Stefan Kuhl explains that progressive eugenicists "understood Nazi policies as the direct realization of their scientific goals and political demands."[26]

Another example of progressive enthusiasm for Hitler's sterilization program involves Charles Goethe, founder of the Eugenics Society of Northern California, who, upon returning from a 1934 fact-finding trip to Germany, wrote a congratulatory letter to his fellow progressive Eugene Gosney, head of the San Diego-based Human Betterment Foundation. "You will be interested to know," Goethe's letter said, "that your work has played a powerful part in shaping the opinions of the group of intellectuals who are behind Hitler in this epoch-making program. Everywhere I sensed that their opinions have been tremendously stimulated by American thought, and particularly by the work of the Human Betterment Foundation. I want you, my dear friend, to carry this thought with you for the rest of your life."[27]

Covering Its Tracks

It was Hitler, historian George Fredrickson notes, who "gave racism a bad name."[28] Indeed Fredrickson points out that the very term "racism" did not come into widespread use until the 1930s, in connection with the ascent of the Third Reich. While the old progressives relished their association with Hitler, progressives since World War II have worked assiduously to cover their tracks and bury all connections between their cause and that of the Nazis.

One major document in this big lie project is historian Richard Hofstadter's book *Social Darwinism in America*. Interestingly Hofstadter's book was published in 1944, before the Allies liberated the concentration camps and Nazi atrocities were fully exposed. Even in 1944, however, links to the Nazis had become politically radioactive, and Hofstadter got to work to redefine Social Darwinism, sever its link with progressive eugenics, and link it instead to the political Right.

Hofstadter was a leftist who had once been a member of the Communist Party. Hofstadter said he joined because "I don't like capitalism." Even after breaking with the party, he retained his animus. "I hate capitalism and everything that goes with it."[29] Hofstadter's big lie scheme involved redefining Social Darwinism as the philosophical foundation of free-market or laissez-faire capitalism. This would ensure that in the future Social Darwinism could be blamed on the "right-wing."

Hofstadter built his case around the English sociologist Herbert Spencer's phrase, "survival of the fittest." This, Hofstadter insisted, is the essence of laissez-faire capitalism. And precisely this dog-eat-dog aspect of the Darwinian ideology, Hofstadter continued, is what American businessmen find most congenial about Social Darwinism. Hofstadter devoted a large part of his book to Spencer and the American sociologist William Sumner, who did indeed invoke survival of the fittest rhetoric to make his case for capitalism.

Sumner, however, was virtually unique in doing this. Hofstadter seemed unable to locate any other American examples. Nor did Hofstadter bother to survey American businessmen. Had he done so, he would have surely discovered that most of them had never heard of Social Darwinism. If they had any philosophical basis for their profession, it was much more likely to be based on Adam Smith or Friedrich Hayek than on Charles Darwin or Herbert Spencer.

Toward the end of his book, Hofstadter makes a few passing references to the connection between Social Darwinism and eugenics. Even so, he gives the clear impression that this was a minor and largely accidental association; at one point, he calls American eugenics a "fad."[30] It was, as we have seen, far more than that. Hofstadter says nothing about how progressive eugenics inspired sterilization laws and modeled euthanasia schemes in America that provided the acknowledged framework for Nazi sterilization and euthanasia programs.

Progressives rushed to praise Hofstadter's big lie, proclaiming his book a masterpiece, which helped it become the standard work on the subject. Since then, even historians sympathetic to Hofstadter—like progressive historian Eric Foner, Hofstadter's former student at Columbia University—recognize that *Social Darwinism in America* is deeply flawed. Even so, it continues to define conventional wisdom on the Left.

Subsequent works on eugenics, such as Daniel Kevles's *In the Name of Eugenics*, make barely any references to the progressive foundations of eugenics and the close ties between progressive and Nazi eugenicists. Even Stefan Kuhl's *The Nazi Connection*, which documents the close influence of American eugenics on Nazi eugenics, falls for the Hofstadter deception that eugenics itself is largely a right-wing cause. So Hofstadter's influence lives on in that his work still supports and advances the big lie.

Under ordinary circumstances, Hofstadter's deception would have been sufficient. Through its efforts, the Left would have buried the eugenic program and transferred the stigma of Social Darwinism to the political Right. In this case, however, the Left intended to continue with its eugenic agenda. Consequently, it became necessary to redefine eugenics itself so that it could now travel on a different passport. Even this would not be enough. If the Left called eugenics something else and still explicitly targeted minority populations in the old Nazi mode, this would be too obviously connected with Nazism.

The challenge for the Left was to formulate a new agenda that renamed eugenics and incorporated its program into a new and broader framework. As historian Angela Franks points out, that framework was initially identified as "population control" in the 1960s and 1970s.[31] Even some prominent Nazi eugenicists like Otmar von Verschuer declared themselves population control researchers and were reintegrated into the progressive activist community promoting that cause. For the past few decades, however, eugenics has marched under a new banner, the banner of "pro-choice."

While Margaret Sanger was an avid eugenicist, today Planned Parenthood celebrates her as a champion of "choice." One is hard pressed to find references to eugenics in Planned Parenthood brochures featuring Sanger's pioneering role in the organization. This is all part of the big lie; the real Sanger opposed choice. As we have seen, she demanded that rich, educated, and "fit" populations must have more children and poor, uneducated, and "unfit" populations must have fewer children. Sanger, like Hitler, believed that reproductive choices must serve the larger interests of society and the species.

If Sanger rejected "choice," how can Planned Parenthood's pro-choice agenda continue to advance Sanger's original objectives? After all, a genuine pro-choice agenda seems to transfer the decision about abortion to the mother. And here we see the profound tragedy of abortion, which is not only that a mother kills a child, but that a mother kills *her own* child. The role of the state is simply to authorize the killing, to make it legal.

While the mother makes the choice, her choice is not made in a vacuum; Planned Parenthood avidly propagandizes for abortion and also lobbies for federal funding of abortion. If the government doesn't pay, the Left insists, then poor women will have trouble getting abortions. With government subsidy, however, the Left can ensure not only that the poor get abortions but—what is in fact the case—also that the majority of abortions in this country are performed on poor and minority offspring. Incredibly the old eugenic objective is once again satisfied, but this time within the apparently neutral framework of "choice."

To see the radicalism of the Left's support for federally funded abortion, consider that abortion as a right is nowhere mentioned in the Constitution. Yet even if one considers it a constitutional right, none of our other fundamental rights are funded by the government. We have a First Amendment right to speak our minds and practice our religion, yet the government subsidizes neither of these rights. We have a Second Amendment right to bear arms, but the government doesn't pay for our guns. We have a constitutional right to assemble, but the state doesn't pay for us to do so. Thus the Left wants a level of federal financial support for abortion that none of these other fundamental rights enjoys. And federal support transforms abortion from state-sanctioned killing to state-sponsored killing.

To date, more than fifty million unborn children have been killed in America in the aftermath of the Supreme Court's *Roe v. Wade* ruling in 1973. Let's be honest: this is genocide on a scale that exceeds the Nazi Holocaust. What is abortion other than euthanasia for infants? So the Left has succeeded beyond Sanger's wildest dreams, even while divesting Sanger of her eugenic record and making her into a cultural icon, the way Mengele would have liked to be remembered. How proud and even jealous Sanger and the Nazis would have been, had they lived to see it. For progressives, the big lie has paid off big time.

Where did the Left get this new eugenic strategy? I've been thinking about this a long time, and finally it hit me. They got it by digging into their own past. They got it from a century-old Democratic approach to dealing with slavery. "Choice," after all, was the rallying cry of the Northern Democrats led by Illinois Senator Stephen Douglas. Douglas used his "choice" doctrine to support the institution of Southern slavery while still being able to assure his Northern constituents that he was not himself advocating slavery.

Let's recall the core meaning of Douglas's infamous doctrine of "popular sovereignty." Douglas argued for letting each state, each territory, and each community decide for itself whether it wanted slavery. Douglas said he didn't personally endorse slavery, but his opinion on the subject was irrelevant. We live in a big country, he said, in which people hold different opinions. So let's agree to disagree and place the power of the decision in the hands of each state or community. In this way, the right to choose becomes supreme. Popular sovereignty, in other words, is a pro-choice ideology.

Douglas's argument is identical in form, and very nearly in substance, to the pro-choice ideology now employed by the Left to champion abortion as a right. The entire cadence of Douglas's rhetoric is entirely, and eerily, familiar. Of course today's Left speaks in terms of the individual making the choice, while Douglas spoke in terms of each community making a choice for itself. But this is the only difference, and it is an insignificant one.

Otherwise, the two positions are the same. We see now in the Left, as we saw almost a century ago in Douglas, the same affirmation of "choice" without regard to the content of choice. Just as Douglas ignored the rights of slaves, presuming that they have no stake in their freedom, so too does the Left ignore the right to life of developing offspring, presuming they have no stake in whether they live or die. The unborn child of today, just like the slave of old, is considered a tool for someone else's benefit and convenience. He or she is a non-person or at least an entirely disposable person. In this respect, the lethal and dehumanizing Nazi mindset lives on.

Seven

American Führers

Many passages in President Roosevelt's book
could have been written by a National Socialist.
One can assume he feels considerable affinity with
the National Socialist philosophy.[1]

Nazi newspaper *Völkischer Beobachter* review of
Franklin D. Roosevelt's book *Looking Forward*

In the early 1930s, the newly inaugurated Roosevelt administration made a fateful decision. It decided not to attempt to make America into a socialist country. Socialism, of course, would require extensive nationalization of industry. In effect, the government would take over the private sector: banking, communications, energy, healthcare, education, and so on. Strictly speaking, socialism involves workers owning the means of production. In seeking to overcome the Great Depression, clearly Franklin D. Roosevelt and his progressive team rejected the socialist road.

But what road did they choose instead? Here the leftist narrative kicks in. According to progressive biographers of FDR, he chose a "middle path" between socialism and capitalism, the path of the welfare state. In doing so, he turned progressivism into the savior of American capitalism. Progressivism—this story goes—rescued the American economy and gave it the wherewithal to win World War II. In this respect, FDR is the canonized hero of American progressivism. Subsequent Democratic presidents, from Lyndon Johnson to Obama, have all sought to expand the power of the state by invoking the FDR model.

Johnson's Great Society self-consciously built on FDR's New Deal. And Obama officials over eight years never tired of appealing to FDR not only in pushing for Obamacare, but in likening Obama's actions in the wake of the 2008 mortgage crisis to FDR's actions in the wake of the Stock Market Crash of 1929. Essentially Obama engineered a federal takeover of the banking and finance industries—again, not an actual nationalization but a state-directed capitalism in which the government in effect controlled these industries and told them what to do.

Through Obamacare, progressives established state control over the health care industry, one sixth of the entire economy. Through the regulatory powers of the EPA and other agencies, the federal government actively manipulates—though it does not yet control—the energy industry. During the 2016 campaign, both Hillary and Bernie advanced proposals that would increase government control over higher education. Through the public school system, the government of course already controls much of elementary and secondary education.

While progressives continue to portray these measures as a "middle path" between socialism and capitalism, there is actually a technical name for them: fascism. This is what fascists like Giovanni Gentile and Mussolini actually advocated. They were not in favor of socialist state ownership; Gentile and Mussolini knew their fellow socialists had no idea how to run industries. Instead they advocated state-run capitalism, putting the industrial might of the private sector at the behest of the state. The Nazis had their own term for this, *Gemeinnutz vor Eigennutz*, which means the common good over the individual good. FDR, like most modern progressives, understood the sentiment and shared it.

Now at this point, we must pause to acknowledge a progressive eruption. How can you even suggest—the argument goes—that FDR was some kind of a fascist? Wasn't it FDR who fought the fascists? Wasn't it America under FDR's leadership that defeated Hitler and the Nazis? From the Left's viewpoint, it is downright obscene for any responsible person to allege a relationship between the sainted FDR and the geno-cidal fascists and Nazis. While Hitler murdered Jews by the millions, FDR liberated the death camps and brought the Jewish survivors of the Holocaust home.

"He saved America from the Depression and the Nazis." This is how FDR is remembered. This is why progressive historians like Arthur Schlesinger Jr. and William Leuchtenburg list him as one of the greatest, if not the greatest, presidents. Even some on the Right have fallen for this narrative. "How FDR Saved Capitalism" is the title of an article by Seymour Martin Lipset in the *Hoover Digest*. The *Economist* sums up FDR's legacy in the following headline: "The Man Who Saved His Country and the World."[2] From this perspective, far from being a fascist or Nazi, FDR must be seen as the forerunner of today's progressives who call themselves anti-fascists.

This progressive narrative contains a molecule of truth amid a whole slew of bunkum. I agree that FDR is the forerunner of today's self-styled progressive anti-fascists. I simply insist that both FDR and his modern-day progeny are far closer to fascism and Nazism than they care to admit. FDR is the one who set the modern Left on its fascist road. To see this, we must begin by dispelling the miasma of progressive myth-making.

First, FDR did not defeat Hitler. It may be said that America under FDR and later under Truman defeated imperial Japan by taking the lead in the battle for the Pacific and ultimately by dropping the two atomic bombs on Hiroshima and Nagasaki. But as historian Richard Evans writes in *The Third Reich in History and Memory*, "The Soviet Union was the decisive force in the defeat of Germany."[3] As Evans notes, the Wehrmacht was destroyed in its failed effort to take Moscow and Stal-ingrad, and in the subsequent Soviet counterattack. At most, FDR helped accelerate Hitler's ultimate defeat by opening up a new front in the European theater and by providing the Soviet army with Lend-Lease aid and shipments of American military supplies. None of this is to depreci-ate the heroism of America's "greatest generation." It is, however, to deny credit to FDR where credit is not due.

True, America liberated German concentration camps, but these were labor camps and that's why they had survivors, although most of those survivors were not Jews. As historian Timothy Snyder shows in *Bloodlands*: *Europe Between Hitler and Stalin*, America didn't liberate any death camps; they were all in the territory the Soviets occupied. "The Red Army liberated Auschwitz," Snyder writes, "and it liberated the sites of Treblinka, Sobibor, Belzec, Chelmno and Majdanek as well. American and British forces saw none of the major killing sites."[4] There were virtually no survivors of these camps, nor could the Soviets preserve the camps, since the Germans destroyed the structures before they evacuated.

Next, FDR and the Depression. Today even progressive historians like Ira Katznelson concede that FDR didn't save America from the Depression, which grew wider and deeper through FDR's presidency. "Even when economic recovery began," Katznelson writes, "it proved fitful, remaining well below late 1920s levels for most of the 1930s."[5] What actually lifted America out of economic Depression was not New Deal policies but rather the entrepreneurial vigor, manufacturing prowess, and sheer work ethic of Americans in the postwar era.

Of course FDR did lead America into the fight against Hitler's Germany and Mussolini's Italy, but this hardly proves that FDR had no affinities with Nazism or fascism. By way of analogy, Martin Luther led the Protestants in a fight against the Catholic Church but can we conclude from this that Martin Luther had no affinities with Christianity? On the contrary, Luther and his followers were devoutly Christian, no less so than the Catholics. The Reformation was an intramural fight between two contending groups of Christians—a fight, one may say, within the house of Christendom.

Along the same lines, the fight between the Shia and the Sunni factions hardly proves that one or the other is not Islamic. Both are Islamic, and in fact their theological beliefs are virtually identical. The main difference is over the line of succession from Muhammad. Yet this seemingly trivial difference has not prevented bloody conflicts from erupting between the two Muslim sects. And again, in Russia, the bitter skirmishes between Leninists and Trotskyists in the early twentieth century

If conservatives had violently disrupted Obama's or Hillary's rallies or attempted to violently prevent his inauguration, the media would apoplectically denounce such fascist tactics. Yet when the Left did exactly this to Trump, the media turned around and blamed...Trump. *Getty Images*

The twenty-five-point Nazi Party platform, with a few small modifications, reads like the platform of today's Democratic Party and would undoubtedly provoke thunderous applause if read at a Democratic national convention. *Wikimedia Commons*

Die Ziele der Nationalsozialisten Nr. 7
Aus dem Programm der NSDAP

Die 25 Punkte

Both Hitler and Mussolini were socialists. Hitler changed the name of the German Workers' Party to the National Socialist German Workers' Party. Mussolini was a socialist organizer who moved seamlessly from Marxism to fascism. All the founders of fascism in Germany, Italy, France, and England were from the political Left. *Library of Congress*

The masked protesters at Berkeley illustrate how the Left has learned to use Nazi tactics of censorship, intimidation, and violence while posing as the ones fighting Nazism. *Getty Images*

Unlike the Nazis, who set ten thousand books ablaze in Berlin on May 10, 1933, the American Left simply doesn't assign books or hire professors that contradict its ideology and big lies. *Library of Congress*

The Nazis invented the technique of turning street thugs into ideological saints. Joseph Goebbels turned Nazi brownshirt Horst Wessel—who was killed in an urban brawl—into a martyr much in the same manner that the American Left would later turn street hoodlum Trayvon Martin into a martyr. Unlike Obama, however, Goebbels did not say that Horst Wessel could have been his son. *Wikimedia Commons*

Freud identified "transference" as a phenomenon involving the shifting of blame and responsibility; this describes how the Left and the Democrats blame their own practices of enslavement, genocide, racism, and fascism on the very conservatives and Republicans who have fought these evils from the beginning. *Wikimedia Commons*

The first concentration camps were Democratic slave plantations, and both slave camps and Nazi camps were closed systems that not only exploited the labor of racial "inferiors" but also disfigured their moral personalities. *Library of Congress*

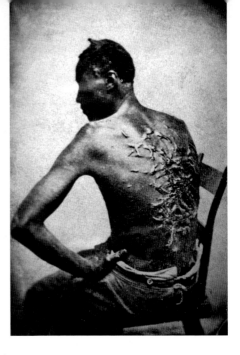

Hitler drew his inspiration for *Lebensraum*—which is to say land seizures in eastern Europe, as well as his attempted genocide of their native populations—from Democratic Party founder Andrew Jackson's forced relocation, land-stealing, and genocide against the American Indians. *Library of Congress*

INDIAN LAND FOR SALE

GET A HOME
OF
YOUR OWN

EASY PAYMENTS

PERFECT TITLE

POSSESSION

WITHIN

THIRTY DAYS

FINE LANDS IN THE WEST

IRRIGATED
IRRIGABLE

GRAZING

AGRICULTURAL
DRY FARMING

IN 1910 THE DEPARTMENT OF THE INTERIOR SOLD UNDER SEALED BIDS ALLOTTED INDIAN LAND AS FOLLOWS:

The Ku Klux Klan was, in the words of progressive historian Eric Foner, "for 30 years the domestic terrorist arm of the Democratic Party." It can be considered a sister organization of the Nazi brownshirts, another private terrorist militia that used similar tactics to intimidate and murder political opponents and racial minorities. *Library of Congress*

We all know the founder of Marxism, Marx, and the philosopher of capitalism, Adam Smith. Giovanni Gentile, shown here, was the philosopher of fascism. Progressives have buried him so that no one will see that his tireless advocacy of the centralized state—we are the state and the state is us—is virtually identical to what the modern Left advocates. *Wikimedia Commons*

Josef Mengele killed young children and performed macabre experiments on their body parts at Auschwitz. Later he became an abortionist in Argentina. His counterparts can be found among Planned Parenthood officials who offer fetal body parts for sale, and in the practice of the Philadelphia abortionist Kermit Gosnell. *Wikimedia Commons*

Young John F. Kennedy returned from his trips to Germany in the 1930s effusive about Hitler and Nazi Germany. JFK echoed Hitler's claims of Nordic superiority and accused people who were critical of Hitler of being jealous of him. Even as late as 1945, JFK described Hitler as a "legend." *Wikimedia Commons*

Philosopher Martin Heidegger—a favorite among leftists because of his advocacy of atheism, environmentalism, and anti-capitalism—was a lifelong anti-Semite, a devoted fan of Hitler, and champion of the Nazi *Gleichschaltung* to bring German cultural institutions into line with the führer. *Getty Images*

The introduction of fascist tactics to the American university came in 1969, when armed leftist thugs took over the library, student union, and radio station at Cornell and threatened the lives of professors who did not submit to their "nonnegotiable demands." Today some of those same thugs run Cornell. *AP Images*

Hitler hated Jews in part because he saw them as greedy capitalists from the shady world of finance who didn't contribute their fair share to the larger society. This sounds very familiar, and indeed it echoes the Democratic Left's denunciations of Wall Street and the top 1 percent. *Library of Congress*

Cartoonist A. F. Branco drew this one specifically for this book. *A. F. Branco*

reflected an intramural quarrel within the same ideological camp. As these examples show, unremittingly bitter fights can erupt among ideological relatives, just as unremittingly bitter fights sometimes erupt among actual blood relatives.

So, too, the fight between FDR, Hitler, and Mussolini was an intramural fight and a struggle for power among once-amicable leftist leaders with a shared collectivist ideology.

But to see this, we have to remove our post–World War II blinders that have been put there by left-wing historiography. We have to recover FDR's world before the war, before everything was blown to smithereens and the debris—I mean the ideological debris—cleared away in a progressive janitorial operation. We have to listen to what FDR and his brain trust and to what ideological allies actually said about fascism and Nazism, and we have to hear also what the fascists and Nazis—Mussolini and Hitler included—said about FDR. This investigation produces a completely different picture from the one in progressive textbooks and popular media.

Before we embark on the investigation, I'd like to preview one of my conclusions by answering the following question: is progressivism really a middle path between socialism and capitalism? Of course not, any more than fascism is. The whole middle path nonsense is part of the big lie. In reality, socialism, fascism, and progressivism are three similar—though not identical—forms of leftism. All three march in the same direction, away from liberal capitalism, so there is no middle path at all.

Of the three leftist paths, one, socialism, has been largely abandoned although it is still trodden, if only in theory, in leading American universities. As for fascism, official fascism is dead although I will show in this chapter that fascism lives on today through American progressivism. Progressive economics is essentially identical to fascist economics, and the whole fascist conception of government and the fascist subordination of the individual to the state are today the *cause celebre* of the American Left. This is as true today as it was in the 1930s.

FDR, in this respect, was the inventor of American fascism, our first Duce or führer, although the ground for him was paved by his

proto-fascist predecessor, Woodrow Wilson. I make my case by showing the fascist elements of Wilson's and FDR's actions and exposing the
mutual admiration society of the 1920s and 1930s between American
progressives on the one hand, and Italian fascists and German Nazis
on the other. Along the way I'll expose progressive big lies, such as
historian William Leuchtenburg's claim that "Mussolini's corporate
state did not find an American following."[6] As we'll see soon enough,
nothing could be further from the truth.

It Did Happen Here

Returning to the United States from Rome, where she had been the
correspondent for the *New York Times*, Anne McCormick noticed
something very striking. The atmosphere in Washington two months
after the inauguration of President Franklin D. Roosevelt, she wrote in
the May 7, 1933, *New York Times*, "is strangely reminiscent of Rome
in the first weeks after the March of the Black Shirts." McCormick found
this odd—and delightful. She mentioned the similarity not to criticize
FDR but to praise him. What she liked best about FDR was that he was
acting like Mussolini and patterning the New Deal state after Italian
fascism.

In Rome, McCormick had a reputation for being one of the many
progressive foreign correspondents infatuated with Mussolini's regime.
She routinely reported on the "solidarity" that Italians felt under the
"elan" of the Mussolini dictatorship. "You see here," she wrote a few
weeks after Mussolini's Ethiopian incursion, "a remarkable manifestation—a nation moving in a kind of trance—enchanted into a conviction
of invincible strength." Of McCormick, historian John Diggins writes
in *Mussolini and Fascism* that "for almost 20 years she carried on a
political love affair with an idealized Italy and its noble leader."

Back in America, McCormick was similarly enamored of FDR. The
FDR administration, she wrote, "envisages a federation of industry, labor
and government after the fashion of the corporative State as it exists in
Italy." Congress had passed legislation that "vests the president with the

authority of a dictator." This was "a sort of unanimous power of attorney" in which "all the other powers—industry, commerce, finance, labor, farmer and householder, State and city—virtually abdicate in his favor." The national mood, like McCormick's mood, was in favor of dictatorship. "America today literally asks for orders. Nobody is much disturbed by the idea of dictatorship."[7]

Around the same time, others in the media compared FDR with Germany's new leader, Adolf Hitler. Hitler, like FDR, rose to power through the democratic process. Of course by then he had become, like Mussolini, a dictator, but that term didn't have the bad odor it does now. McCormick and others did not hesitate to call FDR a dictator or urge him to become one. Dictators were viewed as resolute figures who got things done. They claimed to represent the genuine will and spirit of their people.

The view on the Left in Germany, Italy, and the United States was that planned societies function best under the firm hand of a single leader. "Hitler is Germany and Germany is Hitler," Rudolf Hess liked to say. This was the classic expression of the leader principle or *Führerprinzip*. In the same vein, the Italians liked to say that "Mussolini is Italy and Italy is Mussolini." FDR and the progressives liked this way of thinking. The *Führerprizip* in Germany and its equivalent in Italy closely mirrored FDR's own view—echoed in the progressive media—that FDR is America and America is FDR.

These sentiments on the part of McCormick and others were not those of outliers or cranks. Rather, they reflected progressive, and to some extent mainstream, sentiment in the early FDR era. Even the *Saturday Evening Post* and *Fortune* magazine spoke in similar terms. We get a sense of this in the reception accorded to Mussolini's flamboyant aviation minister Italo Balbo when he came to America in 1933 to attend the Chicago World's Fair.

Balbo had been one of the original Italian blackshirts. Coming of age as a fascist organizer in his home region of Ferrara, he was one of the principal organizers of Mussolini's March on Rome. None of this prevented Balbo from being featured on the cover of *Time* on June 26,

1933, with an accompanying article that presented fascist triumphs in aviation technology as an example America could learn from.

On July 20, 1933, President Roosevelt hosted a White House luncheon in Balbo's honor and presented him with the Distinguished Flying Cross. Balbo told FDR he was heading home, but FDR prevailed upon him to stay longer and undertake a nationwide American tour. According to the *New York Times*, the "Air Minister left the White House with his face wreathed in smiles."

FDR's aides organized a massive downtown ticker-tape parade for Balbo in New York, after which Balbo delivered a stirring speech about the virtues of fascism to 65,000 New York Democrats at Madison Square Garden. Balbo wired Mussolini to say, "The existence of anti-fascist sentiment abroad is a myth" that had been "exploded by the enthusiastic welcome my air squadron has received in America."[8]

While the progressive mass media was whipping up public sentiment in favor of Mussolini's regime, progressives at America's elite universities were courting Adolf Hitler. Seven months after the notorious Nazi book burning in 1933, Columbia University invited the German ambassador to speak on campus where he was introduced by the university's president Nicholas Murray Butler. Political scientist Paul Hollander writes that Columbia "maintained friendly relations with Nazi academic institutions and representatives of Nazi Germany."[9]

In 1934, Harvard president James Conant hosted a tea at his house for Ernst Hansfstaengl, head of the Nazi Press Bureau under Joseph Goebbels's Propaganda Ministry. Hansfstaengl was a close friend of Hitler who frequently dined at his house. Hitler liked to have Hansfstaengl do his piano renditions of rousing Harvard football marches. Hitler especially liked the final cheer "Harvard, Harvard! Rah! Rah! Rah!" Hitler gave Hansfstaengl the affectionate nickname "Putzi" and Hansfstaengl's son Egon warmly referred to Hitler as "Uncle Dolf."

During Hitler's rise to power, Hansfstaengl helped finance the publication of *Mein Kampf* as well as the purchase of the *Völkischer Beobachter*, which became the Nazi Party's official newspaper. While a Boston rabbi mobilized a Jewish protest, the *Harvard Crimson* pooh-poohed the critics and called for Hansfstaengl, a Harvard alumnus, to be awarded an honorary degree "appropriate to his high position" in the government of "a great and profound nation."[10]

That same year prominent Harvard faculty, administrators, and student leaders visited the Nazi warship *Karlsruhe* when it docked in Boston harbor, flying the swastika flag. The Harvard group also attended a gala reception at which the warship captain praised Hitler. And in 1936 Harvard sent an academic delegation to celebrate the anniversary of Heidelberg University. The event was boycotted by British universities because it was highly politicized to feature Nazism in a positive light. In attendance, mingling with the Harvard delegation, were Nazi theorist Alfred Rosenberg, Propaganda Minister Joseph Goebbels, and SS chief Heinrich Himmler.[11]

On the cultural front, another FDR admirer, the songwriter Cole Porter, penned a catchy tune in 1934 with the following lyrics: "You're the top! You're the Great Houdini! You're the top! You're Mussolini." That's not how the song is performed today, but that's because Porter later changed the words. He did so once progressives recognized it would be embarrassing for them, as it would for anyone in America, to be associated with Mussolini. So Cole Porter became party to the big lie. His original lyrics, along with McCormick's oeuvre, the Balbo tour, and the Harvard-Hitler connection, have as a consequence of progressive labors simply disappeared into the fog of history.

The Proto-Fascist

While this chapter focuses on FDR—our unacknowledged American führer—the story would be incomplete without beginning with the progressive president who preceded him nearly two decades earlier, Woodrow Wilson. FDR, it should be noted, was navy secretary in the Wilson administration, and never during his tenure nor in subsequent years did he publicly dissent from any of Wilson's actions described here.

Indeed, FDR and his team openly spoke of the New Deal as a continuation of Wilson's policies. As I'll show, it was a case of the proto-fascism of Wilson maturing into the more full-blown fascism of the FDR era.

Wilson, of course, preceded Mussolini and Hitler. That's why I call him a proto-fascist. I'm not saying he would have been a fan of actual fascism, but I am saying he was a precursor of fascism in that his regime reveals fascist strains even before there was an official name to describe them. To understand proto-fascism, consider the academic debate over whether the philosopher Nietzsche was a proto-fascist. Nietzsche died in the 1880s so obviously there is no direct association between him and fascism. Had he lived, he would most likely have been appalled by Hitler and Mussolini. Nietzsche detested German nationalism, and he was not an anti-Semite.

On the other hand, Nietzsche was one of Mussolini's favorite thinkers, and Mussolini declared in his time "the Will to Power in Europe in represented solely by fascism." Hitler visited the Nietzsche archives at Weimar and was photographed there by his personal photographer Heinrich Hoffman to show his zest for Nietzsche. Hitler also sent Mussolini a newly published edition of Nietzsche's complete works with an autographed dedication; it became one of Mussolini's most treasured possessions.

If Nietzsche explicitly rejected nationalism and anti-Semitism, what was his appeal to these men? Nietzsche spoke in terms of creating not merely an *übermensch*, or overman, but a race of overmen, a superior breed to rule the world. Nietzsche also went on to talk about the *untermenschen*, the lower people who would have to be eliminated or exterminated, through war or eugenics, in an inevitable struggle for power. One can see why these ideas appealed to Hitler.

Unencumbered by the moral restraints of Christianity—which Hitler and Mussolini also reviled—Nietzsche also reveled in the prospect of large numbers of people he considered inferior being wiped off the earth. "May a storm come," he writes in *The Will to Power*, "to shake all this rotten and worm-eaten fruit from the tree." Again, one can envision the Nazis and the blackshirts cheering. And soon, courtesy of Hitler and

Mussolini, the storm did come. Therefore, I can see why Hitler and Mussolini cherished Nietzsche and, with appropriate qualifications, I consider Nietzsche a proto-fascist.[12]

Wilson was a proto-fascist in the same way. What Wilson, a disciple of Hegel, liked best about the German philosopher was Hegel's apotheosis to the all-powerful state. Having studied under German mentors, Wilson's model for government was drawn from the militaristic experience of Bismarck's Prussia. Wilson ridiculed the American founders—he was the first American president to do so—calling their ideas about individual rights, decentralized power, and checks and balances, simple-minded and outdated. Wilson preferred a model of centralized power with him at the helm and all of society in supine obedience to progressive leftist dictates. As Giovanni Gentile would recognize, even without the name this is the essential meaning of fascism.

Admittedly my calling Wilson a proto-fascist may seem hard to believe for people who have been raised on the progressive humbug about Wilson being a champion of global democracy and an advocate of all people having the right to self-determination. Actually, Wilson had a chance to promote both and in fact promoted neither. Had Wilson actively fought for the self-determination of Germany in the aftermath of World War I, he might have prevented World War II.

One of Hitler's most bitter complaints—one that struck a resonant chord with his fellow Germans—is that his country would never have sued for peace in the Great War had they known they would be almost completely deprived of their rights of autonomy and national self-determination. Most historians recognize that more reasonable terms than the ones imposed on Germany at Versailles may have prevented Hitler's ascent to power and thus prevented a second world war. Wilson could have insisted on such a treaty, and gotten one, but he didn't. So Wilson's rhetorical buncombe must be discounted in the face of historical reality.

Let's focus not merely on what Wilson said but on two things that he did. First, in the mode not just of fascism but also of National Socialism, Wilson implemented racist policies throughout the federal government and helped revive the dormant racist terrorist organization the Ku

Klux Klan. Second, Wilson suppressed the civil liberties of Americans in a manner never seen before or since; one would have to go to Mussolini's Italy and Nazi Germany to find closer comparisons.

Progressives know this and profess to be deeply mystified by it. Writing in the *Christian Science Monitor*, Randy Dotinga lists "5 Surprising Facts" about Wilson one of which is that he was "backwards and bigoted when it came to race." Given Wilson's progressivism, Dotinga finds this "the biggest contradiction of all." Here Dotinga, a journalist, is echoing historians like Arthur Link, editor of the Wilson papers, and John Milton Cooper who take a similar line on Wilson. Cooper for instance, terms Wilson's bigoted and tyrannical behavior "puzzling" and a "mystery." He wonders how "such a farseeing, thoughtful person as Wilson let any of that occur."[13]

By this time, I expect my readers to be smiling in full recognition of the big lie territory we are in. The lie is in the pretense that there is something bizarre or anomalous about a progressive like Wilson being a racist, a suppressor of constitutional liberties, and a proto-fascist. The whole point of this book has been to show that this is the predictable, if not inevitable, course of progressivism and the Left. Of course Wilson was a racist, as most of his Democratic predecessors going back to Andrew Jackson were. And of course he engaged in fascist-style suppression of individual liberties; this is how collectivists of all stripes typically behave once they acquire power.

Wilson's racism can be highlighted by his enforcement of segregation throughout the federal government. Many people don't realize that while Democratic-Party-dominated state legislatures had made segregation widespread throughout the South, the federal government in Washington, D.C., had not been segregated since the end of the Civil War. Wilson reversed this and instituted segregation in pretty much every division of the federal government.

Wilson's actions were bitterly protested by the leading spokesman of black America, Booker T. Washington, who was a Republican. When a group of African American leaders including Republican journalist Ida B. Wells confronted Wilson about his actions, he informed them that they should be thanking him because segregation was largely for the benefit of black people. Wilson was, as Chris Myers Asch writes in the *Washington Post*, an "unabashed white supremacist."[14]

Wilson's closest allies in Congress were Democrats who were even more racist than he was. When the issue of America joining the League of Nations came before Congress, Democratic Senator James Reed erupted, "Think of submitting questions involving the very life of the United States to a tribunal on which sit a nigger from Liberia, a nigger from Honduras, a nigger from India."[15] As a good progressive internationalist, Wilson was of course in favor of the League of Nations, but he also blocked a condemnation of racism in the Treaty of Versailles and never uttered a word to chastise his fellow Democrats for their violent racial rhetoric against blacks and other minorities.

Wilson also helped revive the Ku Klux Klan. Oddly enough this was the result of a single screening of a movie, David W. Griffith's *The Birth of a Nation*, which portrays the Ku Klux Klan as the savior of the South. Despite the crude technology of the time, the film is now recognized as a cinematic masterpiece. I regard it as one of the most powerful propaganda films ever made. In this respect, it foreshadowed Leni Riefenstahl's brilliant propaganda films *Victory of Faith* and *Triumph of the Will*, both portraying Hitler as the savior of Germany.

At Griffith's urging, Wilson arranged to have *The Birth of a Nation* screened in the White House, with his cabinet and other influential friends in attendance. After the screening, according to Griffith, Wilson described the film as "terribly true" and "like writing history with lightning." Some progressives today question whether Wilson actually said this, as there is no independent corroboration in the Wilson archive, but there is no reason to doubt Griffith's veracity on this point.

Immediately following the screening there was a Klan revival across the country, which was a testament both to the power of the film and to Wilson's apparent endorsement of it. Previously the Klan had been mostly in the Democratic South; now, according to historian David Chalmers, the Klan spread from "Maine to California." Suddenly, there were Klan chapters in Oregon, Colorado, Wisconsin, Ohio, Pennsylvania, and New

Jersey.[16] I'm not saying Wilson intended this, but most historians agree that the White House showing of *The Birth of a Nation* gave the Ku Klux Klan a new legitimacy and popularity.

During World War I, Wilson created a propaganda ministry that became a forerunner to similar ministries created by Mussolini and Hitler. In terms of its outright bullying and intimidation of the press and the political opposition he faced, Jonah Goldberg writes that Wilson's operation was more effective—by which he means ruthless—than Mussolini's.

Wilson's goons even turned their venom against private citizens, encouraging children to spy on their parents and neighbors to spy on their fellow neighbors. They encouraged vigilantes to threaten and even beat up ideological nonconformists. In a phrase that could easily have been spoken by Hitler or Mussolini, Wilson insisted that "conformity will be the only virtue and any man who refuses to conform will have to pay the penalty."

It's hard to imagine a more illiberal sentiment than this. In line with it, the Wilson administration also instituted a widespread crackdown on civil liberties that would make the McCarthyism of the 1950s seem like child's play; essentially any criticism of the government, even privately uttered to a friend, could send you to jail. And in fact tens of thousands of Americans were arrested and imprisoned under the notorious Palmer Raids. Goldberg writes, "More people were arrested or jailed in a few years under Wilson than under Mussolini during the entire 1920s." Goldberg concludes that during World War I under Woodrow Wilson, "America became a fascist country."[17]

Looking to Mussolini

If Wilson can be considered America's proto-führer, Franklin D. Roosevelt became, at least for a time, America's actual führer. This isn't my term for FDR; it was coined by Germany's leading newspaper, the *Frankfurter Zeitung*, in an article comparing FDR to Hitler. The term führer means nothing more than "leader" or "supreme leader," and the

Frankfurther Zeitung did not mean it as an insult. Although critical of Hitler's policies until it was eventually forced into compliance, the newspaper had praised Hitler's commanding style of leadership, and it intended its reference to FDR as an American führer to be a compliment.

I intend to vindicate this term as applied to FDR through a two-part demonstration. In this section I examine FDR's enthusiasm for Mussolini, which was not unique to him but represented a larger movement of American progressives who looked to Italian fascism as a model for America. Some on the Left even looked to Hitler for leadership. And the enthusiasm was reciprocal: both Hitler and Mussolini praised FDR and saw in the progressive New Deal an at least partial realization of the ideals of both fascism and National Socialism. Let's peek into the windows of this mutual admiration society.

It should be said at the outset that FDR personally had no affection for Hitler. But he did for Mussolini. In a letter to journalist John Lawrence, a Mussolini admirer, FDR confessed, "I don't mind telling you in confidence that I am keeping in fairly close touch with that admirable Italian gentleman." In June 1933, FDR wrote his Italian ambassador Breckinridge Long—another Mussolini admirer—regarding the fascist despot: "There seems no question he is really interested in what we are doing and I am much interested and deeply impressed by what he has accomplished and by his evidenced honest purpose in restoring Italy."[18]

From FDR's point of view, Mussolini had gotten an early start in expanding state power in a way that FDR himself intended. Italy under *Il Duce* seemed to have moved further down the progressive road than America. So FDR urged leading members of his brain trust to visit Italy and study Mussolini's fascist policies to see which of them could be integrated into the New Deal. FDR also dispatched three members of his Committee on Administrative Management to Rome to examine Mussolini's administrative structure for organizing his dictatorial government, again with a view to reorganizing FDR's own administration.

Rexford Tugwell, one of FDR's closest advisers, returned from Italy with the observation that "Mussolini certainly has the same people opposed to him as FDR has." Even so, "he seems to have made enormous progress." Tugwell was especially wowed by how the Italian fascists were able to override political and press opposition and get things done. He quoted favorably from the 1927 charter of Italian fascism, the *Carta del Lavoro*, which seems to have impressed him far more than the American constitution. Fascism, he concluded, "is the cleanest, neatest, most efficiently operating piece of social machinery I've ever seen. It makes me envious."[19]

This sycophantic devotion to fascism, repulsive though it appears today, was at the time characteristic of the way that leading leftists felt about Mussolini both in Europe and the United States. In England, the Fabian socialist George Bernard Shaw praised Mussolini for actually implementing socialist ideals. In 1932, the utopian leftist novelist H. G. Wells actually called for a "liberal fascism" in the West, emphasizing the need for "enlightened Nazis." One finds similar paeans to Italian fascism by progressives in Germany and France.[20]

The American Left, however, was even more devoted to Italian fascism than the European Left. The leftist journalist Ida Tarbell interviewed Mussolini in 1926 for *McCall's* magazine and returned effusive with praise. Muckraker Lincoln Steffens, who famously said of the Soviet Union, "I have seen the future and it works," also praised Mussolini for his leftist sympathies, noting rapturously that "God has formed Mussolini out of the rib of Italy." Steffens seemed unruffled by fascism's deprivation of civil liberties, noting that true liberty is "a measure of our sense of security." FDR had famously said to Americans during the Great Depression that they had "nothing to fear but fear itself." Steffens viewed Mussolini too as attempting to abolish fear.[21]

Progressive writer Horace Kallen, an early champion of multiculturalism, said it was a "great mistake" to judge fascism as merely tyrannical, noting it was an experiment in social justice "not unlike the Communist revolution." Both systems, he said, had given citizens a sense of unity and we should approach them with patience and judge them only by their results. For progressive historian Charles Beard—known for his attacks on the American founders as selfish, landed capitalists—Mussolini's heavy-handedness was one of his positive traits. Beard admired the fascist dictator for bringing about "by force of the State the most compact and unified organization of capitalist and laborers the world has ever seen."[22]

Herbert Croly, editor of the *New Republic*, celebrated Mussolini for "arousing in a whole nation an increased moral energy" and subordinating the citizens "to a deeply-felt common purpose." Another *New Republic* editor, George Soule, praised the New Deal for its kinship to Mussolini's policies: "We are trying out the economics of fascism." This flagship magazine of American progressivism praised the Mussolini regime throughout the 1920s, even publishing articles by fascist intellectuals like Giuseppe Prezzolini, who wrote that true socialism would be realized not in Russia by the Bolsheviks but in Italy by the blackshirts.[23]

In 1934, the leftist economist William Pepperell journeyed from his home base of Columbia University to the International Congress on Philosophy in Prague where he announced the name "Fabian Fascism" to describe the New Deal, which he considered a creative hybrid of socialism and fascism. A few years later, in 1938, when a journalist visited Governor Philip La Follette, he found that this founder of the Wisconsin Progressive Party had two framed photographs in his office: one of Supreme Court Justice Louis Brandeis and one of Benito Mussolini. La Follette admitted that these were his two personal heroes.[24]

Some on the Left went even further and praised Nazism. Writer Gertrude Stein insisted in 1937 that the most deserving candidate for the Nobel Peace Prize was Adolf Hitler. Lawrence Dennis, a foreign service diplomat and author, extolled Nazism for producing "a formula of national solidarity within the spiritual bonds and iron discipline of which the elite and the masses of any given nation...can cooperate for the common good." Dennis called for Americans to embrace fascism, recognizing that it might look quite different here than it did either in Italy or Germany. In 1936 Dennis attended the Nuremberg Party Congress where he shared his enthusiasms with Nazi ideologue Alfred Rosenberg and Hitler's longtime associate Rudolf Hess.[25]

The progressive African-American scholar W. E. B. Du Bois said Hitler's dictatorship was "absolutely necessary to get the state in order." Hitler, Du Bois said, "showed Germany a way out" by making of his country a "content and prosperous whole." In 1937 he wrote, "There is today in some respects more democracy in Germany than there has been in years past." Du Bois even contrasted American racism, which he considered irrational, with Nazi anti-Semitism, which he said was based on "reasoned prejudice or economic fear."[26]

With Compliments from Hitler

So far we've seen what the American Left, both inside and outside the FDR administration, thought of the fascists and Nazis, but what did the fascists and Nazis think about them? I start with Mussolini's review of FDR's book *Looking Forward*. Mussolini noted that the book was a welcome repudiation of classical liberalism. The New Deal, he added, was "boldly interventionist in the field of economics" based on the idea that "the state no longer leaves the economy to its own devices," and in this respect FDR's policies were "reminiscent of fascism." Consequently, FDR's attempt to make the whole economy work for the common good, Mussolini commented, "might recall the bases of fascist corporatism." Indeed FDR's whole approach "resembles that of fascism."[27]

Mussolini and FDR were in touch even before FDR was inaugurated, and Mussolini was initially much more favorable toward FDR than he was toward Hitler. In fact, the Italian press just as frequently compared Mussolini and FDR as did the American media. When journalist Irving Cobb visited Mussolini in 1926 he said to him, "Do you know, your excellency, what a great many Americans call you? They call you the Italian Roosevelt." Mussolini was thrilled. "For that," he replied, "I am very glad and proud. Roosevelt I greatly admired." Mussolini clenched his fists. "Roosevelt had strength—had the will to do what he thought should be done."[28] Here Mussolini is praising FDR basically for being, like him, a political strongman.

In Germany, the Nazi press also had positive things to say about FDR. In his book *Hitler's American Model*—which I have referenced earlier—progressive legal scholar James Whitman notes, "the strange fact that the Nazis frequently praised Franklin D. Roosevelt and the New Deal government in the early 1930s." Big lie alert! This fact is only "strange," it turns out, because scholars like Whitman have been camouflaging the ideological affinities between the American Left and the Nazis. So we can discount Whitman's fake perplexity. Much more interesting is his documentation of enthusiastic paeans to FDR in the Hitler youth magazine *Will and Power* as well as heroic photo spreads of FDR in the Nazi-controlled *Berlin Illustrated Magazine*, accompanied by an article on "the fascist New Deal."[29]

On May 11, 1933, the Nazi newspaper *Volkischer Beobachter*, in an article titled "Roosevelt's Dictatorial Recovery Measures," praised FDR for "carrying out experiments that are bold. We, too, fear only the possibility that they might fail. We, too, as German National Socialists are looking toward America." In a favorable review of FDR's book, the *Völkischer Beobachter* concluded that while maintaining a "fictional appearance of democracy," in reality FDR's "fundamental political course…is thoroughly inflected by a strong national socialism." On June 21, 1934, the same newspaper noted, "Roosevelt's adoption of National Socialist strains of thought in his economic and social policies" and compared his leadership style with Hitler's own dictatorial *Führerprinzip*.[30]

Hitler himself told a correspondent for the *New York Times* that he viewed FDR traveling down the same path as himself. "I have sympathy for Mr. Roosevelt," Hitler said, "because he marches straight toward his objectives over Congress, lobbies and bureaucracy." Hitler, like Mussolini, viewed FDR as a fellow dictator. Hitler added that he was the sole leader in Europe who had genuine "understanding of the methods and motives of President Roosevelt."[31]

Hitler told FDR's German ambassador William Dodd that FDR's insistence that American citizens place the common good above their own personal good "is also the quintessence of the German state philosophy which finds its expression in the slogan 'The Public Weal Transcends the Interest of the Individual.'" Even as late as 1938, Dodd's successor Hugh Wilson reported to FDR that Hitler remained a fan: "Hitler said he had watched with interest the methods which you, Mr. President, have been attempting to adopt for the United States in facing some of the problems which were similar to the problems he had faced when he assumed office."[32]

Ecco Un Ditatore!

Finally, I show how FDR came chillingly close to becoming a fascist dictator during his long tenure in office from 1932 to 1945. If FDR didn't become a full-scale despot, he came closer than anyone else in U.S. history. By this point in the book we can anticipate the outrage that this will provoke on the Left. We are also at the point where we must calmly disregard it. The outrage itself is a tactic to protect the big lie. "How can you say this?" and "how dare you say that?" I dare because it happens to be true.

As we've just seen, the Italian fascists and even the Nazis recognized FDR's dictatorial tendencies and also their ideological kinship with his policies. FDR's Republican predecessor, Herbert Hoover, saw close parallels between the New Deal and fascism, and so from the other end of the spectrum did the socialist Norman Thomas. And in 1933 America's most respected columnist, Walter Lippmann, told FDR that he had "no alternative but to assume dictatorial powers."[33] So I'm not making this up; FDR was widely seen as a fascist dictator or a dictator-in-the-making by many of his contemporaries.

I won't say FDR was a dictator in the Hitler mode, because he never had Hitler's absolute power, nor of course did he murder his opponents, gas the Jews, or start a world war. So when I call FDR an American führer I mean he was a führer in the American way rather than in the German way. A better comparison is between FDR and Mussolini, both of whom viewed themselves as a kind of national boss, overriding the constraints of democracy while still functioning within political limitations imposed by their respective systems. While FDR's legal powers remained short of those of Mussolini, this is not because he "held back"; rather, he was constrained by America's constitutional system which prevented this dangerous man from bringing full-scale fascism to America.

Consider one of FDR's key initiatives that was the centerpiece of the New Deal: the National Recovery Act (NRA). This act essentially spelled the death knell for the free market in the United States. It empowered the federal government to establish coalitions of labor and management in every industry to set production targets, wages, prices, and even minimum and maximum working hours. These agreements would be reviewed by a government-run Industrial Advisory Board answerable to FDR himself. Further, the NRA legislation raised income taxes and corporate taxes and expanded the government's power of eminent domain to confiscate private land for public use. According to FDR adviser Rexford Tugwell, the NRA was designed "to eliminate the anarchy of the competitive system."[34]

No government intervention in the U.S. economy on this scale had ever been contemplated—let alone enacted—before this. The NRA was widely recognized across the political spectrum at the time as a fascist project. The progressive writer Roger Shaw, writing in *North American Review*, stated the NRA was "plainly an American adaptation of the Italian corporate state." The Marxist writer Victor F. Calverton seconded this in *Modern Monthly*, noting, "The NRA is doing part of the job that European fascism has set out to accomplish." And FDR's own Interior Secretary Harold Ickes admitted, "What we're doing in this country are some of the same things that are being done in Russia and even some things that are being done under Hitler in Germany." Mussolini himself, upon hearing of the NRA, offered a single telling comment, "Ecco un ditatore!" which means "Behold a dictator!"[35]

The man FDR picked to run the NRA, General Hugh Johnson, was himself a fascist who loved to associate himself with what he termed the "shining name" of Mussolini. Johnson carried around with him a copy of a propaganda pamphlet, *The Structure of the Corporate State*, which had been written in Italian by one of *Il Duce*'s sidekicks Raffaello Vigone and translated into English by Oswald Mosley's British Fascist Party in 1933. Johnson especially liked to quote the sections about how fascism rode roughshod over the confused apparatus of democracy in order to transfer all authority to the centralized state. Under Johnson, the NRA issued a pamphlet, *Capitalism and Labor Under Fascism*, which acknowledged that "the fascist principles are very similar to those which have been evolving in America."[36]

To FDR's dismay, his NRA was struck down by the Supreme Court in its landmark 1935 *Schechter Poultry Corp v. United States* decision. Other New Deal initiatives were also overturned. The Supreme Court was concerned with the way FDR sought to override private property rights and also the rights of contract. These rights—which can be seen under the umbrella of economic liberty—had been, since the founding, considered just as basic as other fundamental rights like the rights to free speech, religion, and assembly. Acting in its role as the protector of minority rights—part of our system of checks and balances—the Supreme Court blocked FDR from overturning 150 years of economic liberty.

So what did FDR do? In 1937, he introduced his infamous "court packing" scheme. Basically FDR threatened to increase the number of Supreme Court justices from nine to as many as fifteen. This would give him the chance to appoint up to six more justices, giving him an overwhelming majority. The mindset behind this can be seen in what FDR's top aide Harry Hopkins told an audience of New Deal activists in New York. "I want to assure you," he said, "that we have lawyers who will declare anything you want to do legal." This was FDR's approach: if you want to do it, call it legal, and if the Supreme Court says otherwise, stack it. Here we see the classic fascist contempt for the distinctive role of the Supreme Court as the conservator of minority rights in a system of checks and balances.

The Supreme Court, in a panic, did a rapid turnabout and gave in to FDR, a move that progressives somewhat bemusedly call "the switch in time that saved nine." This little witticism was coined to divert attention away from the enormity of what FDR did. He basically threatened to destroy our constitutional system unless he got what he wanted—and so he got what he wanted. FDR's actions here—which hover in that twilight zone between the legal and the illegal—are directly comparable to the intimidation tactics used in Nazi Germany and Fascist Italy to bludgeon the judiciary into conformity.

The effect of the Supreme Court's surrender to FDR was basically the end of economic liberty as a constitutional right. No, FDR was not able to revive the NRA at this point, and his actual trespass on property rights and the rights of contract, through the various New Deal programs, was relatively modest. Essentially FDR gave us the welfare state, and I'm not suggesting the welfare state by itself is a fascist concept. The welfare state in Germany, for instance, originated with Otto von Bismarck's moderate, conservative progressivism and predated fascism by more than half a century. Yet we should not forget that it was the Left—the socialists, fascists, and progressives—who further expanded the welfare state.

My point here, however, is that FDR laid the foundation for future progressive administrations to continually undermine economic liberty. The Leviathan government we have now wasn't all FDR's doing, but it was started by FDR. Before him, we had economic liberty as a constitutional right. After him, we didn't. The main thrust of fascist economics involves the expansion of centralized state power at the expense of individual rights and the liberty of the private sphere. So FDR's actions in destroying economic liberty are fascist in this sense.

While FDR intimidated the Supreme Court, he had no need to intimidate the legislature, since his Democratic Party controlled Congress. FDR convinced his fellow Democrats to give him virtually unchecked control over a large swath of the nation's economy. Basically FDR no longer had to consult Congress and could proceed on his own initiative in huge areas of decision-making. In effect, by invoking the cries of "economic emergency" during the Great Depression and then "national emergency" during World War II, FDR was able to assume quasi-dictatorial powers.

Mussolini, too, subverted the power of the legislature and convinced a pliant parliament to turn over its power to him. The Italian parliament didn't even need to meet during Mussolini's reign, because he made virtually all the decisions. So did Hitler who, in the wake of the Reichstag fire in 1933, convinced the German parliament to pass an Enabling Act turning over legislative authority to him and thus, in quasi-legal fashion, making him the supreme ruler of Nazi Germany. Like FDR, these fascist dictators didn't just overthrow the system but rather persuaded and pressured the system to give them essentially unchecked authority.

How did FDR use that authority? Once again, in the fashion of the classic fascist despot, he used it to intimidate private companies and private citizens into submission to his state initiatives. The most notorious example of this was FDR's Blue Eagle program, symbolized by the image of a blue eagle. Today no one would even recognize this symbol. It has been neatly airbrushed from history by progressives. But at the time it was the most recognized symbol in America and was widely compared to the swastika symbol in Nazi Germany.

The point of the Blue Eagle program was to force companies to come into "voluntary" compliance with FDR's initiatives. Companies that did would hang the blue eagle symbol in their stores or display it in their corporate advertising. The government actively urged the public to shop only in Blue Eagle stores and to boycott companies that did not display the symbol. FDR's goons organized Nuremberg-style rallies to whip the public into a frenzy against those who dissented from Blue Eagle compliance.

Again, this was precisely the function of the swastika symbol: along with the trademark "Heil Hitler" salute, it served as a notice of compliance with the policies of the Nazi regime. Historian Aryeh Unger has a telling term for this; he calls it "voluntary compulsion." A German admirer of Hitler in the 1930s called it "working towards the Führer."[37] Everyone showed their loyalty by orienting their actions toward Hitler, getting as it were into lockstep with him. FDR employed precisely the same voluntary compulsion in order to get the whole country working toward the American führer.

Like Hitler and Mussolini, FDR established a massive propaganda machine within the government and, at the same time, sought to restrict the liberty of the press. In Germany, journalists were essentially forced to join the Ministry of Propaganda. Italy, too, had its National Fascist Syndicate of Journalists to which you had to belong to be a journalist in "good standing." FDR's approach was only slightly more subtle. He installed one of his most devoted henchmen as chairman of the Federal Communications Commission. Under this goon, the FCC required radio stations to submit transcripts of all programs dealing with "public affairs" for FCC clearance.

The FCC also let it be known that criticizing the government could lead to a broadcast license revocation. Many progressive radio hosts were only too eager to serve as FDR lapdogs in much the same manner that our mainstream media willingly became Obama and Hillary lapdogs. Henry Bellows of CBS told FDR that he valued the "cooperation" between the government and his network and "as a lifelong Democrat, I want to pledge my best efforts to making this cooperation successful." CBS and NBC both banned critics of the New Deal from their stations throughout the 1930s and early 1940s. Only a few stations held out, but to save their licenses, they too were soon forced to fall into line.[38]

A Pact with Racism

Finally, FDR cozied up to and made deals with the worst racists in America. I'm not saying that FDR himself was a racist. I don't know if he was or wasn't. But I do know that he worked closely with the racists in the Democratic Party to advance their agenda even as they helped him advance his. This aspect of FDR admittedly draws him closer to Nazism than to fascism, since racism was a trademark not of Mussolini's fascists but rather of Hitler's National Socialists. Again, this is an aspect of FDR that progressives have worked hard to keep out of the textbooks and the national consciousness.

First, FDR appointed Hugo Black, a former Ku Klux Klansman, to the Supreme Court. Black was completely unqualified—his only judicial experience had been eighteen months as a municipal court judge—but he had a reputation as an enthusiastic New Dealer who had publicly endorsed FDR's court-packing plan. Black was also an active Klan member who had spoken at and led Klan rallies and marches throughout his native Alabama. While FDR later claimed he didn't know this about Black, it's hard to see how this is possible since Black listed it on his resume.

When a Pittsburgh newspaper exposed the depth of Black's association with the Klan—he was a Klan lawyer who made openly racist appeals to juries—it caused a big furor. But FDR stood by Black, who later wrote in his memoir, "President Roosevelt told me there was no reason for my worrying about having been a member of the Ku Klux Klan. He said that some of his best friends and supporters were strong members of that organization. He never in any way, by word or attitude, indicated any doubt about my having been in the Klan nor did he indicate any criticism of me for having been a member of that organization."[39]

FDR also supported racist Democrats in Congress in their efforts to thwart anti-lynching laws. This was a key condition the racists put before FDR. They said they would not support FDR's New Deal programs unless FDR supported their effort to block Republican anti-lynching bills. So FDR convinced even northern Democrats and progressives to back their southern counterparts in keeping these bills from coming to the floor for a vote.[40] This is one of the most disgraceful legacies of the FDR presidency and it goes virtually unmentioned in progressive FDR biographies.

In addition, FDR made a deal with racist Democrats to cut blacks out of most New Deal programs including Social Security and unemployment benefits. He did this by writing exemptions into the programs to exclude the occupations, such as agricultural labor and domestic service, in which blacks were heavily concentrated. FDR also left the administration of these programs to local discretion, allowing local Democratic officials to routinely deny benefits to blacks.[41] Not until 1954, when Republicans controlled the presidency, the House, and the Senate did they finally eliminate the exclusions that denied many blacks Social Security and other benefits.

FDR also continued segregation in the federal government even though he had the power unilaterally to reduce or suspend it. Republicans and blacks regularly called for desegregation in the military and promotion by merit. FDR refused. His Federal Housing Authority promoted segregated housing, his Civilian Conservation Corps was segregated, even the atomic bomb research center in Oak Ridge, Tennessee, was segregated, and black journalists were routinely excluded from the president's press conferences.[42] Again, except for suckers of the big lie, none of this is a "surprise"; it is fully in keeping with the racist history of the Democratic Party.

Finally, FDR interned more than 120,000 Japanese-Americans in what he himself called "concentration camps" for the duration of America's involvement in World War II. These camps—which functioned like prisons with daily head counts and curfews—were lined with barbed wire and guarded by military police. Yes, America was at war with Japan, but America was also at war with Germany and Italy. Dramatically fewer German-Americans or Italian-Americans were targeted by the government and forced to relocate from America's coasts. It's hard not to agree with Japanese-Americans who say they were singled out by FDR in the same manner that Hitler singled out the Jews.

Tricksters on the Left

The first trickster in attempting to cover up FDR's ties with fascism was, ironically enough, FDR himself. In his April 29, 1938, message to Congress, FDR said that "unhappy events abroad" had taught America a simple truth: "The liberty of a democracy is not safe if the people tolerate the growth of private power to the point where it becomes stronger than their democratic state itself. That, in essence, is fascism—ownership of government by an individual, group, or by any other controlling private power."[43]

By now we can recognize the big lie in full swing. Fascism is not private control of the government; it is government control of the private sector. While increasing the power of the centralized state in the same manner the fascists did, FDR pretends that he is doing this to save American democracy from fascist control of the government by private business interests. FDR inverts the meaning of fascism to make it look like his Republican opponents are the fascists and he is, well, the anti-fascist.

Today this inversion is simply too much for anyone to believe. So historian Ira Katznelson attempts to cover for FDR using a more delicate approach, a superior form of tricksterism, one might say. In a previous chapter, I showed how Katznelson contributes to the big lie by blaming the Democratic Party's racist atrocities on the South. With FDR, Katznelson employs a different mode of defense.

He candidly admits FDR's racist and dictatorial tendencies. FDR's rule, he says, had the "most profound imperfections." Thanks to FDR, "Eyes were averted when callousness and brutality proceeded." The deals he made with bigots from his own party were a "rotten compromise." Yet in the end Katznelson supports FDR's strain of dictatorial fascism because, in his words, "With it, the New Deal became possible."[44]

Katznelson's objective is to convince progressives and the Left that FDR was a noble statesman willing to get his hands dirty to get a great thing accomplished. Consider, Katznelson says, the limits FDR operated under; unlike in Nazi Germany, "There was no American enabling act."[45] (One wonders if Katznelson would prefer that there had been one.) So FDR had to work with Congress, he had to work within the American political system to get the New Deal done, and that's why he made the deals he did.

I don't think Katznelson realizes that in order to vindicate FDR of the charge of fascism, he has made a classic fascist argument. I am not referring to Katznelson's implication that the ends justify the means. This claim by itself is troubling. Was it really worth decades of blacks being lynched and systematically discriminated against in order to push through a handful of New Deal programs? I for one don't' think so. But however one answers this question, the fascist thrust of Katznelson's argument lies elsewhere.

The core theme of fascism, we can recall from fascism's philosopher Giovanni Gentile and endorsed by fascism's official founder Benito

Mussolini, is the push for the centralized state. In the fascist worldview, as Mussolini never tired of saying, the state is everything and everything else is subordinate to the state. Given this, all measures are permissible—however brutal and heavy-handed, however inconsistent with private liberty or the constitutional system of checks and balances—in order to expand centralized state control and power.

For all his qualms and head-scratching over FDR's fascist tactics of strong-arming the courts and usurping the authority of Congress and fostering the ugliest forms of racism, Katznelson is good with them in the end because they helped achieve FDR's fascist goal of expanded centralized power. And this is the fascism on the Left we live with now, both in the Left's perpetual ideological push for enlarging government power and also in the Left's willingness to use whatever sleazy and base tactics that are necessary to get from here to there. FDR was not only America's original führer, he also helped create armies of American brownshirts on the Left that are very much with us today.

Eight

Politics of Intimidation

*The legitimation of violence against a demonized internal
enemy brings us close to the heart of fascism.*[1]

Robert Paxton, *The Anatomy of Fascism*

alf a year later, the shock of Trump's election has not yet fully sub-
sided for the Left. Bitter, unremitting political battles rage between
Trump and his adversaries. This is resistance of a volume and vehemence I haven't seen before. The adversaries don't just want to thwart
Trump, to defeat and humiliate him, they also want to get him out of
there. The underlying message of Trump's enemies is the following: it is
happening here, and we cannot rest until we've ousted this fascist and
his supporters from the corridors of power.

But where is the opposition to Trump really coming from? Where's its
ground zero? It's tempting to assume it comes from the Democratic Party.
Yet the Democrats are the minority in both houses of Congress, and
Republicans dominate the state legislatures and governorships. Despite the
tenacity of Democratic opposition, there is only so much the minority party
can do. Yet no one can discount the depth and ferocity of the anti-Trump
movement, so the center of the resistance must be somewhere else.

Some Trumpsters on social media speak in hushed tones about a "deep state," a covert state-within-a-state of opposition that is naturally mounted against an outsider president who has vowed to "drain the swamp." These Trump allies point the finger at covert swamp rats, mainly in various government intelligence agencies from the NSA to the CIA to the FBI. Certainly there is bureaucratic resistance to Trump within the government, but this is something he can deal with, as head of that government.

The Left's real power does not derive from any covert conspiracy but rather from a state-within-a-state that is very much in plain sight. The Left doesn't need to rely on the FBI, the CIA, and the NSA because it already has three of the most powerful institutions of our society. The Left dominates academia, Hollywood, and the media. These are the three most powerful megaphones of our culture and they are the primary instruments for disseminating information to people, especially to young people. In a democratic society, whoever controls the flow of information controls public opinion that ultimately decides all questions. This state-within-a-state is the strongest, deadliest weapon of progressivism and the Democratic Party. Without it neither progressives nor Democrats could get as far as they have, or mount the kind of scorched-earth opposition they have against Trump.

While Trump's victory and the GOP's political domination are temporary, the Left's state-within-the-state is permanent. The Left basically owns academia, Hollywood, and the media. We can see this by asking how we could go about changing them. It's virtually impossible. Hollywood is an incestuous insider culture that is largely self-perpetuating. There is a conservative group in Hollywood, Friends of Abe, but it meets in secret and some of its members have to show up in disguise.

Recently one of the rare outspoken conservatives in Hollywood, Tim Allen, created a furor when he told Jimmy Kimmel, "You know, you get beat up if you don't believe what everybody believes." Then Allen added, "This is like 1930s Germany." Shortly after Allen made this statement, ABC cancelled his sitcom *Last Man Standing* despite six years of high ratings.[2] If it can happen to a big star like Allen, it can obviously happen to anyone. When I released my film *2016: Obama's America*, members of Friends of Abe told me they were glad I made that film because had they done so, it would have ended their Hollywood careers. Actually, a few Hollywood insiders did help with that movie but all of them insisted on using aliases in the credits.

Academia hires its own and is largely unaccountable to any outside force; parents, state legislators, and alumni have only a peripheral impact on what goes on there. Sure, conservatives can endow a chair or send a speaker to this campus or that one, but the impact of these measures is surely only marginal. After all, the Left dominates the humanities and social science departments of virtually every university, and the more selective the university, the greater the extent of the dominance.

A recent report by the Oregon Association of Scholars, a conservative group, shows that universities systematically "weed out" conservative professors and refuse to hire new ones. Interestingly the mechanism for doing this is diversity statements. Leftists in the universities insist that conservatives lack commitment to diversity. So diversity becomes the pretext for progressives to root out the little intellectual and ideological diversity that remains on campus.[3] All of this is not merely depressing, it is also unlikely to change. To change it, conservatives would have to start several hundred campuses of their own, which is impossible.

The mainstream media is no less ideologically insular. In fact, right-wing media is not a refutation of this but a confirmation of it. The reason we have independent right-wing media is because conservatives have been systematically shut out of the TV networks, cable networks like CNN and HBO, and newspapers like the *New York Times*, the *Washington Post*, and the *Los Angeles Times*. The right-wing Fox News channel has a big audience compared to other cable networks, but it is under constant siege, and in any case its audience is a tiny fraction of ABC, CBS, and NBC. Conservative talk radio, for all its reach, is collectively smaller than state-run National Public Radio which is an organ of the political Left.

What this means is that the Left can work together, and does so naturally, to get its message widely disseminated. This is how big lies get told and come to be widely accepted as incontrovertible truth. Typically, the lie originates in academia, where one left-wing academic concocts it and other left-wing academics whoop it up. Then the media adopts it, invoking the academic theory for validity and then drumming it into the popular mind as a proven truth. Periodically Hollywood then converts the story into a sitcom or feature film and builds emotional support for the cause while also making it seem fashionable and cool. Finally, all three institutions gang up on anyone who questions the big lie, seeking to discredit them, ruin them, and ideally drive them out of public life altogether.

Culture of Intimidation

How did we get here? Things, after all, were not always this way. The old Hollywood of the 1930s through the 1950s was dominated by Jewish immigrants who believed in the American dream and America as a force for good in the world. Conservatives like Reagan, John Wayne, and Jimmy Stewart had a place in that Hollywood. None of them could break into today's Hollywood. The media has always leaned to the Left but not even during Watergate has it been so aggressive and proselytizing about its left-wing views as it is now. In a sense, the mask of objectivity has come off completely; today's *New York Times* doesn't even pretend to cover news in a neutral or balanced way.

When I was a student at Dartmouth in the early 1980s, there were still classical liberals of the old stripe on the faculty. They are now gone. Then, as a young Reaganite, I could debate political issues with professors and students on the Left. Sure, the Ivy League was left-wing, but it wasn't monolithically so. Today, by contrast, conservative viewpoints have basically been rooted out. Young people today don't reject conservatism; they don't know what it is. If you ask students on even our best campuses, "What are conservatives attempting to conserve?" they give you gaping, uncomprehending stares.

We live today in one of the most closed, exclusionary, repressive cultures in modern history. In a sense, the Left doesn't have to conduct witch-hunts for conservatives and torment them; they just don't hire them in the first place. When conservative speakers show up to campus, they are frequently prevented from speaking by violent leftist protesters, or shouted down by activists with bullhorns. At Trinity University in San Antonio, where I spoke recently, leftists defaced my posters. I turned their action to my advantage by publicizing their intolerance on social media. As a result, a thousand people showed up to my talk and the leftist attempt to thwart my lecture backfired.

But when controversial right-wing podcaster Gavin McInnes showed up to speak at New York University in February 2017, the NYU anti-fascists showed up in force and assaulted McInnes and the students who had invited him, raining blows on the conservatives and hitting McInnes himself with pepper spray. "I'm dumbfounded that NYU would invite somebody who is a hate speaker," said activist Tamara Fine, "He is a fascist." McInnes attempted to speak but was drowned out by protesters. So he interrupted his talk and left, while outside protesters shouted and scuffled with local police.[4]

In April 2017, conservative pundit Heather Mac Donald was prevented from speaking at Claremont McKenna College. Some 250 protesters blocked her entrance to the Athenaeum, with some chanting "fascist" and others chanting "black lives—they matter here." Campus officials cited security reasons for cancelling Mac Donald's public event. Instead they asked her to speak only to the event organizers and livestream the event on social media. "It was decided that I would give the speech for livestreaming to a largely empty hall," Mac Donald said.[5]

It should be remembered that these are conservative voices that are being imported to campus. There is no indigenous conservatism whatever among the faculty of these institutions. Even so, on the rare occasions when a conservative shows up, he or she is assailed and sometimes assaulted and hounded out.

This is the America we live in now. Ours is a culture of ritual abuse and humiliation, in which dissenting voices are hounded, shamed, and terrorized, in some cases not just to silence them but also to destroy the career and lives of the people who hold them. Demonization is the cultural

Left's regular order of business these days. This, by the way, is why so many Republicans in Congress are so timid; they are terrified of the media with its power to humiliate them so badly that their own side will bury them.

By contrast, violent protesters and criminal thugs are celebrated in academia, the media, and Hollywood as icons of idealism and martyrs of a great cause. Consider the case of Bill Ayers and Bernardine Dohrn, leaders of the Weather Underground, and both formerly on the FBI Most Wanted list. Even though neither one has regretted their past involvement in domestic terrorism, both have been rehabilitated and reintegrated into the progressive community. Ayers and Dohrn are now distinguished professors, Ayers at the University of Illinois at Chicago and Dohrn at Northwestern University Law School.

In the progressive universe, thugs also become celebrities. Che Guevara, a murderous communist thug and political prison camp warden who ordered the execution of political prisoners and committed mayhem in Cuba, Africa, and South America before he was killed stirring up trouble in Bolivia, has become a progressive cult hero, featured on countless T-shirts and dorm-room posters. Trayvon Martin was a street hoodlum who got into a violent scuffle with a man who shot him in self-defense. Trayvon immediately became a martyr to the progressive cause, and President Obama validated his sainthood by saying that Trayvon could have been his son.

Where does all this craziness come from? More broadly, how did our cultural institutions—from academia to the media to the movie and music industry—become so deeply perverted? The conventional explanation, offered by Allan Bloom in *The Closing of the American Mind* and then picked up by Jonah Goldberg in *Liberal Fascism*, is that all of this traces back to the 1960s. In the spring of 1969, as Bloom recounts, gun-toting leftists dressed in military uniforms seized the administration offices at Cornell University. They also took over the student union and the local radio station. This was a fascist-style takeover. Political scientist Walter Berns, a friend of Bloom who taught at Cornell at the time, read the protesters excerpts from Mussolini's speeches and the protesters cheered wildly, unaware that they were cheering fascism.

Many conservatives accept Bloom's account that it was the craven submission by the administration and the faculty to the demands of the leftist thugs that symbolizes the subsequent ideological surrender of the American university to the political Left. Some of course didn't surrender; they supported the takeover and embraced the thugs' demands. One such collaborator was Cornell President James Perkins—a former New Dealer in FDR's Office of Price Administration—who was himself a leftist. So were many of the young faculty in the humanities and social science departments.

A band of professors—mostly older classical liberals—did resist the "non-negotiable" demands of the students. Mostly Democrats, they nevertheless believed in the purposes of a liberal education and had no intention of letting undergraduate thugs dictate to them what and how they should teach. So the thugs made them an offer they couldn't refuse: submit or be killed. And they submitted. Only a handful of faculty held out—Bloom included—and nearly all of them left Cornell shortly thereafter.

In this respect, at Cornell and elsewhere, there was in fact a surrender. Today at Cornell and other universities the leftist protesters do not have to take on the establishment; they are the establishment. Today the Left doesn't have to make curricular demands; it controls the curriculum committee. There is no need for the Left to burn or ban politically objectionable books; they simply don't assign them. So today the efforts of the progressives are directed at excluding the few, rare voices of opposition that threaten to prevent them from consolidating a complete monopoly of information and opinion on their campuses.

So Bloom's 1960s explanation has a lot going for it, but taken by itself it is insufficient. It begs the following question: where did the Cornell thugs get the idea of mounting a fascist-style takeover? Who taught them these tactics that have persisted to the present day? Here I show that the real ancestors of the Cornell activists and their successors are those masters of bullying, intimidation, and terror—the Nazis.

We have seen parallels between the American Left and the Nazis throughout this book, but this is the respect in which today's Left most closely resembles its Nazi counterpart. It is the Nazis who created a state-within-the-state and invented the type of systematic cultural coordination, propaganda techniques, and aggressive bullying and intimidation that is now the modus operandi of the progressive Left.

Progressive *Gleichschaltung*

The Nazi term for this was *Gleichschaltung*, which means bringing all of society into line with the leftist priorities of Nazism. *Gleichschaltung* at its core is a doctrine of political uniformity and social control; it is the original form of political correctness. *Gleichschaltung* operates largely through outside pressure and intimidation but the Nazis considered it most successful when it led to *Selbsgleichschaltung* or "self-coordination," as people willingly placed themselves under the sway of Nazism. Here I argue that the American Left is attempting a similar task of bringing society into line with progressivism.

Let's look at two parallel cases in which cultural propaganda was used to turn a street thug into an ideological icon. Horst Wessel was a twenty-one-year-old brownshirt known for his bloody battles against the Nazis' rival leftists in the Communist Party. Wessel was also something of an artiste, having moved into a lower-class bohemian neighborhood and composed a sixteen-line poem for the local Nazi paper. The communists shot Wessel dead in a dispute involving his landlady's attempt to evict his girlfriend, a one-time prostitute named Erna Jaenicke, from his apartment.

Ordinarily, this would be a sordid episode best forgotten. But Goebbels used Nazi media to portray Wessel as a martyr. A group of Nazis set the Horst Wessel poem to the music of an old German tune. Thus was born the Horst Wessel song. Wessel's funeral became a huge Nazi demonstration, with thousands of mourners and Goebbels himself delivering the oration. To tears and applause, Goebbels declared, "Wherever there is a

Germany, you will be, too, Horst Wessel."[6] Then everyone belted out the Horst Wessel song which became a kind of Nazi anthem, sung throughout the 1930s and during the war to rally troop and public enthusiasm.[7]

Wessel's bogus martyrdom is the basis for today's progressive paeans to thugs and criminals from Che Guevara to Bill Ayers to Trayvon Martin. For the Left, as for the Nazis, there seems to be nothing that your own side cannot do and get away with it. In some ways, the worse the offense, the harder the Left fights to legitimize it. Not only do leftist thugs become cultural heroes, but those who criticize them somehow become the bad guys. It's the Horst Wessel story over and over again. The only difference, I suppose, is that we don't yet have a Trayvon Martin song and Goebbels never claimed that Horst Wessel could have been his son.

Yet even as the Left embraces Nazi propaganda and bullying tactics, it insists weirdly enough that its actions are in the name of anti-Nazism. That's where the moral respectability comes from. It's how fascist thugs can be portrayed by their progressive allies in the media and Hollywood as good guys. By contrast, their targets—the victims of their fascist bullying and abuse—are portrayed as fascists who fully deserve to be humiliated and abused in this way. If you're beginning to feel that all of this is horribly sick and inverted, that's because it is.

How did things get this way? This incredible story begins with a Nazi philosopher who happens to be one of the great philosophers of the twentieth century, Martin Heidegger. It continues with one of Heidegger's Jewish students, Herbert Marcuse, who strangely enough learned his most important lesson from the Nazis and brought it to America. For reasons we will soon discover, Marcuse taught the 1960s Left to imitate the fascists while posing as anti-fascists. Finally, we turn to another refugee from Nazism who nevertheless in his youth worked with the Nazis and now directs, in much the same manner Mussolini and Hitler did in their early days, his own private militia. Note that Trump doesn't have a private militia, but this guy does. With him, as with Marcuse, fascist thuggery derives its moral legitimacy and public respectability from a fake anti-fascist pose. His name is George Soros.

The Left's Favorite Nazi

Ever since the publication of his magnum opus *Being and Time*, Martin Heidegger's philosophy has been widely influential. Specifically, it provides intellectual grounding for a whole series of progressive causes. First, Heidegger's root-and-branch attack on Western metaphysics from Plato to the present inspired the leftist academic movement called deconstructionism. Heidegger's fundamental questioning of technology is invoked by the so-called deep ecologists of the environmental movement. His opposition to capitalism and materialism—both of which he associates with "Americanism"—has boosted the spirits of leftist anti-capitalism and anti-Americanism. Heidegger's attack on individualism and his enthusiasm for communities of blood and soil helped provide a basis for modern identity politics in which blacks, Hispanics, and others claim a unique identity based on their membership in a particular ethnic group. Finally, Heidegger's atheism—his assertion in *Being and Time* that we are mortal beings and must find our purpose not in some transcendent order but within the compass of our human morality—has fortified the secular, non-religious basis of modern progressivism.

In light of all this, should we view it as astonishing—or merely appropriate—that Heidegger was an admirer of Hitler and a dues-paying member of the Nazi Party? Heidegger was named rector of the University of Freiburg just months after Hitler became chancellor of Germany in 1933. Later that year, on the eve of the Reichstag elections, Heidegger gave his *Rektoratsrede* or rector's address in which he spoke out in favor of Hitler's German "resurgence." At the same time, Heidegger circulated a manifesto of German academics pledging their loyalty to Hitler and the National Socialist State, thus establishing himself as one of the chief coordinators of Nazi *Gleichschaltung*.

In this now-infamous rector's address, Heidegger mocked the notion of intellectual freedom saying it was a false freedom that should be subordinated to the larger objectives of Hitler's new Germany. Heidegger said that true education isn't merely about books but also involves participation in the Nazi Labor Service. In his words, "The National Socialist State is a workers' state." Heidegger's talk was followed by a rousing rendition of the Horst Wessel song and shouts of *Sieg Heil*. Later Heidegger spoke of Nazism's "inner truth and greatness." Even after World War II, when the monstrous crimes of Nazism were undeniable, Heidegger maintained his silence about what the Nazis did to the Jews and other captive populations.

Despite Heidegger's complicity with Nazism, many progressives rushed to defend him. First, these progressives say that Heidegger was only a Nazi for a brief period in the 1930s and by the middle of the decade he had already begun to distance himself from Nazism. Second, progressives point out that a number of Heidegger's most prominent students, notably Karl Lowith, Herbert Marcuse, and Hannah Arendt, with whom he had an extramarital affair, were Jewish; therefore, he could not have been anti-Semitic. Perhaps, these leftist defenders say, Heidegger was briefly infatuated by Nazism but then quickly saw the error of his allegiance.

Heidegger himself took this line in the aftermath of World War II, in which he minimized his Nazi commitment. Heidegger said his lectures on Nietzsche in the late 1930s and early 1940s were, correctly interpreted, critical of Nazism. Here, however, Heidegger was being disingenuous. The so-called criticisms of Nazism, if they existed, were so obscure that they would be indecipherable to even the most careful reader. Heidegger's disingenuousness, indeed outright dishonestly, can be compared here to the Nazi eugenicists who participated in the sterilization and euthanasia schemes during Hitler's reign but later tried to cover their tracks by denying their past and quietly slipping into the ranks of the population control movement.

The problem for Heidegger and many of his left-wing apologists is that so much has come out to expose Heidegger's close and abiding relationship to Nazism. This is a man who said rhapsodically of Hitler, "The Fuhrer alone is the present and future German reality and law. The Fuhrer has awakened this will in the entire people and has welded it into a single resolve."[8] Not only did Heidegger embrace the Nazis, but he viewed his Nazism as arising out of his philosophy, a political expression of the groundbreaking themes in *Being and Time*. Moreover, the recent publication of Heidegger's black notebooks, written over a forty-year period from 1931 to the early 1970s, show that he was a lifelong anti-Semite.

Faced with this dismaying body of evidence, many of Heidegger's leftist apologists have shifted their line of defense. They now say that Heidegger was a philosopher who may have been a committed Nazi, but that doesn't mean he was a Nazi philosopher. In this respect, the Left distinguishes Heidegger from such intellectual promoters of Nazi doctrine as party ideologue Alfred Rosenberg. The Left's goal here is to jettison Heidegger the man for his despicable politics but retain Heidegger the philosopher as an inspiration for a whole host of leftist causes.

Now it's true that Heidegger was not a philosopher of Nazism in the sense that, say, Giovanni Gentile was a philosopher of fascism. It hardly follows from this, however, that Heidegger's Nazism was not rooted in the premises of his philosophy. Basically Heidegger's thought emerges out of a distinction between tribal society or *Gemeinschaft* and commercial society or *Gesellschaft*. This distinction did not originate with Heidegger—it was first advanced by the German sociologist Ferdinand Toennies—but Heidegger's work built upon it.

Essentially, Heidegger supported Nazism as a "blood and soil" affirmation of tribal *Gemeinschaft*. He detested cosmopolitan *Gesellschaft* which he saw as eroding the bonds of tribal society. Heidegger associated *Gesellschaft* with America, a country based on commerce and trade. He also associated *Gesellschaft* with the Jews. In his black notebooks, Heidegger terms the Jews "worldless," by which he means that they are people without a place, united across the continents by what he saw as the grubby pursuits of finance and trade. Even in this brief account we see how Heidegger's affinities with Nazism spring from the depths of his philosophical commitments.

One of Heidegger's students, Karl Lowith, protested against the effort to evade the connection between Heidegger's philosophy and his Nazism, pointing out decades ago that Heidegger himself viewed his philosophy as leading to Nazism, so it made no sense for Heidegger's disciples to pretend they understood Heidegger better than he understood himself.[9] Yet Heidegger's progressive acolytes refuse to heed Lowith's protestations.

In a recent book, the leftist political scientist Sheldon Wolin attacks his fellow progressives for becoming such persistent, deluded apologists for a Nazi thinker.[10] Wolin sets about to resolve a mystery: how, he asks, could an avowed right-wing Nazi have become the darling of the contemporary academic and political Left? Of course, by this point we know that this is not a mystery at all. Nazism is left-wing, not right-wing. Thus it is hardly a puzzle that the same leftist convictions—hatred of God, technological capitalism and "Americanism"—that drove Heidegger to Nazism are precisely what makes him appealing to leftists today.

What's Wolin up to? Basically he wants his fellow progressives to get back on track with the big lie. Wolin realizes that there is simply no way to win by covering for a Nazi enthusiast, whatever his philosophical pedigree. So Wolin is begging his fellow leftists to get rid of Heidegger, denounce him, stop making him one of their own. If I can put myself in Wolin's place and state his argument in my own words, it goes like this: "So what if Heidegger was one of us? Mussolini was also one of us. Does that mean that we should try and restore Mussolini? Come on, leftists. We've made so much progress blaming Nazism on the right-wing. Let's stick with our theme that Heidegger was on the Right and stay away from him. Let's not blow our cover now, just to save this one guy Heidegger."

Wolin's sense of urgency about detaching Heidegger from the Left can be explained by seeing that Heidegger's larger project and the Left's larger project today are one and the same. Heidegger insisted that everything was political and this is also what the Left believes today. Heidegger said that free speech and academic freedom were myths. What really mattered was the larger community. Ditto for the Left once again. Heidegger favored not merely debate but open ideological indoctrination for young people. Sound familiar? Heidegger knew about and evidently supported the intimidation and eviction of Jews and other "undesirables" from the German campus. The Left today has a new category of undesirables; this time they are not Jews but conservatives. Finally,

Heidegger's goal was conformity or ideological unity, and while the Left blathers on about campus diversity it's quite obvious that this diversity is merely a cover for ideological unity and conformity of precisely the kind Heidegger sought in his time and for his country.

Even more than most other professors in Germany, Heidegger enthusiastically enrolled himself in Hitler's *Gleichschaltung*. In fact, he sought to be the academic leader of *Gleichschaltung* in the German universities. This didn't work out because the Nazis discovered he was a typical incompetent intellectual and gave the position to someone else. Yet Heidegger's *Gleichschaltung* is precisely what the Left is attempting today, not merely with American universities but with all of American culture. Consequently, Wolin doesn't want Heidegger's Nazi fingerprints over the Left's broad and to date highly successful project to create a state-within-a-state.

Brownshirt Tactics 101

In 1925 the Jewish philosopher Theodor Lessing spoke out against the repressive political climate of Weimar Germany. Although Lessing's explicit target was the cravenness of the Weimar regime of Paul von Hindenburg, his real target was the emerging power of Nazism, and he faulted the government for yielding to it. The Nazis immediately recognized the threat posed by Lessing. Hitler youth at Lessing's University of Hanover formed a "committee against Lessing." They encouraged students to boycott his lectures. Nazi youth then showed up and disrupted Lessing's classes. Lessing was forced to give up his academic chair the following year.

In his account of what happened, Lessing acknowledged he could do nothing to prevent being "shouted down, threatened and denigrated" by student activists. He was helpless, he said, "against the murderous bellowing of youngsters who accept no individual responsibilities but pose as spokesman for a group or an impersonal ideal, always talking in the royal 'we' while hurling personal insults...and claiming that everything is happening in the name of what's true, good and beautiful."[11] This was fascism, German style, in the 1920s.

In March 2017, the eminent political scientist Charles Murray—a former colleague of mine at the American Enterprise Institute—showed up to give a lecture on class divisions in American society at a progressive bastion, Middlebury College in Vermont. Hundreds of protesters gathered outside McCullough Student Center where Murray was scheduled to speak and engage in dialogue with Middlebury political scientist Allison Stanger. Murray is a libertarian who leans Republican, although he's no fan of Donald Trump. Unlike Lessing, who taught at the university where he was harassed, Murray doesn't teach at Middlebury, which is virtually devoid of conservative faculty. (Stanger is a moderate Democrat affiliated with the New America Foundation.)

In any event, the discussion promised to be a scholarly and illuminating one, giving students a perspective that they never get. But the Middlebury protesters were having none of it. The activists confronted Murray and Stanger, and at one point they struck Stanger. Inside Wilson Hall, protesters turned their backs to Murray and began to boo and shout. Murray found he simply could not be heard. College officials escorted Murray and Stanger to another location where their conversation had, for safety reasons, to be shown on closed-circuit television.

After the event, according to Middlebury spokesman Bill Burger, Murray and Stanger were "physically and violently confronted by a group of protesters." The protesters were masked in the standard Antifa style. Murray and Stanger ducked into an administrator's car, but the protesters attacked the car, pounding on it, rocking it, and seeking to prevent it from leaving. "At one point," Burger said, "a large traffic sign was thrown in front of the car. Public safety officers were able, finally, to clear the way to allow the vehicle to leave campus."

According to Burger, "During the confrontation outside McCullough, one of the demonstrators pulled Professor Stanger's hair and twisted her neck. She was attended to at Porter Hospital later and is wearing a neck brace." Murray praised campus security officers for the protection they provided but described what he experienced as "scary, violent mob action."[12] This is so-called progressive anti-fascism, American style, circa 2017.

Why does this purported anti-fascism on the part of progressives so closely resemble the fascism that it claims to be opposing? More profoundly, what is anti-fascism as the term is now used on the American Left? To answer these questions, we turn to the founders of the so-called anti-fascist movement on the progressive Left, the sociologist Herbert Marcuse and his colleague Theodor Adorno of the Frankfurt School or the Institute for Social Research in Frankfurt am Main, Germany.

In the last year or so, we've been hearing a lot about the Frankfurt School. Here are two recent articles: one by Sean Illing in *Vox* titled "If You Want to Understand the Age of Trump, You Need to Read the Frankfurt School," the other by Alex Ross in the *New Yorker* titled "The Frankfurt School Knew Trump was Coming."[13] The leftists who wrote these articles clearly want us to see the relevance of the Frankfurt School— and they're right, but not for the reasons they think.

The man who became the Frankfurt School's most influential figure, Herbert Marcuse, was a student of Heidegger at Freiburg, where he also became Heidegger's assistant. Marcuse was a young Marxist, and what attracted him to Heidegger was that he saw Heidegger as a revolutionary just like Marx. One of Marx's central themes, alienation, is also central to Heidegger. Both were men of the Left who despised technological capitalism. Marcuse, in his work, sought to integrate Marx and Heidegger. The *Stanford Encyclopedia of Philosophy* terms Marcuse's project an attempt to create "Heideggerian Marxism."[14]

Marcus recognized Heidegger's burgeoning fascism, but this, by itself, wasn't a problem. Fascism, as we have seen, is not inherently anti-Semitic. Marcuse knew that Heidegger's hatred for individualism, capitalism, and "Americanism" were shared by both fascists and Marxists. Precisely for this reason, Marcuse believed a fusion of Marxian socialism and Heideggerian fascism was a logical synthesis. We see in young Marcuse's intellectual project a confirmation of my earlier demonstration of the leftist and socialist roots of fascism. But Marcuse saw that Hitler was also a raving anti-Semite. As a Jew, Marcuse understood the peril that German National Socialism posed for him personally.

So Marcuse broke with Heidegger and fled the country. He joined the Frankfurt School, which had been formed in 1922 but most of its scholars during the Hitler era became German Jewish exiles living and working abroad. One of Marcuse's colleagues was Theodor Adorno. Both Marcuse and Adorno came to the United States. Adorno worked at the Institute for Social Research, the Frankfurt School's branch in New York City, and then moved to California for several years before returning to Europe in 1949. Marcuse worked at Columbia University, and then he moved during World War II to Washington D.C. to work with two government agencies, the Office of War Information and then the Office of Strategic Services, forerunner to the CIA. Marcuse subsequently taught at Brandeis and then at the University of California at San Diego, where he remained until his death in 1979.

The Deceitful Origin of "Anti-Fascism"

These two men had an enormous influence on both academic culture and popular culture and gave progressivism its anti-fascist credentials. But not at first. At first, the Frankfurt School tried to peddle its various brands of Marxism and socialism in America and found few takers. Who wanted to listen to a group of tedious Germans babble on about the evils of capitalist consumer culture? While such rhetoric was common in the socialist parties and movements of Europe, Americans did not respond well to it. Here people like nice homes and cars and pools in their back yard.

So Marcuse and Adorno put their thinking caps on and had a joint epiphany. They realized that they could market themselves as anti-fascists. This, after all, was the post–World War II era. America had just waged war against the Nazis, and after the war Nazism became the very measure of evil. So Marcuse and Adorno knew that anything associated with Nazism or fascism would automatically be tainted. They set about putting this obvious fact to political use on behalf of the political Left.

Not much was known about fascism and Nazism, outside of super-ficial newspaper and radio coverage. In academia and the media, there was an acknowledged ignorance of what had attracted so many people to fascism and Nazism, with its attendant anti-Semitism. Marcuse and Adorno were German scholars. They were Jewish, and so they could be expected to know about anti-Semitism and the fate of the Jews. And they were refugees from Nazi Germany, so they could claim to be speaking about Nazism, as it were, "from the inside."

The marketing strategy worked. Marcuse was actually hired by the U.S. government to offer insights into how to combat Nazism ideologi-cally. After the war, Marcuse was instrumental in shaping reeducation programs in Germany that were explicitly aimed at eradicating residual Nazi allegiances from the people. Together with Adorno, Marcuse also shaped what was considered anti-fascist education in the United States. Adorno and Marcuse's work was embraced by the American Jewish Committee, which naturally felt that these two German Jewish exiles would know precisely the nature of Nazism, fascism, and anti-Semitism and how to overcome them.

In reality, neither the U.S. government nor the American Jewish Committee understood that Adorno and Marcuse had their own agenda: not to fight fascism per se, but to promote Marxism and a leftist political agenda. Marxism and fascism are, as we have seen, quite close; they are kindred collectivist ideologies of the Left. Their common enemy is, of course, free markets and the various institutions of the private sector, including the church and the traditional family. Marxism and fascism both sought to get rid of capitalism and remake the social order. So did Marcuse, Adorno, and the Frankfurt School.

So the Frankfurt School decided to repackage fascism as a form of capitalism and moral traditionalism. In effect, they reinvented fascism as a phenomenon of the political Right. In this preposterous interpretation, fascism was remade into two things that real fascists despised: free mar-kets and support for a traditional moral order. With single-minded deter-mination, the Frankfurt School launched a massive program to uproot nascent fascism in the United States by making people less attached to the core economic and social institutions of American society.

The classic document in this regard is Adorno's famous F-Scale. The F stands for fascism. Adorno outlined the scale in his 1950 book *The Authoritarian Personality*. The basic argument was that fascism is a form of authoritarianism and that the worst manifestation of authoritarianism is self-imposed repression. Fascism develops early, Adorno argued, and we can locate it in young people's attachments to religious superstition and conventional middle-class values about family, sex, and society.[15]

With a straight face, Adorno produced this list of questions aimed at detecting fascist affinities: "Obedience and respect for authority are the most important virtues children should learn.... Homosexuality is a particularly rotten form of delinquency.... No insult to our honor should ever go unpunished.... No matter how they act on the surface, men are interested in women for only one reason." Basically, a yes answer to these questions showed that you were a budding fascist.

The underlying logic of Adorno's position was that German and Italian fascism were, at their core, characterized by internal psychological and sexual repression. A moment's reflection, however, shows why this position is nonsense. By and large, social attitudes toward religion, the family, and sexuality were quite similar across these countries, allowing for some modest variation. One might speculatively argue that the Germans of the time were more uptight than, say, the French, but who would argue that the Italians were more repressed than, say, the English?

So Adorno's F-Scale had no power to explain why fascism came to power in Germany and Italy but not elsewhere. Most real fascists, historian Anthony James Gregor dryly observes in *The Ideology of Fascism*, "would not have made notably high scores."[16] The one question that would in fact have uncovered fascist affinities—do you support increasing the power of the centralized state over individuals, families, churches, and the private sector?—Adorno left off his F-Scale, presumably because it would have brought enthusiastic yes responses from progressives and Democrats.

Given the patent absurdity of Adorno's anti-fascism, with its obviously fraudulent and pseudo-scientific F-Scale, why did the mainstream of American academia fall for it? Why did they go along with Adorno and proclaim his work the definitive basis for anti-fascist education? The short answer is that even then academia had a strong progressive tilt, and the progressives were looking for a way to cover up progressive complicity in fascism and Nazism.

The progressives were already in the process of burying their associations with Mussolini and Hitler. They were actively concealing FDR's link with fascism and Nazism. Right in the middle of this, they saw, to their amazement and relief, that here was a German Jewish scholar declaring fascism a phenomenon of the Right. Clearly he was sticking fascism on conservatives who supported capitalism and affirmed religion and traditional families. This was a lie—real fascists detest those institutions and want to destroy them—but it was a politically convenient lie.

So the progressives delightedly climbed aboard the bandwagon and cheered him on, and the cheering continues. In 2005, for example, the progressive sociologist Alan Wolfe admitted flaws in Adorno's work but praised *The Authoritarian Personality* as "more relevant now" because it "seems to capture the way many Christian-right politicians view the world."[17] Adorno's value to such people is that he empowers them to say, "Down with fascism! Now let's get rid of conservatism and expose those evil people on the Right."

The Sex Pervert as Anti-Fascist

Now we turn from Adorno to an even bigger culprit, Marcuse, who made two signal contributions to giving progressivism its anti-fascist reputation, each of them significant in its own right. The first contribution is, in a sense, derivative. It proceeds from a corollary of Adorno's thought. If as Adorno held, fascism is defined by internal psychological and sexual repression, then anti-fascism means the opposite of that—it means internal psychological and sexual liberation.

This is the message of Marcuse's first important book, *Eros and Civilization*. Marcuse made the case for sexual freedom by inverting Freud's famous argument in *Civilization and Its Discontents*. Freud argued that civilizations are built by repressing our erotic and sexual impulses. These impulses are overflowing, and if unchecked they can produce social chaos. But when we control them, when we defer gratification, as it were, we can channel those energies into productive enterprises.

Marcuse argued the opposite. Modern technological capitalist society, he argued, had established elaborate systems for controlling our sex organs, what Marcuse terms the "sacrifice of libido." Marcuse blamed not merely the free market system for supposedly codifying and merchandizing sex—turning it into a commodity—but he also blamed religious and social mores for repressing and enslaving the sex instincts. Unfortunately, Marcuse noted, there is currently in America a "channeling of sexuality into monogamous reproduction" and a "taboo on perversions."

In familiar and by now unintentionally humorous fashion, Marcuse proclaimed that this "suppressed sexuality" was indicative of an emerging American fascism. Without being released, he wrote, it "manifests itself in the hideous forms so well known," including the "sadistic and masochistic orgies" of prison inmates and "concentration camp guards." Marcuse's mantra was "away with all this." Liberate the libido. Let it all hang out. Marcuse termed what he was promoting as "polymorphous sexuality."[18]

Marcuse's celebration of outright perversion was a mantra that could not be more perfectly timed in the 1960s, when a generation of young activists became alienated from their parents, their preachers, and the norms of their society. They were looking for a sex guru, and Marcuse became their apostle of sexual freedom. Marcuse formally rejected this description of himself—he liked the pose of the disinterested scholar—but he also understood that this was precisely the basis for his celebrity status in the 1960s counterculture. What the children of the sexual revolution liked most about Marcuse was that he gave a lofty basis for their genital adventures. Basically Marcuse made sexual bohemianism into a valiant expression of anti-fascism.

As with his colleague Adorno, Marcuse was pulling off a major scam. While the rutting bohemians of the 1960s had no idea, Marcuse surely knew that the Nazis and the Italian fascists were themselves— almost to a man—bohemians. Hitler himself was a painter and artiste before he went into politics. Historian Richard Evans does not hesitate to call him a "bohemian."[19] He was obsessed with music and regularly attended the Bayreuth Festival. Wagner's music, Hitler said, reflected the triumph of art over life. He was also a vegetarian. Hitler had a secret mistress Eva Braun whom he only married the day before the two of them committed suicide. In their case, "till death do us part" was literally a matter of hours.

Hitler despised Christianity as a kind of disease and regularly spoke of seeking its eventual eradication in the Third Reich. "Pure Christianity," Hitler said, "leads quite simply to the annihilation of mankind.... Let's be the only people who are immunized against the disease." While he recognized the political inadvisability of openly attacking Christianity, privately Hitler called it "an invention of sick brains: one could imagine nothing more senseless." Of Christianity, Hitler said, "The catastrophe for us is that of being tied to a religion that rebels against all the joys of the senses."[20]

Himmler, Hitler's number two man and head of the SS, was an atheist who took his secretary Hedwig Potthast as his mistress. Although he is sometimes portrayed as an uptight moral traditionalist, nothing could be further from the truth: Himmler envisioned human breeding farms in which selected Aryan types would promiscuously breed with selected Aryan women to produce, in the words of historian Sarah Helm, "a constant supply of perfect Aryan children."

Himmler was also a natural food guy who was an eager proponent of organic farming. He insisted on organic food being grown in concentration camps and once stopped by Auschwitz for no other reason than to visit the vegetable garden there. Many of the top Nazis condemned the congestion of the cities and affirmed the value of living in communion with nature. Historian Stanley Payne writes that we find in Nazism "the first major expressions of modern environmentalism."[21]

Goebbels was also an atheist and philanderer who had a series of notorious affairs, one with the Czech actress Lida Baarova. He also wrote a play and an autobiographical novel. He fancied himself a romantic and wrote his doctoral thesis at Heidelberg University on the German romantics. Before Goebbels entered politics, he wanted to be an artist and writer. Had he lived today, it is easy to envision him living in Greenwich Village and teaching romance languages at Columbia University or NYU.

Mussolini too was a bohemian who wrote a play and considered himself an accomplished violinist. He was also an atheist and, though married, famously and even boastfully promiscuous. Historian Richard Evans notes that "Mussolini spent huge amounts of time on his sex life, his official image as a loving and faithful family man paralleling an unofficial one as a man of uncontrollable priapic urges."[22] Bourgeois religious and moral traditionalists these men were certainly not.

Progressives and leftists sometimes seek to vindicate Adorno and Marcuse and prove the moral traditionalism of the fascists by claiming the fascists were anti-homosexual. While it's true that homosexuals were one of the groups later rounded up for the concentration camps, this had nothing to do with moral reservations. Rather, it was based on the Nazi idea that it was imperative for Germany to multiply its Nordic or Aryan population, and homosexuality was seen as impeding that process. Two flamboyant Nazi homosexuals—the party's legal specialist Helmut Nicolai and Achim Gerke who served in Hitler's Interior Ministry—were purged in 1935 on that basis.

As was widely recognized in the 1920s and 1930s, a significant number of the Nazi brownshirts, including the group's head Ernst Röhm were, "like so many of the early Nazis,"[23] homosexuals. William Shirer tells us that the head of the Munich brownshirts, Edmund Heines, was not only a convicted murderer but also a homosexual. The communists and social Democrats derided the Nazi brownshirts by calling them names like the Brotherhood of Poofs in the Brown House.

Himmler and Goebbels, fearful that a gay reputation would hurt the political prospects of the Nazi Party, urged Hitler to reduce the homosexual presence among the brownshirts. But Hitler refused, saying that these things were "purely in the private sphere." The brownshirts, he emphasized, were not a "moral establishment" but rather a "band of fighters." Why, Hitler asked, should he care what they did in the bedroom when they did the job they were meant to do?[24]

The brownshirts only became a problem when they threatened to displace the German police and the armed forces as the country's enforcement brigade. Hitler needed the army and the police, and so he reluctantly agreed to suppress the brownshirts. When Hitler showed up to arrest Röhm and his top lieutenants at the Hanselbauer Hotel, he found himself in the middle of a gay orgy. The first door Hitler kicked open revealed Heines naked in bed with an eighteen-year-old brownshirt troop leader. Hitler told him, "If you are not dressed in five minutes, I'll have you shot on the spot." Heines jumped from under the sheets and did the Heil Hitler salute.

When Hitler's men opened Röhm's door, the brownshirt leader feigned a very casual attitude. Hitler simply told him, "You're under arrest." One by one, doors opened and brownshirt couples came streaming out, in various stages of undress.[25] This was the Nazi atmosphere in those days and it far more closely resembles that of the *Village Voice* or the Democratic National Convention than it does the *National Review* or the Trump White House.

Repressive Intolerance

Marcuse was active on all fronts. In his book *One Dimensional Man* he blasted American capitalism for reducing all values to market values and human beings to consumers manipulated by corporate advertising. Marcuse's solution was to combat corporate advertising with political propaganda, aimed at raising public consciousness and mobilizing it against capitalism. Marcuse also wrote *An Essay on Liberation* which showed the

Left in America how it could help socialist revolutions in Vietnam, Cuba, and around the world: essentially by becoming part of a guerilla resistance in the United States. Again, this was music to the ears of the activist Left in the 1960s. They no doubt thought, "You mean that I too can be a guerilla like Che Guevara right here in Ann Arbor, Michigan?"

Here I want to focus on the idea that Marcuse is probably best remembered for, one that could not be more pertinent today. This idea was unveiled in a famous essay he wrote called "Repressive Tolerance." This essay was published in 1970 along with several others in a book called *A Critique of Pure Tolerance.*

Let's follow the argument of the essay because it provides the basis for the vicious intolerance that the Left currently unleashes against all forms of dissent in our culture. The bullying and terrorizing of conservatives on campus, the shaming of Republicans in the media, the defilement of the American flag, the disruption of Trump rallies—all of this behavior receives its moral justification in Marcuse's notorious essay.

Marcuse begins by admitting that all other things being equal, classical liberal virtues like tolerance and free speech are desirable. But, he says, given the class structure of society in which ruling groups have most of the power and disenfranchised groups have very little, "the conditions of tolerance are loaded." To extend tolerance to intolerant groups, Marcuse argues, "actually protects the already established machinery of discrimination."

Therefore, Marcuse argues that a general principle of liberal tolerance—tolerance toward all viewpoints—should be abandoned: "Tolerance cannot be indiscriminate and equal with respect to the contents of the expression, neither in word nor in deed; it cannot protect false words and wrong deeds which demonstrate that they contradict and counteract the possibilities of liberation."

In society, Marcuse insisted, "Certain things cannot be said, certain ideas cannot be expressed, certain policies cannot be proposed, certain behavior cannot be permitted without making tolerance an instrument for the continuation of servitude." Marcuse was nothing if not blunt about what he advocated: "the systematic withdrawal of tolerance toward regressive and repressive opinions."

What specifically did Marcuse seek to repress? He cited "the withdrawal of toleration of speech and assembly from groups and movements which promote aggressive policies, armament, chauvinism, discrimination on the grounds of race and religion, or which oppose the extension of public services, social security, medical care, etc." Moreover, Marcuse added, his approach "may necessitate new and rigid restrictions on teachings and practices in the educational institutions," including the suppression of certain types of "scientific research."

Marcuse bluntly calls for "intolerance against movements from the Right, and toleration of movements from the Left." He admits his goal is one of "shifting the balance between Right and Left by restraining the liberty of the Right," and in this way "strengthening the oppressed against the oppressors." Marcuse's argument has been summed up in this phrase: no toleration of the intolerant. In the 1960s, Marcuse acolytes used a similar chant—"No free speech for fascists."

Marcuse reminds his readers that when the fascists planned a massacre, "the speeches of the fascist and Nazi leaders were the immediate prologue to the massacre." Yet, he says, "The spreading of the word could have been stopped before it was too late." In fact, had tolerance been withdrawn from the Nazis early enough, "mankind would have had a chance of avoiding Auschwitz and a world war." Marcuse calls on fellow leftists and fellow progressives to give the right wing in America what may be called the fascist or Nazi treatment—a strong dose of repression and intolerance.[26]

At first glance, "no free speech for fascists" sounds like an unobjectionable idea. But upon reflection, it becomes problematic. Don't all citizens under the Constitution have equal rights, and if so don't they have the same rights to free speech, free assembly, and so on? If so, then fascists have those rights too. So on what basis can fascists in America be denied rights? Since Marcuse intends this, he obviously does not believe in equal rights for all citizens, and neither, apparently, do his modern-day followers.

Moreover, not once does Marcuse demonstrate that the groups he intends to repress are in fact fascist. Marcuse's targets are not Nazis but rather patriots, Republicans, and conservatives. The real meaning of Marcuse's essay is the following: no free speech for patriots and conservatives! No toleration for capitalists and Christians! Of course, the fascists and Nazis themselves sought to undermine the institutions of liberal democracy, such as free speech and tolerance, in precisely the way Marcuse recommends.

To fight fascism with intolerance is one thing. But to fight classical liberalism and modern American conservatism with intolerance is, well, fascist. Historian Stanley Payne—who is no conservative—clearly has gotten the message. In *A History of Fascism* he reviews Marcuse's argument for repressive tolerance and concludes, "Rather than presenting an interpretation of fascism, Marcuse seems simply to reflect the kind of thinking that made up fascism in the first place."[27] In other words, if you're looking for a fascist, start with Marcuse.

I've sometimes wondered how Marcuse, a refugee from Nazism, could so glibly recommend the very Nazi tactics that he ran away from in Germany. Reading Marcuse—his Machiavellian admiration for the cunning use of force, his Nietzschean exaltation of power—I think I've figured it out. Whatever his revulsion of Nazi anti-Semitism, Marcuse also observed that the Nazi use of terror tactics was effective. The Nazis got the job done: they beat their opponents into submission. In short order, they produced their *Gleichschaltung*. So Marcuse figured, why don't we, who are also on the Left, apply some of those same successful tactics in the United States?

Marcuse's ultimate objective in this essay is quite clear. He intends to license progressives and leftists to use every sort of tactic, from discrimination to repression to outright violence, to shut down their conservative opposition. Don't worry about being intolerant, he tells them, just remember you are fighting intolerance! Here one can see how Black Lives Matter, Antifa, and every other thuggish group on the Left gets its marching orders and its moral sanction.

There is a final corollary to Marcuse's thesis that often goes unnoticed. Not only does Marcuse license indiscriminate tactics of intimidation and terror against the Right. He also gives an implicit assurance to people on the Left that they can get away with anything, that whatever conduct they themselves engage in will be protected because, after all, they are on the side of humanity and liberation.

Consider for a moment why Bill Clinton's predatory behavior is routinely excused on the Left, even by purported feminists who would go berserk if a Republican or conservative did anything remotely similar. Let's recall that Bill wasn't merely a philanderer; multiple women accused him of harassment, assault, and even rape. The clear explanation for Bill's immunity is that he is politically on the side of the angels, which is to say, he is in the progressive camp, and therefore there are no limits to the level of protection that he is permitted.

The left-wing media was carefully protective about exposing Democratic donor Jeffrey Epstein's orgy island and showed no interest in covering Anthony Podesta's "spirit cooking" perversities. Even Anthony Weiner's scandalous communications with underage girls would have been fine with the Left if it hadn't caused such a big ruckus and made standing up for Wiener politically calamitous.

I conclude my section on Marcuse by returning to those leftist articles I mentioned earlier which insist that the writings of the Frankfurt School are critical to understanding Trump and our current moment. I think we can see now that they are. What they show is not that Trump and the GOP are dangerous fascists. On the contrary. What they show instead is that Marcuse and Adorno and the others were intellectual and political frauds. They were con artists of the Left who originated their own version of the big lie and supplied a bogus rationale for how to engage in fascist thuggery while posing as an anti-fascist.

George Soros's Venture Thuggery

Finally, we turn to the third miscreant in the trilogy, the investor and financier George Soros. Like Heidegger and Marcuse, he too is part of a progressive *Gleichschaltung* and all three of them seem to go about it the same way. The Hungarian-born Soros became a billionaire through shrewd global investments and currency manipulation; his Quantum Fund is one of the world's first private hedge funds. While Heidegger and Marcuse may be considered intellectuals behind progressive fascism, Soros is clearly its largest financial backer.

Soros is the main funder of some 200 leftist groups, including Planned Parenthood, MoveOn.org, and various left-wing environmental and human rights organizations. All are resolutely opposed to Trump and the GOP. The Women's March, billed by the media as a spontaneous eruption against Trump, was heavily subsidized by the Soros network. Soros also backs so-called anti-fascist groups and Black Lives Matter. In 2015, for example, Soros's Open Society gave $650,000 to support Black Lives Matter agitation in the wake of the Freddie Gray killing in Baltimore. This year the Soros-backed group Alliance for Global Justice gave $50,000 to the militant thugs associated with the group Refuse Fascism.[28]

How does Soros see his role in shaping America and the world? I'll let him speak for himself. "I fancied myself as some kind of god," Soros said. "If truth be known, I carried some rather potent messianic fantasies with me from childhood." Asked by Britain's *Independent* to explain that strange assertion, Soros elaborated, "It's a sort of disease when you consider yourself some kind of god, the creator of everything, but I feel comfortable about it now since I began to live it out."[29] One would have to go back to Hitler's remarks in the aftermath of his early victories to hear such talk, which even garden-variety despots generally abstain from.

And what in this case is "god's" agenda? What, in other words, do the Soros-funded groups actually do? One group, the Revolutionary Love Project, dispatches activists to town hall meetings with scripts for how to humiliate Republican congressmen and senators. The whole idea is to create an artificial impression—then hyped in the media—that there is a groundswell of public opposition to Trump and the GOP. Another favorite tactic of Soros's funded groups is the fake racial incident. There have been dozens of these in recent years, mostly on college campuses.

Leftists post racist slogans on walls or in bathrooms and then, when an uproar ensues, the very perpetrators organize rallies to protest what they claim is a Trump-inspired resurgence of hate.[30]

Soros doesn't merely fund activism, he also funds disruptive violence. His costumed, baton-wielding squadrons amount to a private army. He has created a militia of paid thugs quite similar to the Italian blackshirts and the Nazi brownshirts. Soros's strategy is to launch dozens, even hundreds, of groups and then see which ones deliver the goods. Borrowing from the field of venture capitalism, my term for what Soros does is venture thuggery, operating through paid protesters.

The paid protester is something of a new phenomenon in American politics. In the 1960s we had protesters on the Left, even violent ones, but they weren't being rented out by the hour for money. Soros's groups, by contrast, advertise for disrupters and looters. On one ad I saw on Craigslist, protesters are promised $15 an hour to cause trouble. Leftists can thus imagine they're fighting Hitler and get paid for their thuggery. No mention in the ad as to whether Soros also provides health benefits.

David Brock, who runs several Soros-funded groups, including Media Matters, is the quintessential Soros henchman. I knew Brock from the old days, when he professed to be a conservative. Even then, he was known as a sleazy, dishonest guy. He boasted about his unscrupulousness, his willingness to lie for a cause. When Brock's deceitfulness was exposed, he fessed up. Yet far from trying to clean up his act, he presented himself to the Left as one who would be willing to offer his unscrupulousness to their cause.

Brock pretended that his political "conversion" had been forced upon him, because Reagan conservatives disapproved of his homosexuality. Actually Brock's homosexuality was well known among us young Reaganites, and we didn't have a problem with it as long as Brock maintained public discretion, which he did. Even so, when Brock broke ranks and sold his services to the Left, part of what recommended him was his homosexuality.

Emails released by *Wikileaks* show the left-wing activist Neera Tanden, head of the Center for American Progress, describing Brock as "shady" and a "menace."[31] With Brock, as with so many young Nazis, viciousness and opportunism seem to go together. Whatever their politics, everyone who knows Brock can see how well he would have fit in with the original gay brownshirts. Occasionally I envision him jumping to attention and giving a raised-arm salute whenever Soros walks in the door.

It may seem crude, even insensitive, for me to use such language when talking about Soros, who is Jewish and who was after all a refugee from Nazism. Moreover, Soros claims to be a devotee of philosopher Karl Popper, and he named his Open Society Institute after one of Popper's best-known books. Popper is a champion of classically liberal ideas of free speech and open debate, which makes him and Soros very strange bedfellows. I have scoured Popper's work to discover what Soros might see in it and have come up empty-handed. I'm forced to conclude that this Popper business is, for Soros, a complete front. It enables him to pretend to be a friend of liberty while he works to undermine it.

Hitler's Collection Boy

Soros loves to play the Nazi card, as when in the aftermath of 9/11 he flayed President Bush's attorney general, John Ashcroft, for questioning the patriotism of its critics—a tactic that Soros likened to the Nazis. "It reminded me of Germany under the Nazis," Soros said, "It was the kind of talk that Goebbels used to use to line the Germans up. I remember, I was thirteen or fourteen. It was the same kind of propaganda."[32]

This reference to his youth makes the transcript of a 1998 CBS *Sixty Minutes* interview with Soros especially revealing. Here is what Soros told interviewer Steve Kroft about those fateful days in Hitler's Germany:

> Kroft: You're a Hungarian Jew.
> Soros: Mm-hmm.
> Kroft:...who escaped the Holocaust.
> Soros: Mm-hmm.
> Kroft:...by—by posing as a Christian.

Soros: Right.

Kroft: And you watched lots of people get shipped off to the
death camps.

Soros: Right. I was 14 years old. And I would say that's when
my character was made.

Kroft: In what way?

Soros: That one should think ahead. One should understand
and anticipate events when one is threatened. It was a
tremendous threat of evil. I mean—it was a very personal
experience of evil.

Kroft: My understanding is that you went out with this protector of yours who swore that you were his adopted god-
son.

Soros: Yes. Yes.

Kroft: Went out, in fact, and helped in the confiscation of
property from the Jews.

Soros: Yes. That's right. Yes.

Kroft: I mean, that's—that sounds like an experience that
would send lots of people to the psychiatric couch for
many, many years. Was it difficult?

Soros: Not—not at all. Maybe as a child you don't—you don't
see the connection. But it was—it created no, no problem
at all.

Kroft: No feeling of guilt.

Soros: No.

Kroft: For example, that "I'm Jewish and here I am, watching
these people go. I could just as easily be there. I should be
there." None of that?

Soros: Well, of course I, I could be on the other side or I could
be the one from whom the thing is being taken away. But
there was no sense that I shouldn't be there, because that
was—well, actually in a funny way, it's just like in mar-
kets—that if I weren't there, of course I wasn't doing it, but
somebody else would—would be taking it away anyhow.

And it was the—whether I was there or not, I was only a
spectator, the property was being taken away. So the—I
had no role in taking away that property. So I had no sense
of guilt.[33]

What interests me here is not what young Soros did—I'm not going
to attach much weight to the conduct of a fourteen-year-old—but rather
how the mature Soros retroactively interprets his previous actions as a
collection boy for Hitler. Evidently Soros believes that accompanying an
official from a fascist government that is collaborating with the Nazis
for the purpose of serving confiscation notices to Jews to steal their
property and possessions is not something to feel guilt or regret about.

Why? Because just like a market transaction, the outcome would
have happened anyway. Where have we heard this before? Oh yes. Recall
Josef Mengele's response when his son Rolf confronted him with his
crimes. Mengele insisted he was not responsible for what happened at
Auschwitz because the captives there had already been marked for death.
Here we have Soros mounting what may be termed the Mengele Defense.
The only difference is that Mengele didn't get away with it while Soros's
explanation seems fully satisfactory to the political Left.

In a profile of Soros in the *New Yorker*, Jane Mayer notes that
Soros once described 1944—the year that Hitler dispatched more than
500,000 Jews to extermination camps—as "the happiest year of my
life." Mayer adds that this was the year Soros's father saved his family
by supplying them with false identity papers. Soros's father apparently
did the same for other Jewish families, but he sold them the papers and
thus profited from the endeavor.

Mayer asked Soros about this and he said, "I was lucky to have a
father who understood that this was not normalcy, and if you go by the
normal rules you are going to die. Many Jews did not take evasive action.
What I learned during the war is that sometimes you can lose everything,
even your life, by not taking risks."[34] Once again, Soros evades the issue.
Precisely because this is not a normal time, it would seem that you
shouldn't make money on helping your fellow Jews get out of Germany.

Soros doesn't see it that way. He doesn't see anything wrong with what his father did. On the contrary, he views him as a personal hero. He seems to blame the Jews who weren't as far-sighted as his dad. Why shouldn't those who thought ahead not profit from those who didn't? And once again, Soros callously likens the whole deal to market and investment decisions. See what happens when you don't take the right kinds of risks!

We see in Soros the kind of base amoralism that puts him into the same company as Heidegger and Marcuse. These three men had a deeply intimate relationship with Nazism, and their whole outlook was formed in response to it. Consequently, the leftist movement that they have shaped in America is also a product of that engagement. And we are the victims of this demon-possession. In a sense, fascism drove these three men crazy, and now they are trying to make us crazy.

We see how this trio of Heidegger, Marcuse, and Soros put its talents and resources behind thuggish leftist causes. Heidegger openly backed the Nazis. Marcuse and Soros promote Nazi tactics on behalf of a purportedly anti-fascist Left. Together this horrid trio played a big role in the destruction of our universities, the shameless leftist propaganda of the media, and the brownshirt tactics of progressives today.

Nine

Denazification

This is not the end. It is not even the beginning of the end.
But it is, perhaps, the end of the beginning.[1]

Winston Churchill, November 10, 1942

In 1945, American, British, and Soviet forces converged in Germany nine months after the Allied landing at Normandy. Holed up in his bunker in Berlin, Hitler, accompanied by his new wife Eva Braun, saw that defeat was now a *fait accompli*. On April 30, 1945, he made his final resolution. Rejecting the advice of Nazi loyalists to flee the city, Hitler and Braun withdrew to a private section. There, Eva Braun swallowed cyanide. Hitler did the same, while also—just to make sure of the outcome—putting a bullet through his head. Nazi loyalists then burned Hitler's body beyond recognition to prevent it being recovered by the Allies.

Three days earlier, Mussolini disguised himself, got into an Alfa Romeo sports car, and attempted to flee Italy with his mistress Claretta Petacci. The disguise didn't work; Mussolini's features were too distinctive. He and his mistress were apprehended at the Swiss border. Both were machine-gunned the next day by local partisans, and Mussolini's body was hung upside down in the Piazzale Loreto in Milan. Within the space of a few days Mussolini and Hitler perished, and thus did fascism and Nazism come to an ignominious end.

Reluctant though we may be to believe it, fascism is now back, not in Europe but in the United States. To paraphrase Sinclair Lewis's book, it is happening here. Through the relentless pounding of Trump from all quarters, the Left is basically attempting a fascist coup. By a fascist coup I mean the exertion of power by the unelected arms of the Left—mainly the media Left—to overturn the outcome and the mandate of a free election. If the coup succeeds, America will effectively cease to be a democracy. The fascists—dressed in anti-fascist garb—will have proved that they are fully capable of canceling the will of the electorate. In a sense, there will be no point in even holding elections anymore because the Left would have established veto power over the results.

We should let this realization sink in. If we truly believe America is facing a fascist threat—if we recognize that the argument of this book is correct—then it follows that we can't do things in the same way as before. In other words, normal, lackadaisical politics is largely obsolete. It makes no sense to carry on as if what is happening is not happening. Instead, we must face up to the reality of the situation and devise a response adequate to the danger we are facing. In this concluding chapter, I show how to do this.

The old fascism was defeated through military force from the outside. It took a world war with tens of millions of casualties to accomplish this. The new fascism can be vanquished without military force from the inside. Historians agree that had the Italians and Germans responded differently, they could have prevented Mussolini and Hitler from coming to power. The Italian military and police, for example, were much stronger than Mussolini's blackshirts and could have thwarted Mussolini's triumphal March on Rome. At various stages in his ascent, Hitler could have been stopped and his brownshirts dispersed or locked up. In other words, Mussolini's and Hitler's countrymen could have stopped fascism and Nazism before it was too late.

Why didn't they? Speaking of Italy, historian Renzo De Felice says that the Italian ruling class made the catastrophic mistake of continuing with normal politics, "They acted with a complete lack of political imagination and with a complete incapacity of assuming true responsibilities. They adopted a policy of constitutionalizing fascism, while at the same time attempting to emasculate it." This complacency, historian Anthony James Gregor writes, "was born of an indisposition to take fascist doctrine seriously."[2]

Precisely the same complacency and pusillanimity characterized the political establishment in Germany. Hindenburg, the Reichstag, and the rival political parties all tried to "accommodate" Hitler, not recognizing that he wasn't playing by the same rules they were. In doing so, the very people who were in a position to stop Hitler facilitated his assumption of complete power and the sway of Nazism over the whole society. Then came the deluge, in which most of these enablers were themselves swept away.

The appeasement of Hitler continued on the foreign policy front. Here the key figure was England's befuddled prime minister, Neville Chamberlain. For Hitler, Chamberlain was symbolized by his umbrella. Hitler concluded that Chamberlain was weak. This was no longer, he mused, the swashbuckling England of Sir Francis Drake. Had Britain and France fought Hitler at the outset, they could have defeated him. By coddling him, they gave him a chance to grow stronger, until France itself was overrun and England was very nearly reduced to rubble. The accommodation of fascism, it seems, carries a very high cost which may include survival itself.

Through Both Sides of Their Mouth

Today conservatives and the Republican Party, who are now the nation's governing powers that be, are also taking a very big risk if they seek to appease the fascism of the political Left. Admittedly today's left-wing fascism differs in one important respect from Hitler's and Mussolini's left-wing fascism. The old fascists at least used the name; they called themselves what they were. Our fascist Left, by contrast, purports to be anti-fascist. I know, it's crazy. The very people who champion the centralized state, have a long history of racism and racial terrorism, used the power of the government against their political opponents while they could, and continue to use cultural intimidation and street thuggery to enforce their ideology, insist they are the ones who are anti-fascist.

At the same time, recognizing that fascism and Nazism are now toxic labels—the most toxic labels in Western culture—these self-styled anti-fascists have foisted the fascist label on the Right. Crazier still, they are calling fascists the very champions of limited government and individual rights who wouldn't dream of using state power against their critics or engaging in fascist-style cultural exclusion and intimidation. In this respect, the Left is like the vicious sibling who punches you in the face and then starts wailing that you have been punching him. Consequently, we are in a bizarre situation where the real fascists pretend to be anti-fascist while accusing the real anti-fascists of being fascists.

The Left's mechanism for producing this inversion is the big lie. The big lie is not merely about fixing the fascist and Nazi labels on Trump and the Right—this is the superficial part of the lie, and I disposed of it in a single chapter—but more profoundly it is aimed at concealing the fascist and Nazi roots of the American Left. Even today, the agenda and tactics of the Left are deeply shaped by fascism and Nazism. To conceal this obvious relationship, leftists lie thorough both sides of their mouth, by which I mean, they lie about who the fascists and the Nazis were, and then they lie about who they are.

Let's catch this process at work. Here's how the Left lies about the Nazis in order to create a false contrast between the Nazis and them. The Left says, the Nazis were capitalists while the Left is anti-capital-ist. The Nazis were Christians while the Left is secular. The Nazis were anti-abortion while the Left supports the right to abortion. The Nazis were repressed and sexually conventional while leftists are sexually liberated bohemians. In fact, on every one of these points, the views of the Left and the National Socialists are essentially the same:

anti-capitalist, anti-Christian (in belief and in sexual ethics), and opposed to a right to life.

Now let's watch the big lie operate from the other end. Here's how the Left lies about itself in order to camouflage its ideological and tactical proximity to the Nazis. The Left says, the Nazis were the party of racism while the Left is the party of anti-racism. The Nazis enslaved people while the Left is the party of anti-slavery. The Nazis perpetrated genocide and racial terrorism while the Left would never ever do that. The Nazis were viciously intolerant of dissenting views while the Left is unbelievably tolerant. In fact, in America it was the Democratic Party that was the party of slavery, segregation, racism, and the Ku Klux Klan. It remains the party of racial identity politics to this day, while the Republicans were founded as an anti-slavery party, continue to favor a color-blind society, and are tolerant in a polite, respectful, old-fashioned American way that politically correct speech-banning progressives cannot stand.

Clearly, any strategy to defeat the fascist Left must begin by unmasking, as I have done in this book, the full dimensions of the big lie. The so-called anti-fascists must be exposed as the fascists they are. The Left's efforts to oust Trump by any means necessary should be recognized for what it is: an attempted fascist coup. We, who are accused of being fascists, must understand that we are the true anti-fascists. We are vindicating the results of a free election and putting into effect the mandate of that election. This is the starting point; from here we can get somewhere.

Trump, to his credit, knows that something's up, that he needs to do things differently, and that he must take decisive action against an extreme, and even sometimes violent, Left that deems itself "the resistance." Trump recognizes the fight is not merely legal and political, it is also cultural. That's why Trump, while he's getting his Supreme Court justices through, signing executive orders, and working to repeal Obamacare and pass tax reform, also puts his multitasking skills to work in swatting Meryl Streep, *Saturday Night Live*, and the cast of the Broadway play *Hamilton*, not to mention the "failing" *New York Times* and "low ratings" CNN.

Right now Trump, whatever his failings, is the most fearless man in the country. Unlike virtually all previous Republicans, he refuses to walk within the parameters that the Left has carved out. Far from being intimidated by the cultural assaults of the Left, he seems to revel in using his bully pulpit as well as his social media megaphone to repel them. Being a pop culture icon himself, he knows how to do it. Trump is a larger-than-life figure who, the more they pelt him, the larger he becomes. The Left has now digested this. Having first derided and ridiculed him, they are now mortally afraid of him and much of their rat-like cunning is devoted to figuring out a way to destroy him.

To prevail—perhaps even to survive—Trump needs allies. And where are his allies? Happily, there are the Trumpsters, fiercely committed to their man, but they by themselves cannot sweep Trump's ideas to victory. The only way to do that is with a unified conservative movement and a unified GOP. The bad news is that much of the conservative intelligentsia and the GOP establishment remain in la-la land. Some of them still have their political guns aimed at Trump. These so-called Never Trumpers seem to have accepted the Left's big lie that Trump is the fascist. How can we possibly win with such a confused, slack-jawed crew?

By and large, the Right and the national GOP refuse to take seriously, or even to understand and recognize the dangers of, the fascist doctrines of the Left. How to undo the fascist elements of progressive ideology and scale back the power of the centralized state? They have no idea. In fact, establishment Republicans don't mind trimming government programs but aren't so sure they want to eliminate them altogether. How to counter the progressive *Gleichschaltung*, which seeks to enforce a uniformity of thought across the culture? Beats them. In fact, they'd rather go along with the bad guys in the futile hope that they can avoid becoming targets. How to respond to left-wing street thuggery? Cowering and avoidance is the only way they know how to fight back. Clueless and invertebrate, these hollow Republicans seek to moderate the fascism of the Left by accommodating it.

Already their actions are having the opposite effect. The fascism of the Left shows no signs of abating. In fact, it grows stronger. Having taken over the culture, it has its sights resolutely focused on taking over the country. Its goal is to get rid of Trump—and the sooner the better—and also to use the fascist smear to permanently discredit the GOP. Ultimately the Left seeks to do what all fascists do: effectively eliminate all opposition. They want to discredit us and reduce us to pariahs, destroying our careers and breaking our spirits if they can. Then they will begin the familiar fascist process of "reeducating" us, to the point where we don't just stop resisting them but actually pay them obeisance.

We should learn the lesson of history and not make the same mistake the Italians and the Germans did. We should uproot fascism before it becomes unstoppable from within, and then we should carry out our own denazification just as the Allies did in postwar Italy and Germany. Our grandparents and great-grandparents routed fascism from the outside, but they evidently didn't destroy it once and for all. We can rout it from the inside and finally deposit it on the ash-heap of history.

An Anti-Fascist Agenda

What would an anti-fascist agenda look like? Here my approach is simple. First I identify the main ideological doctrine of left-wing fascism, then I recommend policy measures to undo it by moving things in the opposite direction. Next I turn to the progressive *Gleichschaltung* in the cultural arena where the Left enforces fascist-style conformity through political correctness and big lies. I show how to break this institutional monopoly, end the regimentation of thought, and explode the big lie. Finally, I turn to the Left's fascist thuggery, which is aimed not merely at forcibly subduing the opposition but also at intimidating and terrorizing potential opponents into submission. Here I get tough and show how the Right should fight fire with fire. To modify a line from Marcuse that I now apply to Marcuse's own ideological progeny, "No free ride for fascists."

Fascism, at its core, is the construction of the all-powerful Leviathan state. As Mussolini reminds us in his *Autobiography*, "The foundation of fascism is the conception of the State. Fascism conceives the State as an absolute, in comparison to which all individuals or groups are relative, only to be conceived of in their relation to the State. For us Fascists, the State is not only a living reality of the present, it is also linked with the past and the future, and thus transcending the brief limits of individual life, it represents the immanent spirit of the nation."[3] I believe if a leading Democrat said this at the party's national convention, replacing the word "fascism" with "progressivism," the whole audience would rise to its feet applauding.

In keeping with Mussolini's description, fascist theoreticians like Giovanni Gentile spoke of the fascist state as a single body and of individuals as cells within that body. Each cell by itself is meaningless; the cells are only valuable to the degree they serve the body. In Gentile's words, "the legitimate will of the citizens is that will that corresponds to the will of the state."[4] In the economic sphere, as we have seen, the fascist state through mandates and regulation controls the operations of private corporations and private entities, especially critical industries like banking, health, energy, and education. And this Leviathan state, of course, is also the core ideological blueprint of modern American progressivism.

The anti-fascist project, therefore, is to dismantle the Leviathan state. I'm not suggesting that conservatives or Republicans should get rid of the state. This is neither possible nor desirable. Rather, we should restore the government to the limited powers and limited sphere delineated by the Constitution. Under progressive rule, the state has become too large; it has become ravenous and tyrannical. We must starve the beast, lop off some of its organs, and cut it down to size.

How to do this? The first step, of course, is to get rid of the Obama legacy. This means overturning Obamacare, a progressive seizure of one-sixth of the U.S. economy, and replacing it with a health care system that restores private control and encourages private initiative. Second, repeal Dodd-Frank and return the banking and investment industries to private control. Third, let's tighten eligibility requirements so that food stamps only go to the small population of people who are truly needy. Obama deliberately swelled the ranks of people who receive food stamps in order to make more Americans dependent on the government.

Trump and the Republicans, however, should go beyond repealing what Obama did. They should pass comprehensive tax reform, which ideally involves a steep reduction in the corporate tax rate and a flat rate for individual income taxes in the 15 to 20 percent range. For individuals, why not have a simplified tax form with very few deductions that can be filled out on a single page? Tax reduction and simplification are two of the best ways to curb Leviathan and therefore constitute an antifascist master stroke. The Right should also steeply reduce federal regulations, privatize government functions as much as possible, and sell off the large tracts of land the government currently holds for no apparent reason.

One of the essential features of both fascism and Nazism was the elimination of regional autonomy and the transfer of all power to the center. In Germany, William Shirer writes, "Hitler achieved what Bismarck, Wilhelm II and the Weimar Republic never dared to attempt—he abolished the separate powers of the states and made them subject to the central authority of the Reich." Hitler's interior minister put it bluntly: "The state governments from now on are merely administrative bodies of the Reich."[5]

Here in America, mirroring what the Nazis did, the progressive Left has worked for more than half a century to strengthen the authority of the federal government at the expense of the states. This project has been carried out partly in the name of administrative uniformity and partly in the name of eliminating the alleged racism that is implied in the concept of states' rights. States' rights, after all, was the rallying cry of secession and later segregation and state-sponsored discrimination.

This leftist attack on states' rights is a fraud. First, the reason the founders created a system of dual sovereignty in which separate powers are assigned to the federal government and the states is precisely because they didn't want—and the people of the sovereign states, who largely ruled themselves, would not accept—a dull and potentially tyrannical uniformity of rules for all citizens. Rather, they wanted what the economist Friedrich Hayek once termed a "framework of competing utopias," each state experimenting with different rules. This way people could see what worked best. If you didn't like the way things were run in your state, you could always move to another state. In short, the founders wanted true diversity and this is what the Left—by imposing a national set of rules—seeks to stamp out.

Yes, states' rights were invoked to defend slavery and segregation, but let's remember who did that—the Democratic Party. So the Democrats today profess to stand against states' rights in order to prevent the atrocities that they committed. One may say that they are trying to save the country from themselves. I guess their motto is "Stop us before we go racist on you once again." Contrary to leftist propaganda, there is nothing wrong with the concept of states' rights. The problem is with the ideology of the Democratic Party, and the remedy for preventing future Democratic atrocities is to never, under any circumstances, vote for a Democrat.

Trump and the Republicans should restore the integrity of the original constitutional division of power by returning large swaths of federal power to the states. I recognize this is a long-term project that will long outlast the Trump presidency, because the Left has, with the shameful complicity of the courts, so thoroughly distorted the constitutional arrangement. Still, I say, let the restoration begin.

Built to Last

Even if Trump and the GOP do these things, however, how can they be sustained? How can we have a victory built to last? One way they are sustained is by making sure we have a Supreme Court made up of people on our team. During the Gorsuch hearings, Republicans kept stressing that Gorsuch is a good constitutionalist. I'm good with that. But the question I wanted to have answered was a different one—is Gorsuch a good Republican? I hope Trump's team investigated that one before nominating this guy.

Here's why, quite apart from his judicial philosophy, Gorsuch's political ideology and GOP commitment are important. For the past decade, a decisive majority of Supreme Court justices have been Republican nominees. Yet the Court remains precariously balanced between the Left and the Right. How is this possible? It has come about because the Left can count with Euclidean certainty on its four votes. Republicans, by contrast, are always in limbo. How is Justice Kennedy going to vote? And even when he votes Right, we often say, "Yay, we got Kennedy! Oops, we lost Roberts."

So while Republicans come to the Supreme Court looking to decipher the original intent of legislators, or with a solemn eye to respecting precedent, Democrats come to the Supreme Court looking to serve the Democratic cause. Our guys cherish the Constitution and try to avoid even the appearance of partisanship. As with Roberts, they will bend over backwards to uphold Obamacare and leave it to Congress to undo, while their guys, with clockwork regularity, engage in judicial activism to enact a leftist agenda. Our team is all about preserving precedent, in effect holding things in place, while their guys are all about moving the dial leftward. In sum, there is a disproportion of ideological commitment between us and them, and the net effect is a steady ratcheting of Supreme Court jurisprudence over time to the Left.

The only way to halt this is to appoint ideologically committed Republicans to take on ideologically committed Democrats. Sure, we can engage in all the highfalutin discourse we want about theories of constitutional interpretation. But in the end it comes down to a simple question of whether our laws are going to be upheld and theirs struck down, or whether their laws are going to be upheld and ours struck down. Better—I say—that ours be upheld and theirs be struck down.

With legislation, as with the Supreme Court, we can only have our way if we keep winning elections. One of the lessons of recent history is that even seemingly durable changes in government—see Obamacare—can be undone when the other party returns to power. Since 1980, America had lived under a divided government; when one party controls the presidency, the other typically controls the Congress. It's hard to get anything done and especially hard to make changes that endure.

Durable changes only occur in American politics when the same party controls the presidency, Congress, and the courts. By the way, there is nothing fascist about this; we are talking about political majorities created through elections and popular consent, such as what would happen under any parliamentary system. And interestingly one-party dominance has been the rule rather than the exception in U.S. history. From the 1820s to 1860, the Democrats were the majority party, controlling for the most part the presidency, Congress, and the Supreme Court. From 1865 to 1932, in the post–Civil War era, the Republicans became the majority. From 1932 to 1980, the Democrats once again became the majority.

This is not to say that, in any of these eras, the minority party was excluded from government—it sometimes even won the presidency—but even then the majority party set and controlled the agenda. Eisenhower was a Republican and had no intention of reversing the New Deal, but even had he wanted to, he would not have been successful. This was the era of Democratic dominance, and Ike was carried by the Democratic tide. During that period the Democrats, starting with FDR, created a semi-permanent shift in the structure of government. Trump must aspire to do the same in the opposite direction.

This means Trump and the Republicans must work to build a lasting GOP governing coalition. This they don't have now. How can they get it? First, Trump must ensure that both his rhetoric and policies are consistently aimed at consolidating and expanding his support among the working class—not just the white working class but among working people generally. Blue-collar workers are critical to the Democratic Party; without them, it's very difficult for the Left to secure an electoral majority. Trump has been given a new opportunity here with Democratic National Committee Chairman Tom Perez's stated desire to purge the Democratic Party of pro-life voters and candidates.

Second, Trump and the GOP should go all-out to win the votes of minorities. As the party of the aspiring middle class, there is no reason the GOP should not get 20 percent of the black vote, 50 percent of the Hispanic vote, and the vast majority of the Asian-American vote. If the Republicans achieved this, the Democrats would never win another national election. Republicans already have many of the right policies—an emphasis on jobs and economic growth—but what has been lacking is having conservative "community organizers" in these communities, showing how Republican policies can revive America's inner cities and provide opportunity for everyone.

These Republican outreach groups need to be every bit as dedicated as the Left's community organizers who try to inflame community grievances and convince minority voters that their only friend is big government (which is really the source of most of their problems). Trump made a stab at this during the campaign—pointing especially to the massive failures of Democratic policies that were supposed to benefit minority communities—but there needs to be a concerted Republican effort to follow up on his overtures and to make the case for school choice, enterprise zones, and stricter "broken windows" policing to ensure safer streets. The American dream is still manifestly a magnet of immigrants—it should be made just as attractive to the minority groups already here. Winning over minority voters is crucial to creating the lasting Republican majority that can finally overthrow left-wing fascism.

The End of *Gleichschaltung*

Finally, we turn to the ugliest face of progressive fascism; namely its effort to establish a uniformity of thought and feeling across the country. The leftist project here mirrors what Joseph Goebbels said about Nazi *Gleichshaltalung*: "National Socialism is not only a political doctrine, it is a total and all-encompassing general perspective on all public matters. We hope the day will come when nobody needs to talk about National Socialism any more, since it has become the air that we breathe. People must get used inwardly to this way of behaving, they must make it into their own set of attitudes. Only then will it be recognized that a new will to culture has arisen."[6]

The Left, seeking precisely the same conformity of thought and feeling across American society, pursues its own *Gleichschaltung* not merely through "fire in the streets" but also through the long march through the institutions. Having largely overtaken the institutions, the Left can now use academia, the media, and Hollywood—their state-within-a-state—for outright fascist propaganda. At the same time, it excludes and expels from those institutions conservative and dissenting voices. Its fascist street thugs—who call themselves "activists"—do not hesitate to harass, intimidate, and beat up anyone who threatens this left-wing *Gleichschaltung*.

This type of fascism requires a new type of response from the Right. So far conservatives have contented themselves with documenting and deploring the bias of academia, the media, and Hollywood. This is scarcely enough. We have to break up this monopoly of information. We have to open up new space for rival and dissenting viewpoints. We have to create rival cultural institutions. And we have to stop the street thugs. This will require, from the Right, a new creativity, a new resolve, and a new willingness to use lawful physical force. Anyone who says that physical force is out of bounds does not know what it means to stop fascism.

The first step is for us on the Right to cultivate a new mindset. We must learn to decode what we read and see and hear. When we hear on CNN, for instance, that Trump is off to a really bad start, we must learn to recognize that this means Trump is off to a really good start—because what is bad from CNN's point of view is good from our point of view. We should become accustomed to treating everything we get from progressive academia, the media, and Hollywood as false. Not in the factual sense of course but in the deeper sense that the facts are being spun to serve a fascist metanarrative. In sum, we should always be alert for the big lie in all its forms.

Step two, we should use all the weapons at our disposal, from conservative media to social media, to publicly flay academia, Hollywood, and the media for its one-sidedness and exclusion. Trump is already on this, and it's one of the things I love most about him. I'd like to see him go further here in the policy direction by cutting off federal funding for National Public Radio and the Public Broadcasting Service. Both are propaganda organs of the fascist Left.

When state universities ban conservative speakers, Republican lawmakers should move quickly to cut off their federal and state funding. In places like Berkeley, where the university chancellor, city mayor, and local police seem to be in cahoots to suppress First Amendment rights, Trump should send in the National Guard, just as Eisenhower did in 1957 to stop another group of bigoted Democrats from suppressing the constitutional rights of black students. Sure, the Left will howl, but let them howl. That's why we're doing it.

Notice that we're not trying to persuade the left-wing fascists. Nothing could be more useless than that. Rather, we're cutting them off as best we can. We're also alerting the public that what they are getting from the Left is not mere "knowledge" or "news" or "entertainment" but rather political propaganda disguised as knowledge, news, and entertainment. This is the original meaning of the hashtag #FakeNews. Once the American people see this, the power of these leftist megaphones will dissolve. Then American politics becomes genuinely competitive. Right now we are fighting with the whole apparatus of mainstream culture against us.

Third, we have to create over time our own rival institutions. I know, of course, that we can't start hundreds of new campuses of our own, but the good news is that, thanks to technology, we don't have to. What we must do, rather, is create one or more world-class online universities that rival the best in progressive academia. If we can figure out a way to provide a high-quality education at a fraction of existing college tuition, we will revolutionize higher education and challenge, perhaps even displace, its existing power structure.

We also have to make our own movies—not merely documentaries but also feature films. In just a few years, I have topped Michael Moore on the documentary charts, making, in succession, the second, sixth, and eighth highest-grossing political documentaries of all time. But that's hardly enough. Hollywood communicates most of its ideological messages via romantic comedies, thrillers, horror films, and animated family movies. The big man in Hollywood isn't Michael Moore; it's Stephen Spielberg. We have to compete in all genres.

Moreover, we have to build media channels that go beyond the relatively narrow reach of talk radio and the Fox News channel. Think of this. In the world of television comedy, the Left has Bill Maher, Jon Stewart, Stephen Colbert, and John Oliver. Currently we have very little to compete with this, and many young people get not only their style and sense of humor but also their political information from these clowns.

The solution, of course, is that we need our own clowns. This will obviously take time—Maher and company started in local comedy clubs, doing in Beatles' fashion their eight days a week—but we should at least get started. Think of how valuable conservative donations would be to some of these innovative new projects rather than going to all the familiar interest groups and think tanks and policy organizations that have long since reached the limits of their effectiveness. Only through such measures, creatively and comprehensively pursued, can we achieve true denazification, because it brings to an end the *Gleichschaltung* of the Left.

We must also take on the Soros brigades, which is to say the street hooligans who use bullying and terror tactics to shut us down and shut us up. When they drive one of our speakers off campus, we must send ten more speakers accompanied by heavy security. If they tear down our posters and street signs, we should tear down their posters and street signs. Some Trumpsters have adopted countermeasures such as tracking down the identities of masked Antifa protesters and releasing their names on social media, or duct-taping Antifa thugs to lampposts and STOP signs. I realize this is not normal Republican activism, but it certainly gives the leftist bullies their comeuppance.

Most important, we should not hesitate to unleash the law and the police on these leftist brownshirts. Reagan set a good example by doing this as governor of California in the 1960s. Every violent disruption today should be aggressively prosecuted. The Democratic Party, we recall, used the Ku Klux Klan as one of its political enforcers. The Klan did not go away of its own accord. It was fought first by Republican President Ulysses Grant during Reconstruction and then later through the legitimate law enforcement power of the FBI. When Antifa "protests" rise to the level of violent crime, riots, or domestic terrorism, they also should be pursued by the full weight of law enforcement.

By way of a test case, some 200 leftists—several of them journalists—who violently disrupted the presidential inauguration were charged with felony rioting, a crime that carries a maximum of ten years in prison.[7] The Left would have us believe that rioting is a noble form of political protest and somehow the law does not apply to them. Typically, these cases come before progressive judges who let the protesters off with a symbolic penalty or none at all. At the Berkeley disruptions, it was even worse: despite a maelstrom of violence, there were almost no arrests as the police stood idly by. But no one should be above the law. Once judges and juries start handing out five and ten year prison sentences, all this nonsense will quickly subside.

Quid Pro Quo

Finally, I take on an issue that has troubled me since Trump's inauguration: how do we stop the Left's use of government power against its opposition? Under Obama, the Left used the powers of the state—the IRS, the FBI, the Justice Department, and government spying—against its conservative critics. We saw this with the IRS harassment of Tea Party groups, with the secret surveillance and harassment of dissident journalists like Sharyl Attkisson and James Rosen, and with my own selective prosecution for exceeding campaign finance laws. No American has ever been prosecuted, let alone locked up overnight for eight months, for doing what I did.

This use of government power as a weapon against dissidents is pure fascist behavior. Gentile described it as a stage in the development of fascism, when fascism is "no longer a revolution against the state but a revolutionary State mobilized against the residue and internal debris that obstructed its evolution and organization." Hitler himself termed this type of fascist state retaliation a form of "physical and spiritual terror." The advantage of such terror, Hitler says, is that its targets are "neither morally not mentally equal to such attacks." So they are taken by surprise "until the nerves of the attacked persons break down." The ultimate point of such terror, according to Hitler, is to produce political conformity: "The defeated adversary in most cases despairs of the success of any further resistance."[8]

As someone who experienced firsthand this use of state-sponsored intimidation, I know how bad this stuff is. Some on the Obama crew that I dealt with would fit in nicely, I'm convinced, on the notorious People's Court in Nazi Germany. We should not think that because this is America, we are immune from such types of people. We too have our scum of the Earth and some of them have government badges. Indeed equipped with the power of the state, as the fascist authorities were, they are much more dangerous than ordinary criminals with courts, jails, and swat teams at their disposal.

So I'm sorely tempted to propose that Trump turn this same deadly apparatus of government on the Left. Why shouldn't we deploy the IRS, the NSA, and the FBI against the Left in the same way that Obama went after the Tea Party? Why not have the IRS investigate Michael Moore in the same way that the Obama administration had the FBI investigate me? After all, if we don't do to them what they have been doing to us, how else are we going to get them to stop? Won't they stop bullying and terrorizing us only when they see that we too can bully and terrorize them? Personally I'd love to see Obama occupy the bunk bed I vacated at my confinement center.

There's even precedent for the approach I'm discussing. During the Civil War Lincoln learned that Confederate soldiers were killing captured black federal troops or selling them into slavery rather than treating them as lawful prisoners of war. Lincoln promptly issued an Order of Retaliation. It said, "It is therefore ordered that for every soldier of the United States killed in violation of the laws of war, a rebel soldier shall be executed, and for every one enslaved by the enemy or sold into slavery, a rebel soldier shall be placed at hard labor on the public works."[9]

Despite the evident harshness of his order, Lincoln knew this was the only way to change Confederate behavior. And it did. But that was wartime, and, upon reflection, we're in a different situation. We're not in a civil war, at least not yet, and we don't want ourselves to become the instruments of lawlessness. Fortunately, we don't have to, and there is a better solution—a solution that worked. Last November we put the gangsterism of Obama and Hillary before the American people and the American people said, "enough," and threw the bums out.

That was a good start. The next step is to investigate and prosecute the abuses of power during the Obama administration. While leftists will scream political vendetta—the only vendettas they want to see are from their own side—in reality we're doing nothing more than holding Obama, Holder, Lynch, Hillary, and Lerner accountable for their actions. In sum, to crush the fascism of the Left, we don't need to fight lawlessness with lawlessness. Rather, we can fight lawlessness with lawfulness. But we have to be firm about it, recognizing the kind of people we're dealing with.

Are we conservatives and Republicans up for the task ahead? Yes, I believe so. Look at our history. We're the party that fought a great war to end slavery, fought lynching and segregation, shut down the Ku Klux Klan, opposed eugenics and forced sterilization, and resisted the incipient fascism of the street thugs in the 1960s. In sum, we're the party that has, for a century and a half, combated the fascism of the political Left. We've won before, and we can win again. We have the power now to stop them. We just have to do it. In the words of that slogan from the 1960s, "If not now, when? If not us, who?"

Notes

One

1. Walter Laqueur, *Fascism* (New York: Oxford University Press, 1996), 3.

2. Hugh Aynesworth, *Conversations with a Killer* (Authorlink: April 2000).

3. Adolf Hitler, *Mein Kampf*, Trans. Ralph Manheim (Boston: Houghton Mifflin, 1999), 231.

4. Lee Lescaze, "Reagan Still Sure Some in New Deal Espoused Fascism," December 24, 1981, *Washington Post*. www. washingtonpost.com/archive/politics/1981/12/24/reagan-still-sure-some-in-new-deal-espoused-fascism/928d80c5-3211-4217-85df-d775e1566c41/?utm_term=.8daa0cefc433.

5. Arthur Delaney and Jeffrey Young, "In 2005, the GOP Apologized for Exploiting Racial Polarization," August 26, 2016, *Huffington Post*, http://www.huffingtonpost.com/entry/gop-southern-strategy_us_57bf5732e4b085c1ff288a4e.

6. Matt Vespa, "Ashley Judd At Anti-Trump Women's March: I Feel Hitler In These Streets," January 21, 2017, *Townhall*, https://townhall.com/tipsheet/mattvespa/2017/01/21/ashley-judd-at-womens-march-i-feel-hitler-in-these-streets-n2274910; Jerome Hudson, "John Legend: Trump's 'Hitler-Level' Rhetoric Could Turn U.S. Into Nazi Germany," November 17, 2016, *Breitbart News*, http://www.breitbart.com/big-hollywood/2016/11/17/john-legend-trumps-hitler-level-rhetoric-lead-nazi-germany/; RuPaul, Twitter Post, November 11, 2016, 6:38am, https://twitter.com/rupaul/status/797086073864134656?lang=en; "Actress Meryl Streep Renews Harsh Criticism of Trump in Emotional Speech," February 12, 2017, *Fox News*, http://www.foxnews.com/entertainment/2017/02/12/actress-meryl-streep-renews-harsh-criticism-trump-in-emotional-speech.html.

7. Dave Urbanski, "Trump-Hitler Comparisons Continue After Inauguration Day—But Experts Call Such Notions Unfounded," January 23, 2017, *The Blaze*, http://www.theblaze.com/news/2017/01/23/trump-hitler-comparisons-continue-after-inauguration-day-but-experts-call-such-notions-unfounded/; Daniel Greenfield, "Every Republican Candidate is Hitler," March 18, 2016, *Front Page Magazine*, http://www.frontpagemag.com/fpm/262157/every-republican-presidential-candidate-hitler-daniel-greenfield; Dinesh D'Souza, *The End of Racism* (New York: Free Press, 1996), xiv.

8. A. James Gregor, *The Faces of Janus* (New Haven: Yale University Press, 2000), 1; A. James Gregor, *Giovanni Gentile: Philosopher of Fascism* (New Brunswick: Transaction Publishers, 2008), xii.

9. Chris Hedges, "Donald Trump: The Dress Rehearsal for Fascism" October 17, 2016, *Common Dreams*, https://www.commondreams.org/views/2016/10/17/donald-trump-dress-rehearsal-fascism; Ben Cohen, "With Trump's Announcement That He Will Censor the EPA, America is Now a Pre-Fascist State," January 26, 2017, *The Daily Banter*, https://thedailybanter.com/2017/01/america-is-now-a-pre-fascist-state/; Deepak Malhotra, "Why Trump's Experiments With Fascism Will Fail," March 20, 2017, *Fortune*, http://fortune.

com/2017/03/20/donald-trump-fascism-america/; Eric Bates, "Beyond Hope," December 13, 2016, *New Republic*, https:// newrepublic.com/article/138951/beyond-hope-barack-obama-legacy-age-trump; Aron Weinberg, "Trump and the Slow Crawl of Hitler's Fascism," October 10, 2016, *Huffington Post*, http://www. huffingtonpost.com/aron-n-weinberg/trump-and-the-slow-crawl-_b_12396024.html; Fedja Buric, "Trump's Not Hitler, He's Mussolini," March 11, 2016, *Salon*, http://www.salon. com/2016/03/11/trumps_not_hitler_hes_mussolini_how_gop_anti_intellectualism_created_a_modern_fascist_movement_in_america/; Joe Concha, "Maddow: I'm Studying Hitler to Prep for Trump," July 13, 2016, *The Hill*, http://thehill.com/blogs/blog-briefing-room/news/287552-maddow-im-studying-hitler-to-prep-for-trump; Juan Cole, "How the US Went Fascist: Mass Media Make Excuses for Trump Voters," February 24, 2016, *Moyers & Company*, http:// billmoyers.com/story/how-the-us-went-fascist-mass-media-makes-excuses-for-trump-voters/; Yohana Desta, "Ken Burns, a Guy Who Should Know, Calls Trump a 'Hitleresque' Fascist," October 13, 2016, *Vanity Fair*, http://www.vanityfair.com/hollywood/2016/10/ken-burns-donald-trump; Tim Hains, "Refuse Fascism Activist vs. Tucker Carlson: Trump is More Dangerous Than Hitler," February 22, 2017, *RealClear Politics*, http://www.realclearpolitics.com/video/2017/02/22/refuse_fascism_now_activist_trump_is_more_dangerous_than_hitler.html.

10. "Deep Concern Over 'Fascist Appeal' Brought to White House," January 29, 2017, RTE, https://www.rte.ie/news/2017/0129/848523-martin-omalley-us-politics/; John Wagner, "Sanders References the Holocaust When Discussing Trump's 'Intolerance' Toward Muslims," April 2, 2016, *Washington Post*, https://www.washingtonpost.com/news/post-politics/wp/2016/04/02/sanders-references-the-holocaust-when-discussing-trumps-intolerance-toward-muslims/?utm_term=.3c88766db51f; Elizabeth Warren, Twitter Post, March 21, 2016, 12:22pm. https://twitter.com/elizabethforma/status/71195110 1524840448?ref_src=twsrc%5Etfw&ref_url=http%3A%2F% 2Ftime.com%2F4266213%2Fdonald-trump-elizabeth-warren-twitter%2F.

11.   Jon Stone, "Donald Trump is a Fascist, Labor MP Dennis Skinner
      Says," January 30, 2017, *Independent*, http://www.independent.
      co.uk/news/donald-trump-fascist-video-mp-dennis-skinner-boris-
      johnson-a7553881.html; Laura Stone, "NDP Leader Tom Mulcair
      Denounces Trump, Calls Him a 'Fascist,'" January 27, 2017, *The
      Globe and Mail*, https://www.theglobeandmail.com/news/
      politics/ndp-leader-tom-mulcair-denounces-trump-calls-him-a-
      fascist/article33790910/; "Two Former Mexican Presidents
      Compare Donald Trump to Hitler," February 28, 2016, *The
      Telegraph*, http://www.telegraph.co.uk/news/worldnews/donald-
      trump/12176464/Two-former-Mexican-presidents-compare-
      Donald-Trump-to-Hitler.html.

12.   Ashley Parker and Maggie Haberman, "Meg Whitman Likens
      Donald Trump to Fascists, Shaking GOP's Brief Truce," June 11,
      2016, *New York Times*, https://www.nytimes.com/2016/06/12/us/
      politics/meg-whitman-likens-donald-trump-to-fascists-at-
      republican-retreat.html; Tom LoBianco, "Christine Todd
      Whitman: Donald Trump Muslim Comments Like Hitler's,"
      December 9, 2015, *CNN*, http://www.cnn.com/2015/12/09/
      politics/christine-todd-whitman-donald-trump-hitler/; Ross
      Douthat, "Is Donald Trump a Fascist?" December 3, 2015, *New
      York Times*, https://www.nytimes.com/2015/12/03/opinion/
      campaign-stops/is-donald-trump-a-fascist.html; Robert Kagan,
      "This is How Fascism Comes to America," May 18, 2016,
      Washington Post, https://www.washingtonpost.com/opinions/this-
      is-how-fascism-comes-to-america/2016/05/17/c4e32c58-1c47-
      11e6-8c7b-6931e66333e7_story.html?utm_term=.395bf6b75278;
      Eric Bradner, "McCain Steps Up Trump Criticism," February 21,
      2017, *CNN*, http://www.cnn.com/2017/02/21/politics/john-
      mccain-trump-criticism/.

13.   Tom Parfitt, "Donald Trump's America is Like 1930s Germany,
      Claims Adolf Hitler Biographer," February 2, 2017, *Express*,
      http://www.express.co.uk/news/world/762356/Donald-Trump-
      Muslim-ban-Nazi-Germany-Adolf-Hitler-Ian-Kershaw; Peter

Walker, "Donald Trump is Behaving like 1930s Fascist Dictator, Explains Yale Historian," March 27, 2017, *Independent*, http://www.independent.co.uk/news/world/americas/us-politics/donald-trump-1930-thirties-fascist-dictator-adolf-hitler-reichstag-fire-trick-yale-historian-timothy-a7651766.html; Charlotte England, "Donald Trump Using Adolf Hitler's 'Mein Kampf' Playbook, Says World Expert on Nazi Leader," February 8, 2017, *Independent*. http://www.independent.co.uk/news/world/americas/adolf-hitler-donald-trump-mein-kampf-bluffed-way-to-power-nazi-leader-germany-fuhrer-us-president-a7568506.html.

14. John McNeill, "How Fascist is Donald Trump? There's Actually a Formula for That," October 21, 2016, *Washington Post*, https://www.washingtonpost.com/posteverything/wp/2016/10/21/how-fascist-is-donald-trump-theres-actually-a-formula-for-that/?utm_term=.9c0ec4c515a2; Isaac Chotiner, "Is Donald Trump a Fascist?" February 10, 2016, *Slate*, http://www.slate.com/articles/news_and_politics/interrogation/2016/02/is_donald_trump_a_fascist_an_expert_on_fascism_weighs_in.html; Kali Holloway, "Trump Is an Eerily Perfect Match With a Famous 14-Point Gide to Identify Fascist Leaders," December 5, 2016, *Alternet*, http://www.alternet.org/election-2016/trump-eerily-perfect-match-famous-14-point-guide-identify-fascist-leaders.

15. Valerie Richardson, "Electoral College Members Harassed, Threatened In Last-Ditch Attempt to Block Trump," November 22, 2016, *Washington Times*, http://www.washingtontimes.com/news/2016/nov/22/gop-electors-harassed-threatened-foes-maneuver-blo/; Peter Beinart, "The Electoral College Was Meant to Stop Men Like Trump From Being President," November 21, 2016, *The Atlantic*, https://www.theatlantic.com/politics/archive/2016/11/the-electoral-college-was-meant-to-stop-men-like-trump-from-being-president/508310/.

16. Chandler Gill, "Maxine Waters on Working With Trump: 'Greatest Desire to Lead Him Right to Impeachment,'" February 13, 2017, *The Washington Free Beacon*, http://freebeacon.com/politics/waters-trump-lead-right-impeachment/; Nikita Vladimirov,

"Gabbard: I'm 'Doing My Homework' on Impeachment Process," April 21, 2017, *The Hill*, http://origin-nyi.thehill.com/blogs/blog-briefing-room/news/329946-gabbard-im-doing-my-homework-on-impeachment-process?amp=1; Richard Cohen, "How to Remove Trump from Office," January 9, 2017, *Washington Post*, https://www.washingtonpost.com/opinions/how-to-remove-trump-from-office/2017/01/09/e119cc36-d698-11e6-9a36-1d296534b31e_story.html?utm_term=.2d39e074816a.

17. Carlo Munoz, "Obama Pentagon Official Says Anti-Trump Military Coup Now Possible," February 2, 2017, *Washington Times*, http://www.washingtontimes.com/news/2017/feb/2/rosa-brooks-obama-pentagon-official-says-anti-trum/; James Kirchick, "If Trump Wins, A Coup Isn't Impossible Here in the US," July 19, 2016, *Los Angeles Times*, http://www.latimes.com/opinion/op-ed/la-oe-kirchick-trump-coup-20160719-snap-story.html.

18. Deroy Murdock, "Trump Haters Call for Presidential Assassination," March 25, 2017, *National Review*, http://www.nationalreview.com/article/446110/trump-assassination-threats-investigate-prosecute; Jeffrey Rodach, "California University Professor: Hang Trump, Execute Republicans," April 12, 2017, *Newsmax*, http://www.newsmax.com/Newsfront/us-fresno-university-professor/2017/04/12/id/784015/.

19. Adolf Hitler, *Mein Kampf*, Trans. Ralph Manheim (Boston: Houghton Mifflin, 1999), 487-492.

20. Tessa Berenson, "Protesters at Donald Trump Rallies Face Increasing Violence," October 28, 2015, *Time*, http://time.com/4090437/donald-trump-violence-protests-republican-debate/.

21. "In the Name of Humanity, We Refuse to Accept a Fascist America," Petition, May 23, 2017, https://refusefascism.org/refusefascism-org-calls-for-mass-defiance-of-fascist-trolls/.

22. Gideon Resnick, "Anti-Fascists Crash Alt-Right Deploraball," January 19, 2017, *Daily Beast*, http://www.thedailybeast.com/anti-fascists-crash-alt-right-deploraball.

23. Theresa Vargas, Taylor Hartz and Peter Hermann, "Inauguration
     Protesters Vandalize, Set Fires, Try to Disrupt Trump's Oath, as
     Police Arrest More than 200," January 20, 2017, *Washington Post*,
     https://www.washingtonpost.com/local/protesters-bring-shouts-
     skirmishes-and-shutdowns-to-inauguration-celebration/2017/01/
     20/00ea4c72-df11-11e6-acdf-14da832ae861_story.html?utm_
     term=.0a910388a3a4.

24. Charlie Nash, "Refuse Fascism Group Behind Berkeley Riot
     Received $50K from George Soros," February 5, 2017, *Breitbart
     News*, http://www.breitbart.com/milo/2017/02/05/refuse-fascism-
     group-behind-berkeley-riot-funded-george-soros/.

25. Peter Dreier, "Trump No Longer Really Running for President,"
     October 20, 2016, *The American Prospect*, http://prospect.org/
     article/trump-no-longer-really-running-president; David Brooks,
     "The View From Trump Tower," November 11, 2016, *New York
     Times*, https://www.nytimes.com/2016/11/12/opinion/the-view-
     from-trump-tower.html.

26. Eric Levenson, "Not My President's Day Protesters Rally to Oppose
     Trump," February 18, 2017, *CNN*, http://www.cnn.
     com/2017/02/20/us/not-my-presidents-day-protests/; Peter King and
     Ruben Vives, "Violence Breaks Out at Pro-Trump Rally in Berkeley,"
     March 5, 2017, *Los Angeles Times*, http://www.latimes.com/local/
     lanow/la-me-trump-rally-berkeley-20170304-story.html; Debra
     Heine, "Trump Supporters and Anti-Trump Agitators Clash at
     March 4 Trump Rallies Across America," March 4, 2017, *PJ Media*,
     https://pjmedia.com/trending/2017/03/04/trump-supporters-and-
     anti-trump-agitators-clash-at-march4trump-rallies-across-america/;
     Eliott McLaughlin, "May Day Rallies Turn Violent in Several
     Cities," May 2, 2017, *CNN*, http://www.cnn.com/2017/05/01/
     world/may-day-celebrations-protests-around-world/.

27. Alex Johnson, "May Day Protests Turn Violence in Portland as
     Police Cancel Permits," May 2, 2017, *NBC News*, http://www.
     nbcnews.com/news/us-news/may-day-protests-turn-violent-portland-
     police-cancel-permits-n753611; Derek Hawkins, "Sen. Tim Kaine's

Son Among Several Arrested After Protesters Disrupt Trump Rally in Minnesota," March 8, 2017, *Washington Post*, https://www. washingtonpost.com/news/morning-mix/wp/2017/03/08/sen-tim-kaines-son-among-several-arrested-after-protesters-disrupt-trump-rally-in-minnesota/?utm_term=.6b57689573a8.

28. Jesse Benn, "Sorry Liberals, A Violent Response to Trump Is As Logical As Any," June 6, 2016, *Huffington Post*, http://www. huffingtonpost.com/jesse-benn/sorry-liberals-a-violent-_b_103161 86.html.

29. Van Newkirk II, "Political Violence in the Era of Trump," June 3, 2016, *The Atlantic*, https://www.theatlantic.com/politics/ archive/2016/06/violence-trump-rallies/485522/.

30. Natasha Lennard, "Anti-Fascists Will Fight Trump's Fascism in the Streets," January 19, 2017, *The Nation*, https://www.thenation.com/ article/anti-fascist-activists-are-fighting-the-alt-right-in-the-streets/.

31. Chauncey DeVega, "Donald Trump is Not the Victim," June 3, 2016, *Salon*, http://www.salon.com/2016/06/03/donald_trump_is_ not_the_victim_the_rights_laughable_spin_as_violence_breaks_ out_in_san_jose/.

32. Kelly Hayes, "No Welcome Mat for Fascism," March 14, 2016, *Truthout*, http://www.truth-out.org/opinion/item/35204-no-welcome-mat-for-fascism-stop-whining-about-trump-s-right-to-free-speech.

33. Friedrich Hayek, *The Road to Serfdom* (Chicago: University of Chicago Press, 2007), 59; Herman Finer, *Road to Reaction* (Boston: Little, Brown and Company, 1945), ix.

34. Jonah Goldberg, *Liberal Fascism* (New York: Doubleday, 2007), 2, 7.

35. Robert Paxton, *The Anatomy of Fascism* (New York: Vintage Books, 2004), 49.

36. Tony Paterson, "A Berliner in 1963—But Did Former President John F. Kennedy Once Admire Adolf Hitler?" May 23, 2013,

Independent, http://www.independent.co.uk/news/world/world-history/a-berliner-in-1963-but-did-former-us-president-john-f-kennedy-once-admire-adolf-hitler-8629991.html; Allan Hall, "How JFK Secretly Admired Hitler," May 23, 2013, *Daily Mail*, http://www.dailymail.co.uk/news/article-2329556/How-JFK-secretly-ADMIRED-Hitler-Explosive-book-reveals-Presidents-praise-Nazis-travelled-Germany-Second-World-War.html.

37. Denis Mack Smith, *Mussolini* (New York: Vintage Books, 1982), 138; Neta Alexander, "Is He a Fascist?" April 2, 2017, *Haaretz*, http://www.haaretz.com/us-news/1.780456.

38. Anthony James Gregor, *The Ideology of Fascism* (New York: Free Press, 1969), 13.

Two

1. Curtis Riess, *Joseph Goebbels* (London: Fonthill, 2015), 64-65.

2. Thomas Jefferson, *Notes on the State of Virginia*, Ed. William Peden (New York: W. W. Norton, 1982), 120.

3. Gabor Boritt, Mario Cuomo and Harold Holzer, eds. *Lincoln on Democracy* (New York: HarperCollins, 1990), 3; Alexander Hamilton, James Madison and John Jay, *The Federalist* (New York: Barnes and Noble, 2006), 53.

4. Justin Baragona, "Chris Matthews Reacts to Trump Firing Comey: 'A Little Whiff of Fascism Tonight,'" May 9, 2017, *Mediaite*, http://www.mediaite.com/tv/chris-matthews-reacts-to-trump-firing-comey-a-little-whiff-of-fascism-tonight/.

5. Amy Goodman, "Father of Fascism Studies: Donald Trump Shows Alarming Willingness to Use Fascist Terms and Styles," March 15, 2016, *Democracy Now*, https://www.democracynow.org/2016/3/15/father_of_fascism_studies_donald_trump.

6. Isaac Chotiner, "Is Donald Trump a Fascist?" February 10, 2016, *Slate*, http://www.slate.com/articles/news_and_politics/interrogation/2016/02/is_donald_trump_a_fascist_an_expert_on_fascism_weighs_in.html.

7.   Robert Paxton, *The Anatomy of Fascism* (New York: Vintage Books, 2004), 202.

8.   A. James Gregor, *The Ideology of Fascism* (New York: Free Press, 1969), 376; Stanley G. Payne, *A History of Fascism* (Madison: University of Wisconsin Press, 1995), 66.

9.   Max Greenwood, "Warren: Trump Win Partly a Result of 'An Ugly Stew of Racism,'" April 19, 2017, *The Hill*, http://thehill.com/blogs/blog-briefing-room/news/329640-warren-trump-win-partially-a-result-of-an-ugly-stew-of-racism; James Whitman, "Why the Nazis Loved America," March 21, 2017, *Time*, http://time.com/4703586/nazis-america-race-law/; Jeet Heer, "Trump's Fascist Roots Lie in the Republican Party," December 10, 2016, *New Republic*, https://newrepublic.com/minutes/133623/trumps-fascist-roots-lie-republican-party; Michael Tomasky, "GOP: A Neo-Fascist White Identity Party?" December 13, 2015, *Daily Beast*, http://www.thedailybeast.com/articles/2015/12/14/gop-a-neo-fascist-white-identity-party.html.

10.   Zolan Kanno-Youngs, "'We Are All Immigrants,' N. Y. Gov. Andrew Cuomo Says During Speech at Harlem Church," November 20, 2016, *Wall Street Journal*, https://www.wsj.com/articles/we-are-all-immigrants-n-y-gov-andrew-cuomo-says-during-speech-at-harlem-church-1479667579; Michael Shear and Ron Nixon, "More Immigrants Face Deportation Under New Rules," February 22, 2017, *New York Times*, http://www.nytimes.com/images/2017/02/22/nytfrontpage/scan.pdf.

11.   Cleve R. Wootson, Jr., "Sen. Al Franken: Donald Trump's New Ad on the Economy is Anti-Semitic," November 6, 2016, *Washington Post*, https://www.washingtonpost.com/news/the-fix/wp/2016/11/06/sen-al-franken-claims-that-donald-trumps-new-ad-on-the-economy-is-anti-semitic/?utm_term=.e099c542a2cd; David Denby, "The Plot Against America: Donald Trump's Rhetoric," December 15, 2015, *New Yorker*, http://www.newyorker.com/culture/cultural-comment/plot-america-donald-trumps-rhetoric; Peter Dreier, "Trump No Longer Really Running for President,"

October 20, 2016, *The American Prospect*, http://prospect.org/ article/trump-no-longer-really-running-president.

12. Ian Schwartz, "Netanyahu: No Greater Supporter of Jewish People and Jewish State than Donald Trump," February 15, 2017, *RealClear Politics*, http://www.realclearpolitics.com/ video/2017/02/15/netanyahu_no_greater_supporter_of_jewish_ people_and_jewish_state_than_donald_trump.html.

13. Andrew Sullivan, "The Madness of King Donald," February 10, 2017, *New York Magazine*, http://nymag.com/daily/intelligencer/ 2017/02/andrew-sullivan-the-madness-of-king-donald.html; Scott Whitlock, "Unhinged Paul Krugman: Nazi Trump is 'Mentally Ill,'" January 26, 2017, News Busters, http://www.newsbusters.org/ blogs/nb/scott-whitlock/2017/01/26/unhinged-paul-krugman-nazi- trump-mentally-ill; "Rosie O'Donnell Calls Trump 'Mentally Unstable' on Twitter and Warns America That There are 'Less Than Three Weeks to Stop Him,'" January 2, 2017, *Daily Mail*, http:// www.dailymail.co.uk/news/article-4080932/Rosie-O-Donnell-calls- Trump-mentally-unstable-warns-America-three-weeks-stop-him. html; Edmund DeMarche. "Democrats Introduce Bill to Take Nuclear Football out of Trump's Hands," January 25, 2017, *Fox News*, http://www.foxnews.com/politics/2017/01/25/lawmakers- introduce-bill-to-take-nuclear-football-out-trumps-hands.html; Nikita Vladimirov, "Dem to Unveil Bill Requiring a White House Psychiatrist," February 8, 2017, *The Hill*, http://thehill.com/ homenews/house/318554-lawmaker-to-propose-a-bill-requiring-a- white-house-psychiatrist.

14. Matt Feeney, "The Book That Predicted Trump," November 1, 2016, *New Yorke*, http://www.newyorker.com/culture/cultural- comment/the-book-that-predicted-trump.

15. Stanley Payne, *A History of Fascism* (Madison: University of Wisconsin Press, 1995), 203; Richard Evans, *The Coming of the Third Reich* (New York: Penguin Books, 2005), 449.

16. Zeev Sternhell, *The Birth of Fascist Ideology* (Princeton: Princeton University Press, 1994), 4.

17. Ruth Ben-Ghiat, "An American Authoritarian," August 10, 2016, *The Atlantic*, https://www.theatlantic.com/politics/archive/2016/08/ american-authoritarianism-under-donald-trump/495263/; Andrew Sullivan, "The Republic Repeals Itself," November 9, 2016, *New York* magazine, http://nymag.com/daily/intelligencer/2016/11/ andrew-sullivan-president-trump-and-the-end-of-the-republic.html; Steven Levitsky and Daniel Ziblatt, "Is Donald Trump a Threat to Democracy?" December 16, 2016, *New York Times*, https://www. nytimes.com/2016/12/16/opinion/sunday/is-donald-trump-a-threat-to-democracy.html; Timothy Snyder, "Donald Trump and the New Dawn of Tyranny," March 3, 2017, *Time*, http://time.com/4690676/ donald-trump-tyranny/.

18. James Hohmann, "The Daily 202: Trump's Warning to Comey Deepens Doubts About His Respect for the Rule of Law," May 12, 2017, *Washington Post*, https://www.washingtonpost.com/news/ powerpost/paloma/daily-202/2017/05/12/daily-202-trump-s-warning-to-comey-deepens-doubts-about-his-respect-for-the-rule-of-law/5915063ee9b69b209cf2b814/?utm_term=.29f8b7dd4e5f.

19. Dan P. McAdams, "The Mind of Donald Trump," June 2016, *The Atlantic*, https://www.theatlantic.com/magazine/archive/2016/06/ the-mind-of-donald-trump/480771/.

20. Mark Y. Rosenberg, "Donald Trump's Use of Fascist Language Forebodes a Dark American Future," January 24, 2017, *Quartz*, https:// qz.com/892091/is-trump-a-fascist-donald-trumps-inaugural-speech-used-fascist-language-to-prime-america-for-a-dark-future-agenda/.

21. Zeev Sternhell, *The Birth of Fascist Ideology* (Princeton: Princeton University Press, 1994), 215; A. James Gregor, *Young Mussolini and the Intellectual Origins of Fascism* (Berkeley: University of California Press, 1979), 98; Denis Mack Smith, *Mussolini* (New York: Vintage Books, 1982), 15.

22. David Niose, "Our Memorial Day Collision Course with Fascism," May 30, 2016, *Salon*, http://www.salon.com/2016/05/30/our_ memorial_day_collision_course_with_fascism_donald_trump_ and_the_new_american_militarism/; Ishaan Tharoor, "The Trump Presidency Ushers in a New Age of Militarism," March 1, 2017,

Washington Post, https://www.washingtonpost.com/news/worldviews/wp/2017/03/01/the-trump-presidency-ushers-in-a-new-age-of-militarism/?utm_term=.843868bacc08.

23. Stanley Payne, *A History of Fascism* (Madison: University of Wisconsin Press, 1995), 11.

24. "Cornel West on Donald Trump: This is What Neo-Fascism Looks Like," December 1, 2016, *Democracy Now*, https://www.democracynow.org/2016/12/1/cornel_west_on_donald_trump_this.

25. Renzo De Felice, *Fascism* (New Brunswick: Transaction Publishers, 2009), 63; George Mosse, *The Fascist Revolution* (New York: Howard Fertig, 1999), 22; Stanley Payne, *A History of Fascism* (Madison: University of Wisconsin Press, 1995), 168.

26. A. James Gregor, *Mussolini's Intellectuals* (Princeton: Princeton University Press, 2005), 5.

27. Giovanni Gentile, *Origins and Doctrine of Fascism* (New Brunswick: Transaction Publishers, 2009), 25.

28. In addition to Gentile's writings, my subsequent account is especially indebted to A. James Gregor, *Giovanni Gentile: Philosopher of Fascism* (New Brunswick: Transaction Publishers, 2008).

29. Giovanni Gentile, *Origins and Doctrine of Fascism* (New Brunswick: Transaction Publishers, 2009), 28, 31, 55, 57, 67, 87.

30. A. James Gregor, *The Ideology of Fascism* (New York: Free Press, 1969), 207, 223.

31. Walter Laqueur, *Fascism: Past, Present and Future* (New York: Oxford University Press, 1996), p. 13.

32. "Father of Fascism Studies: Donald Trump Shows Alarming Willingness to Use Fascist Terms and Styles," March 15, 2016, *Democracy Now*, https://www.democracynow.org/2016/3/15/father_of_fascism_studies_donald_trump; Isaac Chotiner, "Is Donald Trump a Fascist?" February 10, 2016, *Slate*, http://www.slate.com/articles/news_and_politics/interrogation/2016/02/is_donald_trump_a_fascist_an_expert_on_fascism_weighs_in.html.

33. A. James Gregor, *Giovanni Gentile: Philosopher of Fascism* (New Brunswick: Transaction Publishers, 2008), 63.

34. Mark Landler and Helene Cooper, "Obama Seeks a Course of Pragmatism in the Middle East," March 10, 2011, *New York Times*, http://www.nytimes.com/2011/03/11/world/africa/11policy.html.

35. Dennis Mack Smith, *Mussolini* (New York: Vintage Books, 1982), 312.

36. John Toland, *Adolf Hitler* (New York: Anchor Books, 1992), 224-225.

37. Volker Ullrich, *Hitler* (New York: Alfred A. Knopf, 2016), 193.

Three

1. F. A. Hayek, *The Road to Serfdom* (Chicago: University of Chicago Press, 2007), 145.

2. Zeev Sternhell, *The Birth of Fascist Ideology* (Princeton: Princeton University Press, 1994), 208.

3. William Shirer, *The Rise and Fall of the Third Reich* (New York: Simon & Schuster, 2011), 298.

4. Volker Ullrich, *Hitler* (New York: Alfred A. Knopf, 2016), 125.

5. Adolf Hitler, *Hitler's Table Talk*, Intro. H. R. Trevor-Roper (New York: Enigma Books, 2000), xxiv, 10.

6. A. James Gregor, *The Faces of Janus* (New Haven: Yale University Press, 2000), 20.

7. Joshua Muravchik, *Heaven on Earth* (New York: Encounter Books, 2002), 105.

8. Ibid, 101.

9. Ibid, 108.

10. Zeev Sternhell, *The Birth of Fascist Ideology* (Princeton: Princeton University Press, 1994), 39-66.

11. A. James Gregor, *The Ideology of Fascism* (New York: Free Press, 1969), 159.

12. Stanley Payne, *A History of Fascism* (Madison: University of Wisconsin Press, 1995), 84.

13. A. James Gregor, *Young Mussolini and the Intellectual Origins of Fascism* (Berkeley: University of California Press, 1979), 20.

14. A. James Gregor, *Mussolini's Intellectuals* (Princeton: Princeton University Press, 2005), 33.

15. For a discussion of Woltmann, see A. James Gregor, *Marxism, Fascism and Totalitarianism* (Stanford: Stanford University Press, 2000), 183-186.

16. A. James Gregor, *Giovanni Gentile* (New Brunswick: Transaction Publishers, 2008), 100.

17. A. James Gregor, *Young Mussolini and the Intellectual Origins of Fascism* (Berkeley: University of California Press, 1979), 215.

Four

1. Timothy Snyder, *Bloodlands* (New York: Basic Books, 2010), 160.

2. Sarah Helm, *Ravensbruck* (New York: Anchor Books, 2015), 54.

3. Adolf Hitler, *Hitler's Table Talk* (New York: Enigma Books, 2000), 188.

4. Alan Gilbert, "The Cowboy Novels that Inspired Hitler," August 20, 2016, *Daily Beast*, http://www.thedailybeast.com/the-cowboy-novels-that-inspired-hitler.

5. Ira Katznelson, *Fear Itself* (New York: Liveright Publishing, 2003), 282-283.

6. Adolf Hitler, *Mein Kampf* (Boston: Houghton Mifflin, 1999), 139.

7. Norman Rich, "Hitler's Foreign Policy," in Gordon Martel. ed. *The Origins of the Second World War Reconsidered: The A.J.P. Taylor Debate After Twenty-Five Years* (Boston: Allen & Unwin, 1986), 136; see also James Whitman, *Hitler's American Model* (Princeton: Princeton University Press, 2017), 9-10.

8. Volker Ullrich, *Hitler: Ascent, 1889-1939* (New York: Alfred A. Knopf, 2016), 665; Richard Evans, *The Coming of the Third Reich* (New York: Penguin Books, 2005), 111.

9. John Toland, *Hitler: The Definitive Biography* (New York: Anchor Books, 1992), 702.

10. Timothy Snyder, *Bloodlands* (New York: Basic Books, 2010), 160.

11. Gotz Aly, *Why the Germans? Why the Jews?* (New York: Henry Holt, 2014), 2.

12. Marc Buggeln, *Slave Labor in Nazi Concentration Camps* (New York: Oxford University Press, 2014); Alexander Von Plato, Almut Leh and Christoph Thonfeld, eds., *Hitler's Slaves* (New York: Berghahn Books, 2010).

13. Marc Buggeln, *Slave Labor in Nazi Concentration Camps* (New York: Oxford University Press, 2014), 22.

14. Sarah Helm, *Ravensbruck* (New York: Anchor Books, 2015), 244.

15. Timothy Snyder, *Bloodlands* (New York: Basic Books, 2010), xiii, 256, 76, 382.

16. Wolfgang Sofsky, *The Order of Terror* (Princeton: Princeton University Press, 1993), 199.

17. David Stannard, *American Holocaust* (New York: Oxford University Press, 1992), x, 147.

18. Guenter Lewy, "Were American Indians the Victims of Genocide?" September 2004, History News Network, http://historynewsnetwork.org/article/7302.

19. "Convention on the Prevention and Punishment of the Crime of Genocide," December 9, 1948, United Nations Human Rights Office of the High Commissioner. http://www.ohchr.org/EN/ProfessionalInterest/Pages/CrimeOfGenocide.aspx.

20. Steve Inskeep, *Jacksonland* (New York: Penguin Books, 2015), 203-204.

21. Ibid, 205.

22. Andrew Jackson to Rachel Jackson, March 28, 1814, in Harriet Owsley et. al., *The Papers of Andrew Jackson* (Knoxville: University of Tennessee Press, 1980), Vol. 3, 54; Timothy Horton Ball and Henry Sale Halbert, *The Creek War of 1813 and 1814* (Montgomery: White, Woodruff & Fowler, 1895), 276-277.

23. "Andrew Jackson's Speech to Congress on Indian Removal," December 6, 1830, https://www.nps.gov/museum/tmc/MANZ/handouts/Andrew_Jackson_Annual_Message.pdf.

24. David Stannard, *American Holocaust* (New York: Oxford University Press, 1992), 123-124.

25. Jane Lawrence, "The Indian Health Service and the Sterilization of Native American Women," in Devon A. Mihesuah. ed. *American Indian Quarterly*, (University of Nebraska Press, Vol. 24, No. 3, 2000), 400-419.

26. Stanley Elkins, *Slavery: A Problem in American Institutional and Intellectual Life* (Chicago: University of Chicago Press, 1976), 111.

27. Ibid, 130.

28. Eugene Genovese, "Rebelliousness and Docility in the Negro Slave," in Ann Lane. ed. *The Debate Over Slavery: Stanley Elkins and His Critics* (Urbana: University of Illinois Press, 1975), 43.

29. Sarah Helm, *Ravensbruck* (New York: Anchor Books, 2015), 25.

30. Elie Wiesel, *Night* (New York: Hill & Wang, 2006), 52; Sarah Helm, *Ravensbruck* (New York: Anchor Books, 2015), 34.

31. Ibid, 70.

32. Eugene Genovese, *The World the Slaveholders Made* (Middletown: Wesleyan University Press, 1988), 200.

33. Wolfgang Sofsky, *The Order of Terror* (Princeton: Princeton University Press, 1993), 171-172.

34. Marc Buggeln, *Slave Labor in Nazi Concentration Camps* (New York: Oxford University Press, 2014), 37-38, 46.

35. Kenneth Stampp, *The Peculiar Institution* (New York: Vintage Books, 1984), 188.

36. Wolfgang Sofsky, *The Order of Terror* (Princeton: Princeton University Press, 1993), 58.

37. Ibid, 271-274.

38. Kenneth Stampp, *The Peculiar Institution* (New York: Vintage Books, 1984), 11, 420.

39. Orlando Patterson, "Towards a Study of Black America," Fall 1989, *Dissent*, 480, https://www.dissentmagazine.org/article/toward-a-study-of-black-america.

Five

1. George Fredrickson, *Racism: A Short History* (Princeton: Princeton University Press, 2002), 123-124.

2. Michael Burleigh, *The Racial State* (Cambridge: Cambridge University Press, 2013), 23.

3. James Q. Whitman, *Hitler's American Model* (Princeton: Princeton University Press, 2017), 1, 80, 95, 104, 127, 160; James Q. Whitman, "When the Nazis Wrote the Nuremberg Laws, They Looked to Racist American Statutes," February 22, 2017, *Los Angeles Times*, http://www.latimes.com/opinion/op-ed/la-oe-whitman-hitler-american-race-laws-20170222-story.html.

4. Michael Burleigh, *The Racial State* (Cambridge: Cambridge University Press, 2013), 45.

5. George Fredrickson, *Racism: A Short History* (Princeton: Princeton University Press, 2002), 124.

6. James Whitman, *Hitler's American Model* (Princeton: Princeton University Press, 2017), 50, 138, 145.

7. Ira Katznelson, *Fear Itself* (New York: Liveright, 2013), 283.

8. Joshua Muravchik, "Did American Racism Inspire the Nazis?" March 19, 2017, *Mosaic*, https://mosaicmagazine.com/observation/2017/03/did-american-racism-inspire-the-nazis/.

9. James Whitman, "Why the Nazis Loved America," March 21, 2017, *Time*, http://time.com/4703586/nazis-america-race-law/.

10. Volker Ullrich, *Hitler: Ascent 1889-1939* (New York: Alfred A. Knopf, 2016), 84.

11. A. James Gregor, *The Ideology of Fascism* (New York: Free Press, 1969), 246-248; A. James Gregor, *Mussolini's Intellectuals* (Princeton: Princeton University Press, 2005), 214-217.

12. Gotz Aly, *Why the Germans? Why the Jews?* (New York: Henry Holt and Company, 2014), 70, 77-78.

13. Adolf Hitler, *Mein Kampf*, trans. Ralph Manheim (Boston: Houghton Mifflin, 1999), 210.

14. Volker Ullrich, *Hitler, Ascent 1889-1939* (New York: Alfred A. Knopf, 2016), 102-103.

15. Adolf Hitler, *Hitler's Table Talk* (New York: Enigma Books, 2000), 117-118, 373-374.

16. Gotz Aly, *Why the Germans? Why the Jews?* (New York: Henry Holt and Company, 2014), 72.

17. Ibid, 8.

18. John Hope Franklin, *From Slavery to Freedom* (New York: Alfred A. Knopf, 1967), 341; A. Leon Higginbotham, Introduction, Genna Rae McNeil, *Groundwork: Charles Hamilton and the Struggle for Civil Rights* (Philadelphia: University of Pennsylvania Press, 1983), xvi.

19. Ira Katznelson, *Fear Itself* (New York: Liveright, 2013), 90.

20. Ira Katznelson, *When Affirmative Action Was White* (New York. W. W. Norton, 2005), 81.

21. Derrick Bell, *Faces at the Bottom of the Well: The Permanence of Racism* (New York: Basic Books, 1992), 1, 3, 10, 52; Joel Kovel, *White Racism* (New York: Columbia University Press, 1984), xi, 32; Cornel West, *Keeping Faith: Philosophy and Race in America* (New York: Routledge, 1993), 236.

22. Thomas Jefferson, *Notes on the State of Virginia* (New York: W. W. Norton, 1982), 143.

23. Abraham Lincoln, "Speech on the Dred Scott Decision," Springfield, Illinois, June 26, 1857, in Mario Cuomo and Harold Holzer. eds. *Lincoln on Democracy* (New York: HarperCollins, 1990), 90-91.

24. *Dred Scott v. Sandford*, 60 U.S. 393 (1856).

25. John Townsend, "The Doom of Slavery in the Union: Its Safety Out of It," (Address to Edisto Island Vigilant Association, October 29, 1860), http://civilwarcauses.org/townsend.htm.

26. James Whitman, *Hitler's American Model* (Princeton: Princeton University Press, 2017), 59-60.

27. Joel Williamson, *The Crucible of Race* (New York: Oxford University Press, 1984).

28. Kenneth Stampp, *The Peculiar Institution* (New York: Vintage Books, 1984), 193.

29. Volker Ullrich, *Hitler: Ascent 1889-1939* (New York: Alfred A. Knopf, 2016), 672.

30. Michael Burleigh, *The Racial State* (Cambridge: Cambridge University Press, 2013), 82.

Six

1. Editorial from *American Medicine*, Ed. Margaret Sanger, "Intelligent or Unintelligent Birth Control," *Birth Control Review*, May 1919, https://lifedynamics.com/app/uploads/2015/09/1919-05-May.pdf; Richard Weikart, *From Darwin to Hitler* (New York: Palgrave Macmillan, 2004), 135.

2. Gerald Posner and John Ware, *Mengele* (New York: Cooper Square Press, 2000), 9.

3. Ibid, 279.

4. Sarah Kliff, "The Gosnell Case: Here's What You Need To Know," April 15, 2013, *Washington Post*, https://www.washingtonpost.com/news/wonk/wp/2013/04/15/the-gosnell-case-heres-what-you-need-to-know/?utm_term=.61910f9f415c.

5. Alexandra Desanctis, "A Shocking New Undercover Video Exposes the Grisly Reality of Ripping Apart Fetuses," May 25, 2017, *National Review*, http://www.nationalreview.com/article/447939/undercover-video-center-medical-progress-exposes-gruesome-abortion-practices.

6. William Saletan, "The Baby Butcher," January 20, 2011, *Slate*, http://www.slate.com/articles/health_and_science/human_nature/2011/01/the_baby_butcher.html.

7. Nathaniel Nash, "Mengele an Abortionist, Argentine Files Suggest," February 11, 1992, *New York Times*, http://www.nytimes.com/1992/02/11/world/mengele-an-abortionist-argentine-files-suggest.html.

8. Richard Evans, *The Third Reich in History and Memory* (New York: Oxford University Press, 2015), 21.

9. Timothy Snyder, *Bloodlands* (New York: Basic Books, 2010), xv, 257, 261, 382.

10. Michael Burleigh, *The Racial State* (Cambridge: Cambridge University Press, 2013), 142.

11. Angela Franks, *Margaret Sanger's Eugenic Legacy* (Jefferson, NC: McFarland & Co., 2005), 180.

12. Ibid, 70.

13. Paul Popenoe and Roswell Hill Johnson, *Applied Eugenics* (New York: Macmillan, 1918), 184.

14. Edwin Black, *The War Against the Weak* (Washington, D.C.: Dialog Press, 2013), xvii, 258.

15. Margaret Sanger, "My Way to Peace," (Speech, January 17, 1932). *Margaret Sanger Papers*, https://www.nyu.edu/projects/sanger/webedition/app/documents/show.php?sangerDoc=129037.xml; Margaret Sanger, "America Needs a Code for Babies," (Speech, March 27, 1934), *Margaret Sanger Papers*, https://www.nyu.edu/projects/sanger/webedition/app/documents/show.php?sangerDoc=101807.xml.

16. Margaret Sanger to Dr. C. J. Gamble, December 10, 1939, In "Letter From Margaret Sanger to Dr. C. J. Gamble," *Genius*, https://genius.com/Margaret-sanger-letter-from-margaret-sanger-to-dr-cj-gamble-annotated.

17. Linda Gordon, *Woman's Body, Woman's Right: Birth Control in America* (New York: Penguin Books, 1990).

18. Stefan Kuhl, *The Nazi Connection* (New York: Oxford University Press, 1994), 34.

19. Margaret Sanger, "Human Conservation and Birth Control," (Speech, March 3, 1938), *Margaret Sanger Papers*, https://www.nyu.edu/projects/sanger/webedition/app/documents/show.php?sangerDoc=220126.xml.

20. Richard Weikart, *From Darwin to Hitler* (New York: Palgrave Macmillan, 2004), 9.

21. Adolf Hitler, *Mein Kampf*, Trans. Ralph Manheim (Boston: Houghton Mifflin, 1999), 286, 439-440.

22. Otto Wagener, *Hitler: Memoirs of a Confidant* (New Haven: Yale University Press, 1987), 145-146.

23. Adolf Hitler, *Mein Kampf*, Trans. Ralph Manheim (Boston: Houghton Mifflin, 1999), 252.

24. Edwin Black, *The War Against the Weak* (Washington, D.C.: Dialog Press, 2013), 270.

25. Ibid, 259.

26. Stefan Kuhl, *The Nazi Connection* (New York: Oxford University Press, 1994), 36, 46.

27. Ibid, 277.

28. George Fredrickson, *Racism* (Princeton: Princeton University Press, 2002), 2.

29. Eric Foner, "Introduction," in Richard Hofstadter, *Social Darwinism in America* (Boston: Beacon Press, 1992), x-xi.

30. Richard Hofstadter, *Social Darwinism in America* (Boston: Beacon Press, 1992), 161.

31. Angela Franks, *Margaret Sanger's Eugenic Legacy* (Jefferson, NC: McFarland & Co., 2005), 141.

Seven

1. *"Volkischer Beobachter,"* May 11, 1933, in Jonah Goldberg, *Liberal Fascism* (New York: Doubleday, 2007), 148; Wolfgang Schivelbusch, *Three New Deals* (New York: Henry Holt, 2006), 19.

2. Seymour Martin Lipset and Gary Marks, "How FDR Saved Capitalism," January 30, 2001, *Hoover Digest*, http://www.hoover.org/research/how-fdr-saved-capitalism; "The Man Who Saved His Country and the World," October 30, 2008, *The Economist*, http://www.economist.com/node/12502823.

3. Richard Evans, *The Third Reich in History and Memory* (New York: Oxford University Press, 2015), 302.

4. Timothy Snyder, *Bloodlands* (New York: Basic Books, 2010), xiv.

5. Ira Katznelson *Fear Itself* (New York: Liveright Publishing, 2013), 38.

6. James Q. Whitman, "Corporatism, Fascism and the First New Deal," 1991, Faculty Scholarship Series, Yale Law School, http://digitalcommons.law.yale.edu/fss_papers/660/.

7. John P. Diggins, *Mussolini and Fascism: The View from America* (Princeton: Princeton University Press, 1972), 47-48; David Boaz, "Hitler, Mussolini, Roosevelt," October 2007, *Reason.com*, http://reason.com/archives/2007/09/28/hitler-mussolini-roosevelt; Ira Katznelson, *Fear Itself* (New York: Liveright Publishing, 2013), 123.

8. Ira Katznelson, *Fear Itself* (New York: Liveright Publishing, 2013), 58-59, 67.

9. Paul Hollander, *From Benito Mussolini to Hugo Chavez* (Cambridge: Cambridge University Press, 2016), 109.

10. Ian Kershaw, *Hitler, 1880-1936: Hubris* (New York: W. W. Norton, 2000), 261; John Sedgwick, "The Harvard Nazi," March 2005, *Boston*, http://www.bostonmagazine.com/2006/05/the-harvard-nazi/; Michael Grynbaum, "Nazi in Our Midst," February 10, 2005, *Harvard Crimson*, http://www.thecrimson.com/article/2005/2/10/nazi-in-our-midst-theres-bound/.

11. Paul Hollander, *From Benito Mussolini to Hugo Chavez* (Cambridge: Cambridge University Press, 2016), 109.

12. Friedrich Nietzsche, *The Will to Power* (New York: Vintage, 1967), 734; Jacob Golomb and Robert S. Wistrich, *Nietzsche, Godfather of Fascism?* (Princeton: Princeton University Press, 2002), 254-255.

13. Randy Dotinga, "5 Surprising Facts about Woodrow Wilson and Race," December 14, 2015, *Christian Science Monitor*, http://www.csmonitor.com/Books/chapter-and-verse/2015/1214/5-surprising-facts-about-Woodrow-Wilson-and-racism; Beverly Gage, "He Was No Wilsonian," December 10, 2009, *New York Times*, http://www.nytimes.com/2009/12/13/books/review/Gage-t.html?_r=0.

14. Chris Myers Asch, "Woodrow Wilson's Racist Legacy," December 11, 2015, *Washington Post*, https://www.washingtonpost.com/opinions/woodrow-wilsons-racist-legacy/2015/12/09/6a27aad4-9937-11e5-b499-76cbec161973_story.html?utm_term=.f703a0772bb4; Arthur Walworth, *Woodrow Wilson* (New York: Longmans, 1958), 325.

15. Ira Katznelson, *When Affirmative Action Was White* (New York: W. W. Norton, 2005), 85.

16. David Chalmers, *Hooded Americanism* (Durham: Duke University Press, 1987), 3.

17. Jonah Goldberg, *Liberal Fascism* (New York: Doubleday, 2007), 11, 80.

18. John P. Diggins, *Mussolini and Fascism: The View from America* (Princeton: Princeton University Press, 1972), 279.

19. Wolfgang Schivelbusch, *Three New Deals* (New York: Henry Holt, 2006), 32; Rexford G. Tugwell, "Design for Government," *Political Science Quarterly* 48 (1933), 323, 326, 330.

20. John P. Diggins, *Mussolini and Fascism: The View from America* (Princeton: Princeton University Press, 1972), 241; Philip Coupland, "H. G. Wells' Liberal Fascism," in *Journal of Contemporary History* 35. No. 4 (2000), 549.

21. John P. Diggins, *Mussolini and Fascism: The View from America* (Princeton: Princeton University Press, 1972), 28, 224.

22. Charles A. Beard, "Making the Fascist State," in *New Republic*, January 23, 1929, 277; John P. Diggins, *Mussolini and Fascism: The View from America* (Princeton: Princeton University Press, 1972), 226-228.

23. Paul Hollander, *From Benito Mussolini to Hugo Chavez* (Cambridge: Cambridge University Press, 2016), 61; Jonah Goldberg, *Liberal Fascism* (New York: Doubleday, 2007), 11; John P. Diggins, *Mussolini and Fascism: The View from America* (Princeton: Princeton University Press, 1972), 213.

24. Wolfgang Schivelbusch, *Three New Deals* (New York: Henry Holt, 2006), 37; John P. Diggins, *Mussolini and Fascism: The View from America* (Princeton: Princeton University Press, 1972), 221.

25. John Toland, *Adolf Hitler* (New York: Anchor Books, 1992), 409; Lawrence Dennis, *The Coming American Fascism* (New York: Noontide Press, 1993).

26. Werner Sollors, "W. E. B. Du Bois in Nazi Germany," November 12, 1999, *Chronicle of Higher Education*, http://www.chronicle.com/article/WEB-Du-Bois-in-Nazi/1896/; Christina Oppel, "W. E. B. Du Bois, Nazi Germany, and the Black Atlantic," *GHI Bulletin Supplement 5* (2008), 109, https://www.ghi-dc.org/fileadmin/user_upload/GHI_Washington/Press_Room/Press_Coverage_of_the_GHI/2009/supp5_099.pdf.

27. John P. Diggins, *Mussolini and Fascism: The View from America* (Princeton: Princeton University Press, 1972), 281.

28. Irving S. Cobb, "A Big Little Man," in *Cosmopolitan*, (January 1927), 145-146.

29. James Whitman, *Hitler's American Model* (Princeton: Princeton University Press, 2017), 6.

30. Wolfgang Schivelbusch, *Three New Deals* (New York: Henry Holt, 2006), 18-19.

31. John Toland, *Hitler* (New York: Anchor Books, 1992), 312.

32. Wolfgang Schivelbusch, *Three New Deals* (New York: Henry Holt, 2006), 19-20.

33. Ira Katznelson, *When Affirmative Action Was White* (New York: W. W. Norton, 2005), 118-119.

34. Ibid, 235.

35. Wolfgang Schivelbusch, *Three New Deals* (New York: Henry Holt, 2006), 28, 33; James Whitman, "Of Corporatism, Fascism and the First New Deal," 1991, Faculty Scholarship Series, Yale Law School, http://digitalcommons.law.yale.edu/fss_papers/660/.

36. John P. Diggins, *Mussolini and Fascism: The View from America* (Princeton: Princeton University Press, 1972), 280; Jonah Goldberg, *Liberal Fascism* (New York: Doubleday, 2007), 156.

37. Wolfgang Schivelbusch, *Three New Deals* (New York: Henry Holt, 2006), 98; Ian Kershaw, *Hitler, 1889-1939: Hubris* (New York: W. W. Norton, 2000), 529.

38. Wolfgang Schivelbusch, *Three New Deals* (New York: Henry Holt, 2006), 79; Thaddeus Russell, "The Surprising History of What Europe's Dictators Thought of the New Deal," August 4, 2011, *Alternet*, http://www.alternet.org/story/151563/the_surprising_history_of_what_europe's_dictators_thought_of_the_new_deal.

39. Howard Ball, *Hugo L. Black* (New York: Oxford University Press, 1996), 98-99; William Leuchtenberg, "A Klansman Joins the Court," 1973, Crosskey Lecture, University of Chicago Law School, http://chicagounbound.uchicago.edu/crosskey_lectures/1/.

40. Ira Katznelson, *When Affirmative Action Was White* (New York: W. W. Norton, 2005), 167-168.

41. Ibid, 22-23.

42. Ibid, 24.

43. Franklin D. Roosevelt, "Message to Congress on the Concentration of Economic Power," (Speech, April 29, 1938), https://publicpolicy.pepperdine.edu/academics/research/faculty-research/new-deal/roosevelt-speeches/fr042938.htm.

44. Ira Katznelson, *When Affirmative Action Was White* (New York: W. W. Norton, 2005), 7, 486.

45. Ibid, 486.

Eight

1. Robert O. Paxton, *The Anatomy of Fascism* (New York: Vintage Books, 2004), 84.

2. Ben Rosen, "Tim Allen, Conservatives in Hollywood, and Nazi Germany," March 22, 2017, *Christian Science Monitor*, http://www.csmonitor.com/USA/Politics/2017/0322/Tim-Allen-conservatives-in-Hollywood-and-Nazi-Germany-video; Daniel Nussbaum, "ABC Cancels Conservative Tim Allen Sitcom 'Last Man Standing' Despite Strong Ratings," May 11, 2017, *Breitbart News*, http://www.breitbart.com/big-hollywood/2017/05/11/abc-cancels-conservative-tim-allen-sitcom-last-man-standing/.

3. David Krayden, "Universities 'Weed Out' Right-wing Scholars, Says Report," April 14, 2017, *Daily Caller*, http://dailycaller.com/2017/04/14/universities-weed-out-right-wing-scholars-says-report/.

4. Tessa Berenson, "11 Arrested While Protesting Conservative Comedian Speaking at New York University," February 3, 2017, *Time*, http://time.com/4659339/new-york-university-protests-arrests-gavin-mcinnes/.

5. Howard Blume, "Protesters Disrupt Talk by Pro-Police Author, Sparking Free Speech Debate at Claremont McKenna College," April 9, 2017, *Los Angeles Times*, http://www.latimes.com/local/lanow/la-me-ln-macdonald-claremont-speech-disrupted-20170408-story.html.

6. Curt Riess, *Joseph Goebbels* (London: Fonthill, 2015), 75.

7. Richard Evan, *The Coming of the Third Reich* (New York: Penguin Books, 2005), 266-268.

8. Richard Wolin, ed., *The Heidegger Controversy: A Critical Reader* (Cambridge: Harvard University Press, 1993), 47, 49.

9. Ibid, 182.

10. Sheldon Wolin, *The Seduction of Unreason* (Princeton: Princeton University Press, 2004).

11. Gotz Aly, *Why the Germans? Why the Jews?* (New York: Henry Holt, 2014), 175-176.

12. Addison Independent, "Middlebury College Professor Injured by Protesters as She Escorted Controversial Speaker," March 6, 2017, *Addison County Independent,* http://www.addisonindependent. com/201703middlebury-college-professor-injured-protesters-she-escorted-controversial-speaker.

13. Sean Illing, "If You Want to Understand the Age of Trump, You Need to Read the Frankfurt School," December 27, 2016, *Vox,* https://www.vox.com/conversations/2016/12/27/14038406/ donald-trump-frankfurt-school-stuart-jeffries-marxism-critical-theory; Alex Ross, "The Frankfurt School Knew Trump Was Coming," December 5, 2016, *New Yorker,* http://www.newyorker. com/culture/cultural-comment/the-frankfurt-school-knew-trump-was-coming.

14. "Herbert Marcuse," *Stanford Encyclopedia of Philosophy,* December 18, 2013, https://plato.stanford.edu/entries/marcuse/.

15. Theodor W. Adorno et al., *The Authoritarian Personality* (New York: Harper & Bros., 1950).

16. A. James Gregor, *The Ideology of Fascism* (New York: Free Press, 1969), 25-26.

17. Alan Wolfe, "The Authoritarian Personality Revisited," October 7, 2005, *Chronicle of Higher Education,* http://www.chronicle.com/ article/The-Authoritarian/5104.

18. Herbert Marcuse, *Eros and Civilization* (Boston: Beacon Press, 1974), xv, 3, 199, 202.

19. Richard Evans, *The Coming of the Third Reich* (New York: Penguin Books, 2005), 189.

20. H. R. Trevor-Roper, ed., *Hitler's Table Talk* (New York: Enigma Books, 2000), 142, 144-146.

21. Sarah Helm, *Ravensbruck* (New York: Anchor Books, 2015), 101; Stanley Payne, *A History of Fascism* (Madison: University of Wisconsin Press, 1995), 33.

22. Richard Evans, *The Third Reich in History and Memory* (New York: Oxford University Press, 2015), 146.

23. William Shirer, *The Rise and Fall of the Third Reich* (New York: Simon & Schuster, 2011), 35.

24. Ian Kershaw, *Hitler, 1889-1936: Hubris* (New York: W. W. Norton, 2000), 348.

25. Richard Evans, *The Third Reich in Power* (New York: Penguin Books, 2005), 32.

26. Herbert Marcuse, "Repressive Tolerance," in Robert Paul Wolff, Barrington Moore, Jr. and Herbert Marcuse, *A Critique of Pure Tolerance* (Boston: Beacon Press, 1970), 81-123.

27. Stanley Payne, *A History of Fascism* (Madison: University of Wisconsin Press, 1995), 454.

28. Aaron Klein, "Hacked Soros Memo: $650,000 to Black Lives Matter," August 16, 2016, *Breitbart News*, http://www.breitbart. com/big-government/2016/08/16/hacked-soros-memo-baltimore-riots-provide-unique-opportunity-reform-police/; Charlie Nash, "Refuse Fascism Group Behind Berkeley Riot Received $50 K from George Soros," February 5, 2017, *Breitbart News*, http://www. breitbart.com/milo/2017/02/05/refuse-fascism-group-behind-berkeley-riot-funded-george-soros/.

29. Rachel Ehrenfeld, "George Soros: The 'God' Who Carries Around Some Dangerous Demons," October 4, 2004, *Los Angeles Times*, http://articles.latimes.com/2004/oct/04/opinion/oe-ehrenfeld4.

30. Aaron Klein, "Soros-Financed Groups Provided Scipr for Anti-Trump Town Halls," February 28, 2017, *Breitbart News*, http://www. breitbart.com/big-government/2017/02/28/soros-groups-provide-word-word-anti-trump-script-protesters-use-lawmakers/; "7 Fake Hate Crimes That the Media Blamed on Trump and His Supporters,"

November 17, 2016, *Twitchy*, http://twitchy.com/twitchys-3831/2016
/11/17/7-fake-hate-crimes-that-the-media-blamed-on-trump-and-his-
supporters/; Elizabeth Nolan Brown, "There Is No Violent Hate
Crimewave in Trump's America," November 16, 2016, *Reason.com*,
http://reason.com/blog/2016/11/11/election-night-hijab-attack-false.

31. Robert Borosage, "The Poisonous Politics of David Brock," January
     19, 2017, *Nation*, https://www.thenation.com/article/the-poisonous-
     politics-of-david-brock/.

32. Jane Mayer, "The Money Man," October 18, 2004, *New Yorker*,
     http://www.newyorker.com/magazine/2004/10/18/the-money-man.

33. Steve Kroft, interview by George Soros, *Sixty Minutes*, CBS,
     December 20, 1998.

34. Jane Mayer, "The Money Man," October 18, 2004, *New Yorker*,
     http://www.newyorker.com/magazine/2004/10/18/the-money-man.

Nine

1. Winston Churchill, "The End of the Beginning," (speech, London,
    England, November 10, 1942), The Churchhill Society, http://www.
    churchill-society-london.org.uk/EndoBegn.html.

2. Renzo De Felice, *Fascism* (New Brunswick: Transaction Publishers,
    2009), 58; A. James Gregor, *The Ideology of Fascism* (New York:
    Free Press, 1969), 167.

3. Benito Mussolini, *My Autobiography* (Mineola, NY: Dover
    Publications, 2006), 236-237.

4. Giovanni Gentile, *Origins and Doctrine of Fascism* (New
    Brunswick: Transaction Publishers, 2009), 53.

5. William Shirer, *The Rise and Fall of the Third Reich* (New York:
    Simon & Schuster, 2011), 200.

6. Richard Evans, *The Third Reich in Power* (New York: Penguin
    Books, 2005), 211.

7. Madison Park, "More Than 200 Protesters Indicted on Rioting
    Charges from Inauguration Day," February 22, 2017, *CNN*, http://

www.cnn.com/2017/02/22/politics/trump-inauguration-protesters-indictment/.

8. Giovanni Gentile, *Origins and Doctrine of Fascism* (New Brunswick: Transaction Publishers, 2009), 20; William Shirer, *The Rise and Fall of the Third Reich* (New York: Simon & Schuster, 2011), 22-23.

9. Abraham Lincoln, *Selected Speeches and Writings* (New York: Vintage Books, 1992), 386.

Index